# IMPROVING READING IN EVERY CLASS

ABRIDGED EDITION

## ELLEN LAMAR THOMAS

*Reading Consultant, University of Chicago*
*Laboratory School*

## H. ALAN ROBINSON

*Professor of Reading, Hofstra University*

Allyn and Bacon, Inc., Boston
Boston · London · Sydney · Toronto

To
Helen M. Robinson
and Nila Banton Smith,
who believe in improving reading
in every class.

# CONTENTS

# FOREWORD

For many years we have been hearing the softly spoken but never realized slogan "Every teacher, a teacher of reading." This book will make a genuine contribution toward reaching that goal.

One of the most distinctive features of the book is its scope. It suggests procedures not only for teaching the fundamental processes in reading, but procedures, also, for teaching reading in almost all high school subject areas. Four chapters present methods for teaching vocabulary, comprehension, rate, problem solving. The succeeding nine chapters are devoted to practical classroom methods for teaching mathematics, science, industrial arts, typewriting and business education, home economics, music, library services, fine arts, and physical education, respectively. Thus, the teaching of reading in a broad range of high school subjects is covered. Just showing through practical examples and procedures how this can be done is a notable accomplishment in itself.

Another distinctive feature of this book is its practicality. The entire content is thoroughly practical and useable. Both elementary and secondary teachers, and more recently college teachers, are clamoring for how-to-do-it ideas and suggestions. They complain that their college courses, textbooks, extracurricular lectures, etc., deal chiefly with theory and research and that rarely are they given help in actual classroom procedures. Very few books in reading have been devoted exclusively to how-to-do-it suggestions and those that have been published are extremely limited in scope. The helps given in this book, in part, grew out of the experiences of teachers in the University of Chicago Laboratory School and were found to be useful and workable by them. Other ideas were gathered from various sources where those who had used them found them to be of practical value. Teachers will greet this veritable potpourri of useable classroom suggestions with enthusiasm.

A third characteristic which should contribute markedly to the usefulness of this volume is wide variety in the types of helps that are provided. There are motivating activities, teaching procedures, and practice exercises. There are examples of lessons, interviews on how to teach reading, directions to students, warnings in regard to "Do's and Don't's," etc. Tests of different reading abilities, both formal and informal, are suggested. Check lists, guide sheets, and work sheets for practice work are provided for the use of students. Certainly with such a wide variety of helps reading teachers and subject teachers should be able to assess needs, spark interest, and provide abundant practice in developing the necessary reading skills in their respective areas of teaching.

The references in this book are worthy of mention, both as to quality and number. While the authors devote their content to practical helps devoid of esoteric discourse on theory and research, the many references which they provide give evidence of their broad acquaintance with literature in the entire field of reading. Carefully selected references in the text and in bibliographies at ends of chapters provide enrichment reading for teachers and others who wish to have more background about topics treated in the book. Particularly noteworthy is the fact that in cases in which research is available, a practical help is reinforced by referring to a study which has indicated that the procedure suggested in the how-to-do-it help is the one that was found to be most effective.

In Chapter 1 the authors state, "We have been trailblazers in preparing this book." Indeed they have been trailblazers, and as such they deserve our high commendation.

*Nila Banton Smith*

# PREFACE

This is a very practical book. The techniques and procedures offered can be put to work to improve reading in every class. Others have used them over a period of time with good results. Many of these procedures were developed or adapted for various disciplines at the University of Chicago Laboratory School. Obviously, adjustments are needed for different students, teachers, subjects, and situations.

We believe this book is unique. We know of no other in which classroom teachers share their "success secrets" for upgrading reading in the regular work of their courses—with important gains for students in their course work besides. The subject areas of these teachers cross the curriculum.

Since our focus is on the subject classroom, the book emphasizes the developmental and corrective aspects of reading instruction rather than the remedial. The efforts of each classroom teacher can be most helpful in working with a severely retarded reader. These efforts should, of course, be supplemented with the help of a trained remedial reading teacher.

This paperback edition of *Improving Reading in Every Class* is an abridgment of a hardcover edition. We have chosen representative sections for this edition. We refer you to the complete edition for many additional resources.

Without question, *Improving Reading in Every Class* would not exist without the interest, efforts, and generous cooperation of certain members of the staff of the University of Chicago Laboratory School. Roy A. Larmee, former director, initiated a reading program which emphasized improving reading within the classroom, and Francis V. Lloyd, Willard J. Congreve, and Carl Rinne, former administrators, assumed strong leadership roles in extending the program. The effort continues with the support of Philip W. Jackson and Margaret Fallers. Donald O. Conway, assistant director, and Betty Hollander, school examiner, have quietly supported the program in important ways.

The internship program in training of reading consultants at the University of Chicago was instrumental in providing help to the Laboratory School's reading consultant by furnishing the school with capable "assistant" reading consultants. A number of them assisted with the development of specific procedures and materials offered in the book; introductory statements explain their contributions. Contributions were also made by the following, who are now reading specialists in public school systems, independent schools, and colleges: James Bigaj, Patricia Cookis, Camille Haegert, Joyce Ann Harris, Kathleen Jongsma, Eileen E. Liette, Margaret McAuliffe, Leitha Paulsen, and Dorothy Burr Woods.

We express most earnest thanks, too, to three uncomplaining, capable, and conscientious secretaries—Ethel Naros of the Laboratory School, who typed some of the original projects for use within the school, and Nicky Barry and Helen Wensley of Hofstra University, who typed, proofread, copied, collated, and did many of the thankless things essential in preparing a manuscript for the publisher. Samuel Weintraub of the reading staff of Indiana University was most helpful with his patient answers to questions.

The contributions of certain members of the faculty of the University of Chicago Laboratory School speak for themselves throughout the book. These dedicated teachers, striving to solve the reading problems of their students, have made reading instruction an integral part of daily learning experiences. Francis V. Lloyd had this to say about the program under his directorship: "Reading is taught in English class, over the cookstove in home economics, even on the basketball court."

The passing of time, the availability of a reading consultant's services to teachers, and the turnover of faculty may alter and increase or decrease the span of the reading effort at the Laboratory School. Some of the faculty members who were most active in the projects reported here are now in other schools. There is no claim to having attained and maintained a model schoolwide reading program.

Through its reading program the Laboratory School has perhaps made its own contribution. A concept sprang to fuller life there and is reflected in this book—the concept of teachers in many different subjects being concerned with reading and skillful at improving it within their classrooms. The descriptions and results presented in this book are proof of the possibilities and in some classrooms the reality of fusing the teaching of reading skills with the teaching of course content.

*E.L.T.*
*H.A.R.*

# HOW TO USE THIS BOOK

If you are reading this book, you may be a reading specialist, a classroom teacher, a curriculum specialist, a language arts consultant, a school administrator, or a college student planning to specialize in one of these fields.

*If you are a reading or language arts specialist,* you will find here approaches and devices that have worked for classroom teachers in helping their students read more competently in a number of subject areas. These subjects span the curriculum from English through physical education. You will find a great many sound insights about improving reading in chapters that talk right to the classroom teacher, free from reading "pedagese." And you will find the enthusiastic comments of subject teachers who talk about their reading effort: "It saves us time." "Students achieve better in the course all year."

*If you are a classroom teacher,* you will find procedures and devices for upgrading reading specific enough to try out in your classroom tomorrow. You do not need to be a reading expert. You will find suggestive answers to these questions: How can you improve the vocabularies of your students through their regular course work? How can you turn on reading power simply by the way you make a reading assignment? How can you equip your students with better techniques for mastering a textbook chapter? How can you give them more of the reading expertise they need for problem solving? You will find suggestions shared with you by classroom teachers who have used them successfully for coping with the range in reading achievement within their class groups and for getting manageable books into the hands of not-so-able readers. And you will find possible ways of reaching the unreached reader, of catching up his enthusiasm for reading—for life.

*If you are a curriculum specialist,* you already have a special interest in the weighty reading demands that different school courses—and different content within those courses—place upon the student reader, and in the varied skills and techniques students must acquire in order to meet these demands. You are probably interested in the specific and often sequential steps essential for developing these competencies. In this book you will meet subject teachers who do not ask, "Isn't reading the English teacher's job?" or "Why didn't students learn to read on a lower level?" These teachers are well aware that in their courses the student may meet patterns of writing never before encountered: the laboratory manual in science, the practice book in typewriting, a theorem in geometry, a recipe and a sewing pattern in homemaking, a musical example in music theory. They realize that perhaps the student in all his years of school has had no opportunity to learn to read these patterns of writing previously. You may wish to share with others the view of these teachers that the classroom is the ideal place to develop the specialized techniques which are essential for—and sometimes unique to—the particular subjects they teach.

*If you are a school administrator,* you will be interested in the possible procedures offered here for helping *all* the readers of a school, not only the retarded but the average and the highly gifted, to approach their maximum potential. And you may wish to examine the procedures and instructional materials that grew out of a reading program aimed at involving teachers in subject classrooms.

*If you are a student* planning to enter one of the fields above, you will welcome insights into the heavy demands in reading which school courses impose upon students. You may be interested in the ideal of a schoolwide developmental and corrective program aimed at meeting those demands. And you will welcome the practical how-to-do-its and why-do-its for helping students read more competently.

### Development of the Procedures and Materials

We would like to share with you in the rest of this chapter how this book grew and why it has its present contents. We would like to suggest how to use the book to fullest advantage for you and for students. And we would like to offer you a subject-area index, which should help you find your way through the book and increase its utility.

Our book is in part a sharing of reading projects developed in the University of Chicago Laboratory School. There subject teachers and their reading consultant, working together, developed some new procedures and adapted known procedures to "new" disciplines. The units "just grew" (as they would in any school) whenever there were needs and teacher recognition of those needs. Such projects, gathered into a book, form an "anthology." They are not intended to constitute a complete or balanced reading program. Some Laboratory School teachers, like teachers elsewhere, observed in their students a special need for close, study reading. Hence you will find an emphasis on teaching reading for information rather than for appreciation. Many Laboratory School teachers were already highly skilled in sparking a fervor for reading, in relating reading to exciting discoveries, and in developing more reflective, more critical readers. Teachers sought the consultant's help in giving students workaday skills for getting certain study-type reading jobs done. A science teacher observed a real need to improve textbook reading. He asked the consultant to develop the comprehensive guidesheets for students which appear in Chapter 3. The home economics teacher sought out the consultant, and together they prepared materials for helping students handle the reading of recipes and sewing patterns. Projects developed in areas where there were not already sufficient existing resources to meet the need at hand. We trust that this filling in of gaps will be a contribution of our book and not a limitation. It is our special hope that the reader will find our "anthology" suggestive and will increase and multiply such materials, extending them into more and more disciplines.

Teachers of English and social studies, for whom there are no separate sections, will find many helps for developing reading competency within their classrooms in Chapters 2 through 5, and elsewhere throughout the book. They may wish to consult an intensely practical guidebook—one suggestive for all levels—*Reading, Grades 7, 8, and 9, A Teacher's Guide to Curriculum Planning* (Curriculum Bulletin No. 11. New York City: Board of Education of the City of New York, 1957). Social studies teachers have an excellent guide available in *Guiding the Social Studies Reading of High School Students* by Ralph C. Preston, J. Wesley Schneyer, and Franc J. Thyng (Bulletin 34. Washington, D.C.: National Council for the Social Studies, 1963).

Someone asked us, "Can you bottle up procedures that have worked successfully in one school and uncork them in another?" Surely the experiences of others cannot offer routines to be followed explicitly in other classroom situations. But successful experiences can offer ideas and guidelines for trial and adaptation. Obviously the strategies, procedures, and materials in this book need to be adapted for older or younger students, for more capable or less capable readers, for particular situations, for a diversity of purposes. Since the Laboratory School has a somewhat select student enrollment academically, adjustments in difficulty and complexity will often be called for. We trust that the reader will make use of the aids most appropriate for each immediate situation, adjusting them as needed.

You will find throughout the book printed materials addressed directly to students and intended to be placed in their hands. For your convenience, student materials have been marked with an asterisk (*) preceding the page number so that they can be quickly distinguished from materials directed to the instructor. You may wish to use these student materials as they now appear if their difficulty is appropriate for your students. You may wish to adjust or simplify them. You have our permission to do this. Or they may serve admirably as a source of ideas for your own class instruction. Certainly extensive printed materials are not a must in giving reading guidance.

The materials specifically directed towards students may be reproduced in xeroxed, dittoed, or printed form for classroom use after obtaining written permission from Allyn and Bacon. If they contain material that other publishers have permitted us to reproduce, it will be necessary for you to obtain reproduction permission from the publisher involved.

When printed materials for students are supplied in this book, they are intended only to supplement and reinforce instruction by the classroom teacher. We cannot emphasize too strongly that printed guidelines in themselves are not likely to effect much of a change in students' habits.

We have applied known insights about reading to the needs of students across a variety of disciplines—indeed, this is a major thrust of our book. We have tried to express these insights in writing free from reading "pedagese," to channel to classroom teachers "know-how" which has too often been the peculiar property of reading experts, and so to help reduce the lag between the lore of reading specialists and the practices that prevail day after day in many classrooms.

## THE SUBJECT-AREA INDEX

The index at the back of this book is like other indexes in directing you to a great variety of topics. The subject-area index that follows is different. The headings for this index, as you will note, are various subject areas—English, mathematics, industrial arts, and others. It is placed at the front of the book to guide you to all the parts of the book that offer help in improving reading in those particular subjects.

You will ordinarily find under each subject heading—mathematics, for example—three sub-headings. The first is *Specific Helps for Mathematics*. Here you will find specialized strategies for mathematics or general approaches that have been tailored for mathematics. The second sub-heading is *General Aids for Improving Reading*. The index entries under this will guide you to broad background information on how to improve reading which you may relate to mathematics. You will sometimes find a third sub-heading, *See Also*. Here you are referred to approaches and techniques which happen to be discussed in this book under other subject-area headings but which are highly applicable or suggestive for mathematics.

This subject-area index should be useful, for example, to a teacher looking for general aids for improving vocabulary in addition to any specific vocabulary techniques offered in the chapter devoted to his subject and to any related material discussed under another subject. The reading specialist, the language arts consultant, the curriculum consultant, or the college student preparing to specialize in one of these fields may wish to peruse the book from cover to cover. On occasions, however, they should find the subject-area index useful in meeting specific needs of their own and/or in giving specific assistance to subject matter teachers who are ready to help students fuse reading skills and course content.

We have been trailblazers in preparing this book. It took courage for the writers, whose field is reading, to venture into areas like typewriting, music theory, and industrial arts. We offer you this book in the hope that you will find our efforts useful, and, with the addition of your own creative efforts, that you will devise other still more effective ways of helping students reach their fullest potential in reading.

## SUBJECT-AREA INDEX

### ENGLISH AND READING

*See Also*

Classroom libraries to turn on readers, 248–250, 291–299, 301–307
Directions, improving reading of, 228–236, 251–261

## MUSIC

*Specific Helps for These Classes*

Musical examples, how to develop skill in reading, 275–280
Vocabulary of music, study techniques for, 281–284

*General Aids for Improving Reading*

Vocabulary, 9–44
Comprehension, 45–134—especially 69–104, how to upgrade the comprehension of a textbook chapter
Flexibility in rate of reading, 135–165
Problem solving and topic development, 167–204

*See Also*

Classroom libraries to turn on readers, 248–250, 291–299, 301–307

## LIBRARY

*Specific Helps for Librarians*

Matching materials to students' reading levels, librarians can lead in, 285–290
Problem solving and topic development, reading skills for, 167–204

*General Aids for Improving Reading*

Vocabulary, 9–44
Comprehension, 45–134—especially 124–133, how to provide materials that match the reading "reach" of students
Flexibility in rate of reading, 135–165

*See Also*

Classroom libraries to turn on readers, 248–250, 291–299, 301–307

## ART

*Specific Helps for These Classes*

Improving reading and selling reading, 291–299

*General Aids for Improving Reading*

Vocabulary, 9–44
Comprehension, 45–134
Flexibility in rate of reading, 135–165
Problem solving and topic development, 167–204

*See Also*

Directions, how to upgrade reading, 228–236, 251–261

## PHYSICAL EDUCATION

*Specific Helps*

How coaches can get boys "hooked on books," 301–307

# 2

# BUILDING VOCABULARY SKILLS

If you are a subject matter teacher—in contrast to a specialist in the field of reading—you may have little or no idea of what an important contribution you can make to the reading improvement of your students. And in no area of reading are you likely to be more effective than in vocabulary.

You can give your students self-help techniques for improving their vocabularies through your regular class instruction—and you need not necessarily take additional class time. You can help them master new terms for their immediate course work and advance in reading ability as well. Special expertise in reading instruction is not needed.

We offer in *A Program for Vocabulary Development* some answers to the following questions—practical enough, we hope, to try out in your classroom tomorrow.*

* The writers appreciate the contributions of the following teachers: science—Lestina Colby, Jerry Ferguson, A. J. Ferrantino, and Jan Housinger; social studies—Margaret Fallers, Dave Stameshkin, and Joel Surgal; mathematics—Paul Moulton and Richard Muelder; home economics—Dorothy Szymkowicz; typewriting—Faynelle Haehn; industrial arts—Herbert Pearson; foreign languages—Milton Finstein and Ruth Schroth; English—Sharon Calk, Sharon Feiman, Ruth Kaplan, Francis V. Lloyd, Darlene McCampbell, James McCampbell, Eunice McGuire, Emily Meyer, Carolyn Parker, Sue Phillips, Hope Rhinestine, Richard Scott, and Edith Tatel. Richard Scott was generous with his counsel when he served as chairman of the Laboratory School English Department. Special thanks go to his teachers for their lively ideas. Mr. Scott served as consultant for this section.

1. What are some beliefs and principles to guide vocabulary growth?
2. What are some characteristics of the "ideal product" of the vocabulary work in your class?
3. How can you gain insights into each student's attainments and needs?
4. What are some ways to motivate vocabulary improvement?
5. How can you invest new words with meaning through experience?
6. How can you encourage vocabulary growth through reading?
7. How can you remove vocabulary obstacles before students read an assignment?
8. How can students make full use of context to get at word meanings?
9. How can your students get vocabulary increments through frequently recurring word parts?
10. How can a teacher work with word origins to fix meanings in mind and stir interest?
11. What dictionary skills are vital to students if they are to continue their vocabulary growth independently?
12. What are some other ways to promote long-term, do-it-yourself vocabulary growth?
13. What is the "hidden consensus" of experts on the steps a student should take when he meets a new word?

## A PROGRAM FOR VOCABULARY DEVELOPMENT
### Rationale

**General Principles**

The following principles, among others, can guide vocabulary growth in every classroom.

1. Direct and indirect experience: trips, TV, films, film strips, models can enlarge the vocabularies of students and invest new words with meaning.

2. Wide reading accounts for much of a competent reader's growth in vocabulary. Through reading he spends countless hours in a world of words. He meets new words repeatedly in similar and different settings, often with some increment of meaning at each encounter, and gradually incorporates them into his vocabulary. All teachers can encourage students to read widely and to approach their

reading with a conscious effort to notice unfamiliar words and to make selected ones their own.

3. Direct attention to vocabulary should supplement vocabulary growth through reading. Major research studies indicate that consistent, systematic instruction results in considerably greater gains than would accrue in "ordinary" reading without this help; that planned instruction is definitely superior to a casual or incidental approach; and that wide reading alone, especially with less able readers, does not insure an adequate vocabulary.

4. Teachers can remove obstacles from the reading road by first searching through assignments for "stopper" words and then pre-teaching these to students.

5. Context clues can be a *major* self-help technique for students in learning the vocabularies of many of their subjects. They should be given all possible help in learning to use context clues as an aid in getting at the meanings of unknown words.

6. A knowledge of frequently recurring prefixes, suffixes, and roots, when used in conjunction with context revelation, can give students another important self-help technique to help them unlock the meanings of words.

7. Today's graduates are facing a new word explosion. Words not yet coined, emerging as a result of new social, political, and scientific upheavals, will confront students after they leave our classrooms. Habitual procedures that will keep vocabulary growing after high school and college are therefore indispensable.

## Characteristics of the "Ideal Graduate"

The "ideal product" of the vocabulary program has acquired many interests, attitudes, and competencies.

1. He demonstrates a lasting enthusiasm for helping himself move toward the development of a superior vocabulary.

2. He views vocabulary growth as a lifetime process, for which he alone can assume the major responsibility.

3. He has been introduced to the "help-yourself" methods which are appropriate for his personal vocabulary development, has practiced using these methods, and has built them permanently into his reading and listening habits. These procedures will serve as lifetime tools for enriching his word resources.

4. He attends to unfamiliar words encountered during his varied reading and, through conscious effort and the use of procedures effective for him, makes selected words permanently his own.

5. *Most importantly,* he evidences a delight in the precision, the power, and the artistry of words. "What is needed for all learning is interest. A sense of excitement about words, a sense of wonder, and a feeling of pleasure—these are the essential ingredients in vocabulary development."*

This ideal will remain beyond the reach of many students. Accordingly, in almost all classrooms, teachers will want to give constant and abundant help with vocabulary development.

## DIAGNOSING VOCABULARY STRENGTHS AND WEAKNESSES

How can you diagnose the attainments and needs of your students in vocabulary? As one teacher comments, "As a general rule, it's unsound to teach a poor reader *gargantuan* if he doesn't know *gigantic.*"

### Standardized Tests

Your school may already have a vocabulary score on record for each of your students. However, you may want the results of more recent and more thoroughgoing testing, or you may want insights into their vocabulary strength in your subject area. The following tests offer some information about a student's vocabulary power in a number of subject fields. It should be noted, however, that most standardized vocabulary tests have certain shortcomings: (1) they measure the student's mastery of a word in terms of a single meaning, and (2) they test his word power in an artificial situation since the words are out of context.

1. *Diagnostic Reading Tests, Section 1: Vocabulary* (Mountain Home, North Carolina: The Committee on Diagnostic Reading Tests, Revised, 1967), intended for grades 7–13; two forms, A and B. This test yields scores in four subject fields: English,

* Lee C. Deighton, *Vocabulary Development in the Classroom* (New York: Teachers College Press, Teachers College, Columbia University, 1959), p. 59.

mathematics, science, and social studies. There are 200 words in all, 50 in each area. The complete test takes 40 minutes; each subject area, 10 minutes. Since the time limit may "contaminate" the vocabulary score with a speed factor, for some students and in certain circumstances it may be advisable to impose no time limit. Of course, disregarding the time limit converts the test into an informal diagnostic device as the norming of the test included the time factor.

2. *Michigan Vocabulary Profile Test* (New York: Harcourt, Brace, and World, Inc., 1939), intended for grades 9–16; two forms, Am and Bm. This is not a recent test but it yields a profile chart of vocabulary scores in eight fields of knowledge—a feature often highly motivating to students. The eight areas are: human relations, commerce, government, physical sciences, biological sciences, mathematics, fine arts, and sports. There are 240 words in all, 30 in each area. No time limit is imposed. The complete test may require more than one hour. Teachers sometimes fit it into a class period by omitting two sections that are less relevant.

## Informal Tests

Teachers can use quick teacher-made tests to assess mastery of the specific vocabulary techniques or the particular words which concern them at the moment. Such a test is described in the section, "Vocabulary Development Through Context Clues."

## Student Self-Appraisals

Using the brief questions below, a teacher can learn in just minutes something about each student's insights into vocabulary development and his habitual procedures:

For technical vocabulary in various subjects:

1. What do you do when you're studying an assignment and meet an important new technical term?

For general vocabulary:

1. Have you ever considered that learning new words may actually be fun and a lifelong activity?

2. Have you ever consciously done anything to build your vocabulary? If so, what methods have you used?

3. Are you using any of these methods at the present time? If so, which?

4. What do you do when you're reading and meet a word you don't know?

## MOTIVATING VOCABULARY STUDY

Daily in subject classrooms, teachers want students to learn the language of their subjects—to master the specialized vocabulary. Tips for motivating students, suggestive for various subjects, are offered in Chapter 11 in the section "Some Study Techniques for the Vocabulary of Music."

### The Teacher's Vocabulary

A science teacher whose own command of words never fails to impress his classes tells how he "turns on" his students. "As my classes read their first selection of the year, Fabre's poetic nature study, 'The Courtship of the Scorpion,' someone is sure to misinterpret a word. I pull out my *own* list of words and the definitions *I* looked up when I read the selection for the first time. I let the class know that I, too, am a dedicated word collector. They realize the joy they missed in this poetic passage because they didn't attend to a word."

### Vocabulary and Job Ability

A teacher might light the fire by reporting ideas adapted from an article, "Do You Know How Words Can Make You Rich?"*

Did you know that big vocabularies and big paychecks seem to go right along together—and the same goes for small ones? More than any other factor studied, vocabulary appears to be related to money making success. That's the finding of the Human Engineering Laboratory, a research institute which for years explored the factors that lead to getting ahead on the job.

They discovered that foremen had better vocabularies than the men who worked under them. Section managers had better vocabularies than foremen. And so on—up the ladder

* Morton Winthrop, "Do You Know How Words Can Make You Rich?" *This Week,* XXIX (October 30, 1960), pp. 6–7.

on the job—all the way to top executives, who had the top vocabulary scores.

Now school teachers in their classrooms did not conduct this study. It was conducted by down-to-earth, hardheaded investigators searching by scientific methods for the secrets of success.

Of course, we can't leap to the conclusion that a superior vocabulary guarantees promotions and a blue chip bank account. Good work habits, initiative, responsibility and, of course, on-the-job "know-how" must go along with it.

Why does vocabulary contribute to on-the-job success? We *do our thinking* with words—*get our thoughts inside the minds of others* with words—*influence others* with words. Napoleon did not mention his armies when he said, "We rule men with words."

## A Good Vocabulary Pays Off at School

A teacher might stir interest with thoughts like these:

What do you recite with at school? What do you write reports with? What goes down to represent you on your tests and exams? Words. When you turn on more word power, there's a plus for you on all of these.

College entrance personnel have found vocabulary to be one of the best predictors of college success. At the University of Illinois, entering freshmen were given a 29-word vocabulary test. Their scores proved useful in predicting how they would fare for the next four years.

## Word Power—a Personal Plus

This personal appeal may be persuasive:

Your word power is always with you in your personal life. Did you ever try to get very far away from your vocabulary?

Riches in your word bank are one form of social security. What happens to self-confidence if you're talking to someone and the words you want won't come, if you falter and can't finish your thought? Most of us have had that experience. And we've all envied the person who makes words behave, who has words right there when he wants them.

## CAN EXPERIENCE ENRICH VOCABULARIES?

Experience, both direct and indirect, can enlarge vocabularies and richly invest new words with meaning. Students who appear not to be school oriented and make little or no effort to learn printed words will learn words when they live them. A field trip for junior high school students to an airport can give meaning to *beacon, ramp, dispatcher,* and *meteorologist.* The visit of a social studies class to a settlement house can give depth of meaning to *deprived area, immigrant, tenement, slum clearance,* and *social reform* (even for those who already reside in depressed areas). A tour of a dairy can give a science class an in depth understanding of *pasteurization.* Of course, appropriate instruction on the new terms before and after such field trips is desirable to refine and strengthen the vocabulary learnings.

A high school or junior college teacher takes a shortcut in teaching *nautilus* when someone brings a many-chambered, spiral nautilus to class—in teaching *iridescence* when the class is shown iridescent sequins with their rainbow of shifting colors—in teaching *diaphanous* when students see a China silk scarf. A film on man against the desert gives the word *mirage* meaning, as words *about* words can seldom do.

Teachers often enlist the recall of student experience, encouraging sharing through discussion. With *charisma,* a teacher asks: "Do you know someone who has this quality? Have you felt the power of it?"

Teachers frequently bring words close to the lives of teenagers. Sophomore teachers enjoy teaching *sophomoric* to sophomores. *Irrepressible* is more easily retained when students consider, "What student in our class is irrepressible?"

## DOES WIDE READING INCREASE VOCABULARY?

Teachers sometimes ask, "How can I teach vocabulary to students who desperately need such help but are not very school oriented? It seems as though they couldn't care less about new words." They also ask, "How can I help a classroom full of students improve in vocabulary when their vocabulary levels vary so greatly?"

Most of a capable reader's vocabulary growth has accrued to him from his reading. He has met new words repeatedly in a variety of context settings. Often a little bit of meaning brushes off each time, and gradually the word becomes a part of his vocabulary.

A teacher remarks, "When I find students who are deficient in vocabulary, I look first of all to their *reading habits.* If they are reluctant readers I try to start them reading—a magazine, if nothing else, at first. I consider this more important, as the initial step, than anything else." Teachers of subjects other than English often have a far better opportunity to do this than the English teacher. The student's interest in the subject—science, industrial arts, homemaking—and his special liking for the teacher are the "handles."

A young English teacher whose students came from homes in which there were few books used to feel twinges of guilt whenever she took time from the prescribed course to win her "I won't read-ers" to a new view of what is between the covers of a book. She stocked a corner of the classroom with fasten-your-seat-belt fiction, displayed bright magazines on a table, and brought *today* into the classroom through the daily paper. There was browsing time on Friday, a day when students were likely to have weekend hours ahead for reading. Soon some of her unreached boys were reaching for their first book—then for another—and another. An experienced teacher reassured her that she was surrounding nonverbal students with powerful verbal stimuli, influencing some of them to spend many hours in the world of words—working indirectly toward gains in vocabulary and comprehension. The older teacher pointed out that an artificial vocabulary push in class may add a few points to the student's scores on the next standardized test, but if he continues to view books as enemies, a year later those gains may be lost.

Of course the word resources of capable readers, too, will be enriched through many hours spent in reading. Top vocabularies usually go hand in hand with far-ranging reading interests.

## PRE-TEACHING "STOPPER" WORDS

Teachers can take down the obstacle course *before* students read an assignment by pre-teaching selected words. They can search through the passage beforehand, pulling out "stopper" words, and then introduce these in context. As the chill is taken off the reading, discouraged readers may take heart.

A mathematics teacher removes the obstacle of *coefficient* as his class comes to a passage on simplifying algebraic equations. A home economics teacher removes the word-block *colander* just before her class prepares spaghetti. An English teacher brings the *Odyssey* within reach by pre-teaching about the *imperturbable* Odysseus, the *stratagem* of the Wooden Horse, and the like—at the same time catching interest through intriguing snatches of plot. A social studies teacher clarifies *indulgence* before students read about the Reformation.

The following guidelines for pre-teaching "stopper" words are likely to prove useful.

1. *Introduce the new word in context.* Lead the student to make full use of any context clues that are present to help him reason out the meaning.

2. *Spotlight an easy root word within a long, forbidding word.* An extremely important service to students is simply to make them aware that long, forbidding words have parts. Left alone, some students meet a word like *imperturbable,* glance at the first few letters, and skip over the rest. It often helps to spotlight an easy root word within a difficult word. With *commutative* a mathematics teacher might ask, "What does commuter mean?" With *exponential* he might ask, "Can you see a part you already know—one you've used many times?" A social studies teacher might direct attention to *total* in *totalitarian.* A science teacher might focus on the building blocks in *interplanetary.* A music teacher might point out *recite* in *recitative.*

Students will "see into" words quickly if, as they analyze words, you mark off root words on the board with vertical lines or highlight them with colored chalk.

extra|territorial|ity

inter**change**able

Now the words may be revealed as not so difficult after all.

3. *Reduce difficult polysyllables to easy-to-manage syllables.* As numerous teachers will substantiate, many students slide over new and difficult words. How easily do you think you could learn *platy-helminthes* for biology class if you had not examined it syllable by syllable all the way to the end? For practical purposes some students seem unaware that syllables exist. They tend to glance at the first few letters of a difficult word and give up. Middles and endings of words thus receive only slight attention.

But a long, formidable polysyllable can be put on the board with its syllables marked off, with accent marks, and perhaps its phonetic spelling. The class or group can pronounce the word part by part with the teacher. They soon see that a word which looks as if it "comes by the yard" can be reduced to a number of short, easy-to-manage, pronounceable parts.

plat′ ē hel min′ thēz

4. *Call attention to accented syllables.* It will often be helpful to mark the stressed syllables with conspicuous accent marks. As you lead students through the pronunciation of a word you can sharpen their awareness of the force of these marks.

As teachers follow guidelines 2–4, their students are learning to divide and conquer—to examine a difficult word for meaningful parts and to work through it syllable by syllable all the way to the end. As teachers direct attention to parts, they are helping to change the habits of those who did not really focus on new and difficult words.

5. *Tap teen experience.* Some new words or terms are made to order for tapping the experiences of teenagers. For example, a topic extremely close to many young people is buying their first car. A type-writing teacher relates new words to this experience as she pre-teaches the terms *promissory note* and *collateral loan.*

6. *Pre-teach multi-meaning terms.* Some words take off one meaning and put on another as the student walks across the doorsill of a classroom! *Law* does so as he walks into science class, *between* and *point* as he walks into geometry, *role* as he walks into social studies. Such words often call for pre-teaching since the student often reacts, "That's easy; I already know that word!" Often he will not know the precise meaning called for in the particular content field.

7. *Help insure retention.* Students should be helped to use all possible senses and strategies in attempting to retain new words. A mathematics teacher observes, "As a key word is pre-taught, my students see the word, say it, hear it, repeat it, and review it. Then in class sessions that follow, I use the word again and again—avoiding the use of pronouns."

8. *Help students move toward independence.* On all levels teachers will want to give appropriate assistance with difficult terms. Sometimes teachers list crucial words as part of a study guide for a reading assignment, giving the page and line where these can be located in the context. They may pre-teach the most difficult words while the others become the special responsibility of the students. Sometimes the students themselves help select the "stoppers" by culling the assignment. How to equip students with long term self-help methods for dealing with difficult words is the subject matter of the rest of this section of the chapter.


## VOCABULARY DEVELOPMENT THROUGH
## CONTEXT CLUES

Many students do not rely on the language surrounding unknown words as sources of definition and clarification. Teachers often observe a tendency to read right on past unfamiliar words. Alerting students to the intelligent use of context encourages them to habitually hunt for meaning instead of passing new words by without a try.

Few students, teachers report, make full use of context revelation. Few are aware of the existence of specific types of context clues. Almost without exception students need help in judging when they can rely on context clues and when they should turn to the dictionary to find or verify the meaning. Extremes are noted. Some students consult the dictionary as a *first* resort with no regard for context. Others rely almost entirely on context and rarely turn to the dictionary. Obviously neither procedure is desirable for any student in all situations.

Since context clues can be a tremendous help to students in learning the vocabularies of almost all their subjects, a strong case can be built for giving students all the help possible in the use of context clues.

1. Context is *the* major tool for students in vocabulary expansion. We can accelerate this growth by sharpening up their context clue power.

2. Students whose habit it was to half glance at important new words can be led to zero in on these.

3. The judicious use of context clues is a long step toward independence in vocabulary growth—a real aid for getting at the meanings of new words during countless hours of reading in high school, in college, and in years thereafter. Used along with other vocabulary methods, it is a lifelong "help yourself" tool.

4. Over-stress on reaching for the dictionary can be a deterrent to both vocabulary development and reading enjoyment. As one teacher comments, "It is neither possible nor desirable for students to deal meticulously with every new word. If we push students to look up *every* one, they may react negatively. One of my seventh graders was reading a circus story in which interest centered on the plot. When asked to underscore the words he did not know, he marked thirty-two!"

"I suggested, 'Come with the story for a conference.' Together we examined the words, deciding in each case whether context revealed enough meaning or whether the dictionary was called for. In the sentence 'The circus wagon was red, gold, and magenta,' the student had underlined *magenta*. Now he said, 'Oh, I guess it's a color.' In a fast-moving story in which interest centers on plot, 'a color' was probably enough. Painstakingly looking up all thirty-two words might have brought the reaction, 'I hate the dictionary! I hate words! I hate English! I hate reading!' "

### Teacher-Made Tests

Using a passage students will actually be reading in the course, teachers can test students' facility with context clues by asking them to make an intelligent guess at the meaning of underlined words. They might also be asked to explain how they arrived at each guess. The words selected should be important to the meaning of the passage, should be unknown, should have fairly revealing context, and should exemplify various kinds of context clues.

One teacher says, "I probe orally using our day-to-day course materials, observing the needs of individuals as they try out their powers of clue detection. Then I ask, 'What led you to the meaning?' Students experience delight when they work out meanings successfully."

McCullough suggests a discussion following the test as a learning exercise. As the students talk over their answers, they are alerted to clues they missed. They become aware that there are clues of various types and conclude that context, while often limited in its revelation, frequently gives some suggestion of the meaning. Those who answered correctly are asked to share the ways they arrived at their guesses. How-to-do-it suggestions from one student to another, McCullough comments, are sometimes more helpful than those of their teachers.* A test with ten parts, one for each type of clue explained on the following pages, will, as McCullough suggests, reveal students' strengths and weaknesses in the various clues.

### Different Types of Context Clues

Students gain in context clue power when they become aware of specific types of clues, and of the mental processes involved as they use all the hints at hand to reason out a strange word's meaning.†

* Constance McCullough, "The Recognition of Context Clues in Reading," *Elementary English Review,* XXII (January, 1945), p. 4.

† Most of the types of context clues explained on these pages were first identified by Constance McCullough in the reference just cited, pp. 1–5. Others have arrived at somewhat different classifications of contextual aids. The reader may wish to refer to W. S. Ames's broad classification in "The Development of a Classification Scheme of Contextual Aids" in *Reading Research Quarterly,* II (Fall, 1966), pp. 57–82. Roger J. Quealy summarizes the classification schemes of major investigators in "Senior High School Students' Use of Contextual Aids in Reading" in *Reading Research Quarterly,* IV (Summer, 1969), pp. 512–533.

The following explanations of ten types of clues, with examples, should be suggestive to teachers as they clarify these clues for students and as they develop their own practice materials *using words of appropriate difficulty*. Much overlap will be noted; clues rarely exist in "pure" form.

In explanations and discussions, students can be led to construe context broadly—to view the page as a "reader's paradise of clues"—to avail themselves of clues that exist in punctuation, word order, idea order, form classes of words, sentence structure, paragraph organization—to draw on all their experience with the language as an aid in discovering meaning.

1. *Direct explanation clue.* Sometimes a writer realizes full well that he has used a word the reader may not know. In that case he may give an outright explanation of its meaning to assist his reader. He may tuck in a clear, unmistakable explanation.

> An *ecologist,* a scientist who specializes in the relationship between living things and their environment, is likely to have authoritative opinions on the problem of pollution vs. man's survival.

The use of the appositive construction (with the word *or* and commas, or with the commas alone) reveals to you beyond doubt that *ecologist* means an *expert on environmental relationships*. There can be no question as to the meaning. Here is one type of context clue that will not let students down.

In the next example, *that is* indicates that the phrase it introduces is an explanation of the word *laser*.

> The development of the *laser*—that is, a device which concentrates high energies from radiation into a narrow, sharply focused beam of light—has practical applications in medicine.

Direct explanation clues are less obvious when they are not clearly marked by the appositive or the *that is* construction and when they are placed at a distance from the new word with a number of words intervening.

> Regardless of his many reforms and arguments, the senator was forced into a *cul-de-sac* by his opponents. What can a man —eminent senator or petty official—do to retrieve himself from a blind alley?*

---

* Adapted from *Learning to Learn,* edited by Donald E. P. Smith (New York: Harcourt, Brace and World, Inc., 1961), p. 129.

2. *Experience clue.* Often our own life experience—or our indirect experience through reading and other learning channels—provides the clue. We know from our own experience how people and things act or react in a given situation. Consequently, we can approximate the meaning.

> Those first bewildering weeks, the thoughts of a college freshman drift back to high school where he was "in," knew everyone, and felt at home. A feeling of *nostalgia* sweeps over him.

3. *Mood or tone clue.* The author sets a mood—gay, somber, frightening, eerie—or the mood might be ironic. The meaning of the unknown word must harmonize.

> The *lugubrious* wails of the gypsies matched the dreary whistling of the wind in the all-but-deserted cemetery.*

Since *lugubrious* reflects the mood of the sentence, the meanings *mournful, gloomy, dismal* readily come to mind.

4. *Explanation through example.* Sometimes, when a writer uses a new word the reader finds nearby an example that helps illuminate the meaning.

> In the course of man's evolutionary development, certain organs have *atrophied.* The appendix, for example, has wasted away from disuse.

> President Lincoln's attitude toward the fallen South was *magnanimous*—"with malice toward none, with charity for all."

> An occasional *respite* during a long evening of study is desirable. Jim often took a short "breather" between chapters or between assignments.

5. *Summary clue.* Here the new word appears to wrap up a whole situation. We can reason out the meaning because we know the circumstances the new word is summing up. Sometimes the situation that the word sums up is found before the unknown word.

> Pete Littlefield, our center, stands six feet three in his stocking feet and weighs an even 210 pounds. His teammates call him "Runt," an obvious *misnomer.*†

And sometimes the situation the word sums up is found after the unknown word.

* Ruth Strang, Constance M. McCullough, and Arthur E. Traxler, *The Improvement of Reading,* 4th Ed. (New York: McGraw-Hill Book Company, 1967), p. 231.

† Example contributed by Edna Hoffman Evans, Phoenix College, Phoenix, Arizona.

The greatest effect of the Renaissance on education was a growing *secularization* in schools. More school curricula focused on man's expression of feelings toward the world in which he lived. Schools became interested in teaching about affairs of the world, not only about religious matters.

6. *Synonym or restatement clue.* Here the reader infers the meaning of an unknown word because it repeats an idea expressed in known words nearby.

Flooded with spotlights—the focus of all attention—the newly chosen Miss Teen Age America began her year-long reign. She was the *cynosure* of all eyes for the rest of the evening.

Students quickly suggest "the focus of attention," "the center of interest." They should be cautioned, though, that synonyms are seldom exact equivalents and that when precision among shades of meaning is essential they will need to consult a comprehensive dictionary. The example below, from history rather than from contemporary experience, might send some students to the dictionary.

Louis XIV kept his nobles constantly involved in rites and ceremonies and certain ways of doing things. Such *protocol* permitted him to keep them busily engaged while he ruled France without interference.

7. *Comparison or contrast clue.* When a comparison clue is present the reader gets some suggestion of a new word's meaning because he compares it with a word or an idea already known to him.

Bob excels in football, photography, and music, and his older brother is even more *versatile*.

When a contrast clue is present the meaning of the new word is obviously in contrast to an idea expressed in familiar words nearby.

When the light brightens, the pupils of the eyes contract; when it grows darker, they *dilate*.

They were as different as day and night. While he was a lively conversationalist, with something to say on every subject, she was reserved and *taciturn*.

8. *Familiar expression or language experience clue.* This clue requires a familiarity with common language patterns—expressions heard every day. In the example below, the reader, already well-

acquainted with the expression *take upon himself,* has a strong clue to the meaning of *appropriate.*

> He took it upon himself—yes, he *appropriated* the entire responsibility for raising money for the class gift.

9. *Words in a series clue.* When reading words in a series, the reader can often get some idea of the meaning of a strange word because he knows the general nature of the items being enumerated. In this example he easily gathers that codlins and biffins are different types of apples.

> The apples had their places all around the room. They were *codlins,* and golden pippins, brown russets and scarlet crabs, *biffins,* nonpareils and queanings, big green bakers, pearmains, and red streaks.*

10. *Inference clue.* Listings of the various types of context clues often include the inference clue. Of course this type overlaps all the foregoing types except direct explanation.

> Sharon told her roommate, "I'm through with blind dates forever. This one topped all! What a dull evening! I was bored every minute. The conversation was absolutely *vapid!"*

## Making Full Use of Context Clues

Many teachers prefer to work with context entirely in natural situations, as students encounter new words in reading. Others prefer working initially with sentences contrived to "sell" the use of clues and to exemplify each type of clue. In either case the habitual examination of context, not the recall of specific types of clues or the drawing of fine distinctions in classification, is of course the objective.

Some teachers use practice exercises with sentences like those in the preceding explanations (but on an appropriate level) to help students become avid clue hunters. They share the following insights or draw them from students. "How have you become acquainted with a great number of the words you know? Not by looking them up or by word study under the supervision of a teacher, but through your own varied reading—meeting words again and again in clue-providing context. You are likely to make leaps and bounds in vocabulary

---

* Louise C. Seibert and Lester G. Crocker, *Skills and Techniques for Learning French* (New York: Harper & Row, Publishers, 1958), p. 52.

growth by sharpening your context clue power. Before you reach for the dictionary, first ask yourself, 'What clues does context give?' "

Students then read silently the first sentence of the exercise. They are given a few moments to make an intelligent guess at the meaning of the stimulus word. Students who already know the meaning are asked not to raise their hands. Volunteers offer their guesses, which are checked or verified by the dictionary definition. Students who arrived at correct meanings share their "success secrets." There is some discussion of specific types of clues.

## Less Direct Clues

In the initial practice work obvious, clear-cut clues can drive home the value of exploring context. In later practices the students should work with less direct clues. Through realistic examples they can be led to conclude that context often gives hints of the meaning of a particular word, but that it seldom clarifies the whole of any meaning and almost never reveals the nuance of meaning. Much practice in natural situations should follow as the teacher directs attention to new words encountered in day-to-day reading.

## Missing or Misleading Clues

Students should become aware that context sometimes has nothing at all to reveal concerning a word's meaning and may, on occasion, even mislead the reader.

In the following example the context is a real fooler. Both the context of the word *noisome* and also its structure suggest the meaning *noisy.* Upon consulting his dictionary, however, the student discovers the meanings *offensive, distasteful, disgusting, ill-smelling.* The word *noisome,* he finds to his surprise, is derived from the same root as *annoy* and is in no way related to *noise.*

> Corbett had lived in this *noisome* slum for only two weeks, but he would never forget the screaming voices, the angry quarreling, and the fighting that made slum life so unbearable.*

As one teacher sums it up for her classes, "Context is a magnificent help—*but beware!*"

* Richard Corbin, Marguerite Blough, and Howard Vander Beek, *Guide to Modern English for Grade Nine* (Chicago: Scott, Foresman and Company, 1960), p. 98.

## Attacking Assignment Words

In an article, "Clues in Context, a Reading Project on New Words," Sarah Roody tells how she worked with context clues in Rachel Carson's *The Sea Around Us.**

> One day the class walked in to find some difficult words on the board. "Why are all those words on the board?" demanded William suspiciously. "Do we have to learn them?"
>
> "If I were a gambler," replied the teacher, "I would bet a nickel that you will know most of them without even looking them up." William was doubtful—one of the words was *ichthyologist.*
>
> The teacher passed out a passage from *The Sea Around Us.* Written after each word on the board was the page and line where students could find it in context. The class was asked, "Read the paragraph containing *cachalot,* and try to guess what the word means." William made the discovery: "The book says 'the cachalot or sperm whale.' The definition is right here. You don't even have to guess."
>
> Next the students practiced the synonym-type clue, one of the easiest types to guess. Then they proceeded to example clues. In one passage Rachel Carson uses the word *paradox* in referring to the fact that fragile creatures like the jelly fish and glass sponge are not crushed by the immense pressure of the deep water where they live. With a little assistance in the form of additional examples, most of the students were able to deduce that a paradox is "strange but true" or "it's impossible but it's a fact." Then the class turned to the dictionary for a more exact definition.
>
> They moved on to more subtle clues—the use of one's own experience or knowledge, for example. Sea Scouts came closer than others to reasoning out the meaning of the word *sessile* in the context, "Barnacles are sessile." As the mental processes became more difficult, fewer students demonstrated ability to use the clues.

## Words in Context Versus Words in Isolation

Students are sometimes sent to the dictionary with a list of words in isolation. They are to record and learn each word's meaning—but *which* of the meanings? Send a student to look up *abstract* in isolation, and he may be bewildered by a dozen different meanings.

Context is a tremendous help to students as they try to learn to

* Sarah I. Roody, "Clues in Context, A Reading Project on New Words," *Clearing House,* XXVII (April, 1953), pp. 478–480.

use their new words. A sadder but wiser English teacher reports this classic how-*not*-to-do-it. She sent a class of seniors to the dictionary to look up the meanings of words on a list. They were to write original sentences for each. One of the words was *trite*. A student came up with, "The miners who have gone on strike are trite." He defended his answer staunchly, "I can prove it; the dictionary says it means *over-worked!*" Another volunteered, "The bread is trite." "Why, it's right here—it says that *trite* means *stale.*" One other offered, "The shoes I am wearing are trite." "But it says right here it means *worn out.*" What an immense help introducing the word in this contextual setting would have been: "Busy as a bee is a *trite* expression."

### Teachers Strive for a Delicate Balance

Teachers want students to become aware as they work with context clues that context often supplies at least a hint of a word's meaning. On the other hand, they hope that students will realize that the meaning they arrive at through context is almost always tentative or general, that the dictionary is indispensable, and that it should often be consulted to verify or reject a context guess that may have significance for further reading. Teachers will wish to emphasize frequently and strongly that no single context revelation will illuminate all the future uses of the word which the student will meet. They should help students recognize that many situations require the utmost precision of meaning, while for others a general meaning is quite sufficient. Teachers should guide students in making the distinction.

Students may wish to arrive at their own guidelines for using context clues. In the chart on page 29 are a few that have already been generated.

Many students, as we have already noted, tend to slide over unfamiliar words. Teacher help with context clues should accustom the student, by himself, to zero in on important new words, to make the context reveal what meaning he can, and then to reach for the dictionary when appropriate. When he does this frequently and deliberately he has added an important self-help skill to his repertory of vocabulary methods. And he may well be more intent upon comprehending the meaning of the passage than he was in the past.

## VOCABULARY BUILDING THROUGH WORD PARTS

When we give students a working stock of common word parts and teach them to use these in combination with context revelation,

## DO'S AND DON'T'S FOR USING CONTEXT

| *Do Rely on Context Clues* | *Don't Rely on Context Clues*<br>*(Turn to Your Dictionary)* |
|---|---|
| 1. When you have an "unmissable clue"—a direct explanation. | 1. When you require a precise meaning. It almost always takes the dictionary to pin the meaning down. |
| 2. When you have highly revealing clues and the meaning you arrive at definitely "clicks" with the rest of the passage. | 2. When the word is a key word, one crucial to your understanding, and full comprehension is important to you. |
| 3. When, in view of your purpose for reading the selection, you need only a general sense of the meaning. | 3. When the clues suggest several possibilities—the meaning might be one of several—and you must know which. |
| | 4. When you don't know the nearby words. |
| | 5. When you have encountered the word a number of times, realize that it is a common, useful one which you will meet again, and want to master it thoroughly for future reading. |

we are helping them acquire numbers of new words. And we are giving many of them a self-help technique through structural analysis —an added means of increasing their word power in an ongoing, life-long process.

The social studies instructor who teaches the prefix *anti-* when, for example, his students meet *antilabor,* gives them a key which may help them later to unlock *antitrust, antiwar, antislavery,* and *anti-imperialist.* The mathematics teacher who teaches each number prefix at the time it is needed gives his students a hold on *pentagon, hexagon, octagon,* etc.—as well as on hosts of their mathematical and scientific relatives.

Nowhere do Greek and Latin word parts pay off more richly than in science. *Micro-* pays dividends in easier learning of *microscope, microbe, microorganism, micrometer. Hydro-* is a jackpot word part which pays off as the student meets *dehydrate, hydrosphere, hydrographic, hydraulics,* and many others. As one science teacher points out, "Breaking down words makes the vocabulary of science less awesome. The ability to find word parts and use them for meaning is a major vocabulary tool in science."

### Looking for Meaning-Revealing Parts

We have mentioned spotlighting an easy root word within a long, forbidding word as one device for pre-teaching "stopper" words. Of course, the goal for each student is on-his-own competence in analyzing words. Much can be accomplished as needs become apparent in genuine reading situations—each word takes just minutes.

With *unconstitutionality* you might inquire "Can you see a word within a word—a root word—in this word?" printing it on the chalkboard. With guidance students should mentally snip off the *un-* and the *-al* and the *-ity,* discovering *constitution*—and then note the effect of the prefixes and suffixes. When they mentally reassemble the parts and return to the context, they are likely to have arrived at the meaning.

As other words come up as hurdles in the regular readings of the course, these can go onto the chalkboard: "Can you strip this one down to its root word?" Words like these invite this strategy: *reunification, incombustible, proclamation, reactivation, consolidate, mismanagement.* Of course, independence in word analysis calls for familiarity with frequently recurring prefixes and suffixes. As you guide each analysis you are adding to your students' working-stock of these parts. "Can you take this apart—break it into its building-blocks?" (*micrometeoroid, supersonic, altimeter, sharecropping, transcontinental, calorimeter, chemotherapy*) As already noted, students will see into words more quickly if as they work with them, you mark off the root word on the board with diagonal lines or highlight it with colored chalk.

de/humid/ify

unalienable

With each and every analysis you are building a working knowledge of common affixes—their identities, their meanings, their variations in meaning.

### Discovering the Meanings of Parts

Teachers often use an inductive approach through which students discover the meaning of Greek or Latin parts as strange words confront them in their reading. When word analysis serves an immediate purpose, students seem to view it as practical and productive.

When science students come upon the suffix *-lysis* in words like *analysis, hydrolysis,* and *electrolysis,* the stage is set for learning a high-yield word part. They discover, "All those words mean breaking up in some way." Now they have a "handle" on hosts of other words, among them *photolysis, thermolysis, autolysis,* and *biolysis.*

A class group was puzzled when they encountered *microcosm* in a poem. The teacher asked, "Is there a part you know?" The students quickly noticed *micro-.* "How many other words do you know that have that part?" As *microscope, microbe, microfilm,* and *microgroove* went up on the board, the meaning was apparent. An examination of the part *-cosm* suggested *cosmos* to a few. Someone suggested, "Does the word mean something like a very small universe?" With the aid of the context and some assistance from the teacher, the group arrived at the meaning "a world in miniature." Then the teacher helped the students refine and extend the meaning.

The word *graphology* confronted a class of students. Students suggested other words containing *graph,* and these were splashed all over the board. *Logy* was easy—they had met it before. Someone quickly offered, "Oh, it's the study of writing!" Only a check with the dictionary, however, clarified the fact that it is a study of handwriting, particularly in regard to an expression of the writer's character.

### "Selling" Word Part Study

Carefully selected Greek and Latin word parts provide a tool, useful especially for average and superior students, for learning words in families.

A teacher might give a sales talk: "How would you like a method to help you to learn new words not one by one but several— even dozens—at a time. You may find this method your best vocabulary 'bargain.' Did you ever try to lift an unabridged dictionary—all 750,000 words? More than half of all those words entered our language from Greek and Latin. And, luckily, they did not come singly—they came in families. Learn one 'ancestor,' and you'll have a tool to help you learn an entire family of related English words.

"What a step ahead you make when you learn *poly.* You'll find 95 of its relatives in one small high school dictionary. What a giant stride you make when you learn *pseudo.* An unabridged dictionary actually lists 800 derivatives. Though many of those are technical, some are extremely useful."

Students then proceed to do a "bargain counter" practice exercise in which they learn a dozen or so words "for the price of one." The Latin prefix *mal-,* for example, meaning bad, evil, ill, or wrong, lends itself to such an exercise. It provides students with a "handle" to take hold of *maltreat, malodorous, malpractice, malefactor, malevolent, malcontent, malediction, malign, malfeasance,* and numbers of other derivatives.

### Limitations in Using Word Parts

From the first, students should experience the limitations of word part guessing. They should be prepared for deceptive combinations of letters—combinations that are foolers because they resemble a Greek or Latin word element but are completely unrelated. The letters m-a-l, which resemble the Latin prefix *mal-,* are sometimes foolers.

---

#### DO WORD PARTS ALWAYS HELP YOU?

---

Sorry, the answer is no, not always. Some words, for example, contain the letters m-a-l when they do not form a Latin word part.

There's nothing necessarily *bad,* for example, about
          A *mallet*
          A *mallard* duck
          A *male*
          A chocolate *malt*
In these words there is no connection at all between the letters m-a-l and the Latin word part, *mal-,* meaning bad, wrong, or evil.

*A possible check:* Ask yourself, "Does the meaning of the Greek or Latin word part 'click' with the rest of the sentence?"

---

### WORD ORIGINS FIX MEANINGS AND STIR INTEREST

#### Work with Derivations Promotes Vocabulary Growth

Working with the origins of selected words, incidentally as students meet them in reading or in planned activities, has definite values.

1. A not-to-be-forgotten story, the origin of *gerrymander* (below), for example, may fix the meaning of a new word in mind more firmly than anything else.

2. The story of a word may give the word new overtones for the student and enrich and extend its meaning.

3. The romance and excitement of word origins can create word enthusiasts.

Social studies students are likely to remember *gerrymander* when they hear the lively story of Governor Gerry of Massachusetts during whose term an election district was drawn with fantastic boundaries—it was shaped like a salamander!

In any subject classroom, referring to a word's derivation may be helpful in strengthening retention of the meaning. A science student who learns the derivation of *equinox* (from the Latin *equi-*, equal, and *nox,* night) may more easily remember the meaning as the time when the day is equal to the night. A social studies student who learns the origin of *Pantheon* (from the Greek *pan-,* all, and *theos,* god) may more readily remember that this temple served the ancient Romans as a place to worship all their gods. A mathematics teacher might reinforce the meaning of *radius* through its Latin origin, the spoke of a wheel.

Vivid and lasting mental pictures are likely to be formed when students discover

—that *berserk* comes from an Old Norse warrior (or *berserkr*) who in battle worked himself into a frenzy, howled, and bit his shield.

—that *gamut* originally referred to the lowest note of the musical scale. If we "run the *gamut* of emotions," literally we run up or down the scale in a graded series of all the tones.

—that *pandemonium* means wild confusion, as if *all* Hell's *demons* were let loose at once.

—that *flamboyant* is derived from an Old French word meaning flame.

—that *nonplus* derives from two Latin words meaning *not* and *more.* When you're nonplussed, you're at a loss as to what to say, think, or do, literally reduced to a state of "no-more-ness."

## DICTIONARY COMPETENCY IS A MUST

The "ideal product" of the dictionary program runs to the dictionary for the fun of learning about a word. When a student learns to make appropriate and frequent use of the dictionary, he is strengthening his power to keep his vocabulary growing independently for life. To add the dictionary to his vocabulary tool kit, these two strategies (among others) are essential:

1. The student cannot become independent in vocabulary development unless he knows how to use the pronunciation key in a dictionary. If he cannot pronounce a difficult word, he learns it only vaguely, it easily slips from his memory, and he cannot use it in speaking. He must learn how to translate pronunciation symbols into a spoken word—sounding out each syllable, then blending the syllables together into a whole word with the correct accent(s). Students require considerably more practice than one might realize for full mastery of the pronunciation key.

2. The dictionary usually confronts the student with his choice of what may be a confusing array of definitions. He should not select the first one his eyes fall upon, nor the easiest, nor the shortest—but the one that is the best fit in the context setting. In one English class where the students were reading about the *providence* of an animal for its young, every student selected the religious meaning of the word *providence*. A major obstacle blocks vocabulary expansion when, year after year, the student does not habitually find in his dictionary the meaning appropriate for the context in which he finds a word. Practice tied in with genuine reading situations is ideal.

Obviously, thoroughgoing instruction in these competencies is desirable during the elementary and junior high school years. Students in high school and college find it difficult to admit that they don't know how to use the dictionary; instruction in using the dictionary must then become subtle in approach.

### Simplified Dictionaries Meet Individual Needs

To span the broad range in reading achievement among students on each grade level, a supply of multilevel dictionaries within each classroom is of utmost importance. College students who need help with dictionary skills may really learn how to use a dictionary if they practice on one intended for high school students. One teacher asks, "What is gained if a seventh grader who is deficient in vocabulary looks up *inexorable* and finds the meaning given as *relentless?*" Such a student will need guidance in consulting a student dictionary within his reach.

Simplified dictionaries intended for students are listed below.

*Harcourt Brace School Dictionary*—grades 4–8 (Harcourt, Brace & World, Inc., 1968).

*The Holt Intermediate Dictionary*—grades 4–9 (Holt, Rinehart and Winston, 1966).

*Thorndike-Barnhart Junior Dictionary*—grades 5–6 (Scott, Foresman, 1965).

*Thorndike-Barnhart Advanced Junior Dictionary*—grades 7–8 (Scott, Foresman, 1965).

*Thorndike-Barnhart High School Dictionary*—grades 9–12 (Scott, Foresman, 1965).

*Webster's New Practical Dictionary*—grades 4–8 (American Book Co., 1969).

*Webster's New Students Dictionary*—grades 9–12 (American Book Co., 1969).

*Webster's New World Dictionary,* Elementary Edition—grades 4–8 (Macmillan, 1966).

*Webster's New World Dictionary*—grades 9–12 (Macmillan, 1962).

## Dictionary Skills Important for Vocabulary Growth

Systematic and complete coverage of the skills below, among others, will benefit students.

### Selecting Meaning

1. Using guide words to find entries quickly.
2. Selecting the meaning which is the "best fit" in the light of the context.
   (a) Recognizing the order in which meanings are arranged in the classroom dictionary and in other dictionaries.
   (b) Using the information about parts of speech as an aid in selecting the appropriate meaning.
3. Learning that words have different meanings in different subject fields. Making use of such subject labels as med., biol., bot., chem., astron., geol., etc.

### Figuring Out Pronunciation

1. Understanding the pronunciation key of any dictionary, though the keys vary from one to another.
2. Understanding how the dictionary respells words to show pronunciation.
3. Knowing how syllable division is indicated.
4. Understanding accent—primary and secondary.
5. Blending the syllables together into a word with the correct accent.

### Interpreting the Information on Derivation

1. Knowing its location in the dictionary.
2. Appreciating the interest, adventure, romance, and humor to be found within the brackets in the entry for a word.

3. Understanding the meanings of the abbreviations which convey information about derivation.

4. Being aware of the value of studying derivations as an aid in retaining word meanings.

### Using the Information About Synonyms

1. Knowing that the notation SYN in a word entry signals an enumeration and explanation of the word's synonyms.

2. Valuing and utilizing the explanation of the nuances of meaning among those synonyms.

## OTHER WAYS TO PROMOTE LONG-TERM, DO-IT-YOURSELF VOCABULARY GROWTH

A vocabulary program should help students become self-motivated, self-guided, and self-directed—knowing ways to help themselves and assuming responsibility for their own progress. Otherwise they are left dependent, and their vocabulary growth will probably come to a standstill after high school and college.

Daily in subject classrooms, teachers want students to develop on-their-own competence in mastering the technical terms of the course. Tips suggestive for various subjects are offered in Chapter 11 in the section "Some Study Techniques for the Vocabulary of Music." The mastery techniques suggested in the Recite and Review Steps of PQ4R in Chapter 3 are also highly applicable to vocabulary learning.

A personal word collection can be one means of encouraging students in any classroom to take the responsibility for their own vocabulary growth. One teacher reports, "My students lament, 'We look up new words but don't retain them.' I find this the right moment to launch word-collecting. It catches on if I suggest some starting words and make a big deal of the collections."

### Teachers Motivate Voluntary Word Collections

Students often respond to an enthusiastic sendoff.

"Here's a method that can help you lift your vocabulary well above its present level. It's tailored to your individual preferences. *You* decide the words you want and need. You collect them when time is available and not when it isn't. You set your own goals and move toward them as you wish. The method insures not merely the initial learning but also permanent retention.

"You'll find that your added word power will bring rewards in reading. Suppose you're reading this sentence and don't know

*anomaly:* 'Mark Twain's philosophical despair was only an *anomaly.*'
What happens to your comprehension? In this case, context doesn't
help. You may lose the meaning of the entire passage. What happens
to your speed? From perhaps 300 words per minute it may drop to no
words per minute. You may go backward and forward several times
as you struggle, through rereading, to wrest the meaning from the
total context. Each new word you learn helps take down the obstacle
course.

"The method is wide reading, meeting new words, and collecting certain ones with a personal word collection. Small word slips
(or a note pad) go with you everywhere in a convenient kit. When
you find a word that's worth collecting, you record it and the sentence
in which you found it used. When convenient, look up and record the
meaning that fits the context. Record the pronunciation, if it gives you
trouble—and the derivation, if it helps you remember the meaning.

*FIGURE 2–1. Vocabulary slip.*

"Where can you find your new words? [The class suggests textbooks, words teachers and students use in class, personal reading,
conversation, TV.] Listen to TV with a pencil and your vocabulary
slips, and highly articulate national leaders and news analysts will
supply words for your vocabulary.

"You may not want to break your train of thought to fill out a
slip when reading. In that case, check the word in the margin, or make
a light pencil dot, and record it later. If you don't own the book, use
a bookmark to write down words you plan to work on later, together
with their page locations.

"A dictionary should be near whenever you read or study. When you meet a new word important to you, try to reason out its meaning from context clues nearby or from familiar parts. If you can't do so, or if you feel you need a more exact meaning, use your dictionary.

[Students urgently need criteria for word selection.] "You can't collect all the unfamiliar words you meet. Which ones are worth collecting? [Class discusses.] Not *syzygy,* which you'll probably never see again, but words you've seen several times and think you'll see again—words with an aura of familiarity—perhaps *taciturn, paragon, scintillate.* [Possibilities on an easier level: *nocturnal, agile, affluent.*] Chances are you'll run across these a dozen, two dozen— perhaps countless times more.

"A word is likely to be worth collecting if you find it in live contexts—on TV, or in a book, magazine, or newspaper intended for the general reader. You can be confident this word should be deposited in your word bank.

"Collect 'personal words,' words of special usefulness to you. Is it probable that some of you will need different words from those others need? [Class discusses.] Future nurses, businessmen, astronauts need extensive, and quite different collections of technical words.

"You'll want to be on the lookout for vivid, expressive words— with your own conversation and writing in mind. These need not be ostentatious.

"Through your word collection you literally write your own vocabulary builder along the lines of your own interests, uncluttered with words of no use to you.

"You'll probably want to strengthen your technical vocabularies in different subjects—science, social studies, math, business or technical courses, music—by collecting highly important 'official' terms. A simple word slip like the accompanying one, adapted for social studies, is a handy means of recording special terms for special study.

---

**SOCIAL STUDIES VOCABULARY TERM**

Term _____

Definition _____

_____

---

*FIGURE 2–2. Example of content area vocabulary slip.*

"You actually have two vocabularies—your *passive* or recognition vocabulary and your *active* vocabulary. Your active vocabulary consists of those words you have on call for speaking and writing. Your passive vocabulary includes less familiar words, which you recognize and understand in reading but do not use in your own expression. Your passive vocabulary is considerably larger than your active—perhaps three or four times as large. It's far more difficult to add a word to your active vocabulary than merely to recognize it when you meet it in reading.

"But if you wish to improve your fluency in expressing yourself, certain words—those you'll really have occasion to use—will be worth this extra effort. You'll want to practice the correct use of these words by making up sentences of your own. Take care, though, when you make up the sentences. It may be extremely difficult to use a new word with precision. An appropriate dictionary or synonym book offers clear model sentences. In the dictionary entry, the notation SYN guides you to the nuance of meaning. Your teacher, too, is here to guide you.

"You may wish to set a quota—one, two, three, even five new words each day. [Class discusses this.] Or you may prefer to collect your words whenever your reading lends itself. Or you may set a weekly or monthly quota.

"Students say, 'I've collected a hundred words but I can't remember them.' It takes reviews to clinch retention. You've already printed the word at the top of the word slip. Now play solitaire. Cover the meaning and look at the word. Ask yourself the meaning. Try to express it not by rote but with full appreciation of its content. Or test yourself the other way by covering the word and looking at the meaning. Ask yourself the word. Separate the word slips into an I-do-know and an I-don't-know pile.*

"You can put new words on instant call with powerful retention techniques. For long retention, you can use triple-strength learning. If you learn words with your eyes alone, you're using just one-third of your possible learning channels. Why not employ all-out learning— visual, auditory, and kinesthetic?

1. Use your eyes as you *see* and reread the word and definition.
2. *Say* the word—aloud or in a whisper. This is powerful reinforcement.
3. Strengthen learning with your ears as you *hear* yourself say it.

---

* Ruth Strang, class lecture in course on teaching secondary school reading, University of Chicago, summer of 1965.

4. Add kinesthetic (muscular) learning as you *write* out the word and definition with, perhaps, an illustrative sentence.

"Do occasional self-testing. Pull ten or twenty word slips at random from your collection and play solitaire by writing meanings of words. Sometimes write sentences making use of the words.

"Above all, at first opportunity, *use* your new words in conversation or in writing. You might write an imaginative account of some happening and work into it as many new words as possible within reason.

"This is an odd-moment method. You can build vocabulary waiting for a friend, riding in a car, waiting for a bus. You can prop word slips on the sink and learn words while doing the dishes. Such spaced reviews give stronger reinforcement than a single too-long session. When you feel confident that a word is permanently yours, you retire the slip from pocketbook or pocket and file it alphabetically in a file box. Even your 'retired' words should be reviewed occasionally—perhaps every month or so.

"Again, your word kit goes with you everywhere—to class, to the library, to the bus stop, to your home for TV or personal reading. *You* are in the driver's seat. Choose the words that interest you— select your own convenient time—set your own goals."

### Students Set Their Own Goals

One teacher reports: "Collecting words is like keeping a diary— you start off with good intentions. Using the form below, my students make a voluntary commitment to themselves—a definite number of new words to be collected. They fill out two copies, one to keep and the other to hand in. Students who want me to 'nudge' them to keep their commitment add a note to this effect on my copy. I record in my record book each student's pledge and the requests for prodding. I 'nudge' the students through conferences and class announcements. Short-term goals are more effective than long-term with younger and less enterprising students. These students need their enthusiasm periodically rekindled. Frequently 'The Best Word of the Day' might be chosen, the honors going to a word exceptionally useful for other students."

# SET YOUR OWN GOALS FOR VOCABULARY

Only you can set goals for yourself! Only you can move toward them!

If you've decided to start a personal word collection, please set goals for yourself as suggested below. You'll want to consider your test score, your own judgment as to what you need, and any suggestions from your teacher.

The goals you set today are only tentative. You may wish to change them as you make progress. Your goals should be realistic. Planning more than you can possibly attain brings only disappointment.

Your teacher will confer with you about your goals.

| TO IMPROVE VOCABULARY: | PLANNED | FINISHED |
|---|---|---|
| 1. How many words do you plan to have in your personal word collection (and really learn) before the end of this month? | _____ | _____ |
| 2. Have you decided to collect a definite number of words each day? each week? If so, what is your quota? | _____ | _____ |
| 3. Some students prefer not to set a daily or weekly quota but to collect their new words whenever the reading they are doing at the moment lends itself. If this is your decision, indicate by checking here: _____ | | |

### Voluntary versus Compulsory Word Collections

Some teachers who once made collecting words compulsory have dropped the requirement. "When the work is assignment-like, many students react negatively. They abandon the method the minute the year ends and they escape the requirement."

Other teachers express a different view. They say, "We can't expect students to be enthusiastic until they try the method and see the results. Until the junior year in high school, when there's a strong vested interest in PSAT's ahead for some students, they need to be pushed. Word collecting should be required on at least one grade level. Some students appreciate the discipline."

Still other teachers suggest sectioning off a group deficient in vocabulary, dismissing the others to some other project, and giving word collecting a persuasive sendoff.

Whatever the conditions of collection, the word slips for many students are a constant stimulus to be alert for new words and to consciously attend to their meanings. These students are moving toward independence, recognizing that no one can give them a ready-made vocabulary, taking the responsibility for their own collecting, being responsible for retention.

## THE "HIDDEN CONSENSUS" ON VOCABULARY BUILDING

In the preceding discussion of vocabulary building we have considered a number of procedures for vocabulary improvement: using context clues; unlocking new words through Greek and Latin word parts; associating the current meaning with the derivation; consulting the dictionary; recording and reviewing words through a personal word collection. With which of these procedures should the student react when he meets an unfamiliar word? Under what circumstances? In what order?

According to Johnson, there is a "hidden consensus" among vocabulary experts on the strategy below.* The student may, on occasion, stop after Step 1 or Step 2 or Step 3. If examining context clues and word parts yields all the meaning he needs for his present purpose, he should proceed no further. Shaw makes the strategy in-

---

* Harry W. Johnson, "The Hidden Consensus in Vocabulary Development," in *Problems, Programs, and Projects in College-Adult Reading,* National Reading Conference, 11th Yearbook, eds. Emery Bliesmer and Ralph Staiger (Fort Worth, Texas: Christian University Press, 1962), pp. 105–112.

viting to students—makes them want to try it. The persuasive quoted phrasings (in the chart that follows) are his.*

---

### HOW TO CRACK DOWN ON A WORD

---

1. *Always search the context for clues first.*
   Through the context you may catch overtones of meaning. As you do so, you may develop a psychological "set" toward the word—you may "lay the first layer of cement for fixing the term in your vocabulary."

2. *Examine the word for familiar parts.*
   Take the word apart if you can. It may help to sound it out as best you can. Do you recognize any part? Guess all you can from any part you recognize. "When you *do* note a familiar section, your gain is usually great. You develop a strong 'set' toward the word."

3. *Reach for the dictionary,* if Steps 1 and 2 haven't yielded all the meaning you want.
   Now here is where your vocabulary can improve dramatically. Recall any guess you made from context. Now verify—or reject—your guess. This order of things gives you full benefit of the mental set you created by previously trying to deduce the meaning. "The more correct your guess proves to be, the more likely you are to remember the meaning. Nevertheless, if your guess is ridiculously wrong, you may find yourself less likely to forget the word than if you had not guessed at all."

   As you learn the meaning, try to associate the word with its derivation. The derivation is often rich with unforgettable associations.

4. *Record the word,* if it is one you wish to collect to work on further, on a word slip or in your vocabulary notebook.

---

## BIBLIOGRAPHY

Deighton, Lee C., *Vocabulary Development in the Classroom.* New York: Teachers College Press, Teachers College, Columbia University, 1959.

Gainsburg, Joseph C., *Advanced Skills in Reading,* Books 1, 2, and 3, Teacher's Annotated Edition. New York: The Macmillan Company, 1967.

Greene, Amsel, *Word Clues.* Evanston, Illinois: Harper & Row Publishers, Inc. 1962.

Herber, Harold L., *Teaching Reading in Content Areas.* Englewood Cliffs, New Jersey: Prentice-Hall, Inc., 1970.

Petty, Walter T., Curtis P. Herold, and Earline Stoll, *The State of Knowledge About the Teaching of Vocabulary.* Champaign, Illinois: National Council of Teachers of English, 1968.

Seibert, Louise C., and Lester G. Crocker, *Skills and Techniques for Reading French,* "Guessing Word Meanings by Inferences from the Context," pp. 44–56. New York: Harper & Row, Publishers, Inc., 1958.

Shaw, Philip B., *Effective Reading and Learning,* Chapters 5 and 6. New York: Thomas Y. Crowell Company, 1955.

* Philip B. Shaw, *Effective Reading and Learning* (New York: Thomas Y. Crowell Company, 1955), pp. 290–303.

Sherbourne, Julia F., *Toward Reading Comprehension,* pp. 44–74. Boston: D. C. Heath and Company, 1958.

Smith, Donald E. P., and others, *Learning to Learn,* "Vocabulary Development: Context Clues," pp. 125–131. New York: Harcourt, Brace and World, Inc., 1961.

Stauffer, Russell G., *Teaching Reading as a Thinking Process.* New York: Harper & Row, Publishers, 1969.

# 3

# IMPROVING COMPREHENSION

You can upgrade your students' reading comprehension in any classroom where reading is required. You can do this as you go about the everyday activities of the course—as you make the assignment, as you help students master a textbook chapter, as you formulate questions on their reading selections. These routine activities can be designed to turn on reading power.

You can improve the comprehension of your students by the way you make a reading assignment. In the first section of this chapter we suggest six ingredients for an assignment that should help poor readers crack a difficult passage and should enable capable readers to comprehend it even better.

Some powerful reading techniques for mastering a textbook chapter are brought together in the second section. You will find comprehensive guidesheets directly addressed to the student. These suggest procedures specific enough for him to try out as he works on a chapter tonight. Students who in the past have been making a "whip-through" of difficult reading should now have a clear conception of what the thorough study of a textbook chapter demands.

The everyday classroom activity of asking students questions on their reading selections can also turn on reading power. In the section "Questions to Develop Comprehension Skills," we offer a breakdown of comprehension into some component skills. There are also sample questions designed to help students acquire a more complete collection of mastered skills.

The unit "Finding the Key Thought" focuses on one specific and important aspect of comprehension. A rationale is presented for the teaching of key thought or main idea with emphasis on instructional procedures to be used by any classroom teacher.

Of course any progress in comprehension comes to a standstill when the reading is years beyond the student's reach or else so easy for him that he merely marks time. But is it possible and practical to guide the individual student to materials which are on his reading level? Can differentiated materials be supplied within a subject area classroom so that students can work at their own instructional levels? In the last section of this chapter, presented in interview form, classroom teachers of the University of Chicago Laboratory School offer some pragmatic answers to such questions.

## TURN ON READING POWER THROUGH ASSIGNMENTS

*How many reading assignments will you make in a teaching lifetime? Each one of these can help toward better reading.*

You can increase the reading power of your students by the way you make your assignments. You do not need formal training or experience in teaching reading in order to do this.

"Homework for tomorrow" is often the most unpopular announcement of the students' day. The assignment often appears to be "overtime work" with only one purpose—to deprive them of precious free time. It is viewed as the unfinished business that casts its gloom over activities more to their liking.*

However, the assignment can be designed to change resisting readers into enthusiastic readers. It can help discouraged students who "just can't get it" approach their reading with new hope and purpose, and it can enable some of them to handle an assignment that would otherwise have been beyond them.

An effective assignment can salvage countless working hours for students, hours which otherwise would have been wasted in clumsy, inefficient study. Students spend a total of thousands of hours over their books in the course of the school year; effective assignments can help insure that these hours will be spent productively.

Such assignments are not likely to be made at the end of the class

* Harry N. Rivlin, *Teaching Adolescents in Secondary School* (New York: Appleton-Century-Crofts, Inc., 1948), pp. 175–176.

period. Time and thought—both *well rewarded*—go into making an assignment that turns on reading power.

To help toward better reading, an assignment should have several of the components listed below. Not all of these, however, are called for in all assignments. Factors to be considered as an assignment is planned include the interest pull of the selection itself, the preparation the students already have in terms of past experience, the reading skills they have at their command, as well as other factors. The components are far from discrete—there will be much overlap.

1. Capturing interest.
2. Relating the reading to the students' past experience or providing a background of experience.
3. Helping the students have a purpose for their reading.
4. Helping them know *how* to read to accomplish their purpose.
5. Pre-teaching vocabulary and concepts which would otherwise block their understanding.
6. Providing, when appropriate and possible, reading materials on a suitable variety of levels.

We will be concerned here with only the first four components. We have already suggested methods of removing vocabulary roadblocks *before* the students read an assignment. And we will stress later the priceless benefits for students when it is possible to provide materials which span their reading levels. Here it is sufficient simply to point out that Components 5 and 6, too, are often vital if the assignment is to increase reading power.

## COMPONENT 1—CAPTURING INTEREST

An important component of a student's reading readiness for an assignment is interest caught up beforehand—anticipation—zest for the reading. When groups of poor readers were asked, "What makes reading easy?" they answered, "Interest."*

### Giving a Preview

In one English class Poe's "The Pit and the Pendulum" would have been beyond the reach of many students. The opening was

---

* Ruth Strang. Lecture to class in the teaching of secondary school reading, University of Chicago, summer of 1965.

obscure, the setting far away and long ago, the vocabulary beyond them. Was there a way of saving the story? The teacher decided to provide a thumbnail background on the Spanish Inquisition and its extreme cruelty to heretics, then to tell the class the first part of the story—with dramatic flourish.

> Once upon a time an innocent prisoner was condemned—for his religious beliefs—to die by the cruelest tortures of the Spanish Inquisition. After the strain of the long trial, the prisoner fainted. Black-robed figures carried him unconscious —down—down—down—far below the surface of the earth— into a dungeon where the mind of man had excelled itself in devising fiendish implements of torture. When he regained consciousness, he examined his surroundings. On the walls were grotesque carvings—figures of imps and demons—and on the ceiling was the figure of Father Time, pictured, as usual, with a scythe.
>
> Suddenly he observed something startling about the figure. Father Time's scythe was a pendulum—in motion! The sharp blade was descending inch by inch—and he lay, bound securely, *directly in its path*. Now the full meaning of his sentence was clear. He was to die by the cruelest of all tortures, mental torture—for his was to be the anguish of watching death approach by slow degrees.
>
> *Down—down—steadily—steadily down.* Hours passed —perhaps days—he had no way of knowing; and still the pendulum descended. Nearer and nearer—*still nearer and nearer*—until he could feel the rush of the swift blade as it swept past.
>
> Now the blade, as it passed, cut the folds of his garment. One more stroke *and it would reach his heart. Can the fiendish torturers be stopped? Will the prisoner be saved?* If you want to know what happens, read Poe's story, "The Pit and the Pendulum," for tomorrow.

Many of the students could now enjoy Poe's story. A special Poe collection had been trundled on a cart from the library into the class-room. Next day the teacher gave exciting previews of "The Tell-Tale Heart," "The Oblong Box," "Lygeia," and other short stories. These previews took just minutes. That night every Poe book in the class-room went home with a student.

Teachers can often capitalize on the fiction writer's (or the biography writer's) narrative hook, telling or reading a selection up to a point where the audience becomes captive. Similarly, they can search nonfiction assignments for attention-catching content to intrigue the students before they begin reading.

**Never a Dull Moment in Zinch Valley**

In one social studies class, an aura of mystery surrounds the first assignment.* Each student is handed a dittoed sheet, on it, only this:

A group of ten people enters and settles in Zinch Valley. Write an essay answering the following questions:

1. What are the immediate and long-range problems these people face?
2. What are the solutions these people bring to bear on both the immediate and the long-range problems?

That's all! No other information is provided.

But in class there will be an opportunity for questions. For the last 30 minutes of that period, and those 30 minutes only, the students may ask questions. They may have *all* the information they can pull out of their teacher in those 30 minutes.

Questions come pell-mell: "How did they arrive—by jet plane?" "Did they bring guns?" [The students soon begin to realize that they are dealing with very ancient times.] "Where did this happen?" [In the Middle East—Egypt through Mesopotamia.] "When?" [The late upper Paleolithic Age.] "What's the climate of the valley?" "Are there mountains?" "What are the resources?" "What can these people do?" "What do they bring with them in the way of equipment?" [The students are led to understand that clues to these answers have already been given—that the dating clue is the one to research further to discover what prehistoric man of that time and place could do.] "Are they male or female?" "Any children?" "How old?" [Answer: Five males, five females, nine between ages 10 and 45, a mother, a father, one small child.]

The session is lively and the time is up too soon. No more questions are permitted. The students are provoked and frustrated, yet challenged. Of course it is "permitted" to learn more about Zinch Valley through reading! Some of the students react, "I don't *need* all the answers from you—I can find out for myself." A list of readings spanning the reading levels within the class is provided which include everything from easy adventure stories of a Stone Age family menaced by cold, hunger, and wild beasts, to advanced scholarly discourses. What happened in Zinch Valley, the wellspring of some of man's first painting, sculpture, music, and complex social patterns, becomes a

* Edgar Bernstein, University of Chicago Laboratory School social studies teacher. Remarks to Ellen Lamar Thomas, August, 1970.

thrilling chapter in the upward march of human progress. (Years later, students return from college or from the armed forces and ask the teacher, "How's Zinch Valley?")

## COMPONENT 2—USING OR PROVIDING A BACKGROUND OF EXPERIENCE

According to a fundamental law of learning, students learn more easily when a new learning is related to some previous learning. Seemingly remote times and happenings can come close when these are made to touch the students' own experience.

### Long-Ago Lyrics Touch Today

The lyrics of the Sixteenth Century might seem to be moldering in the dust of four hundred years. But one teacher called them "the popular songs of the Sixteenth Century" and compared them with our popular songs.* The students listed the ten most popular songs of today—then ten old-timers that had survived for years. The question arose: "What makes a song survive?" The class reached these conclusions—universality of theme, simplicity, beauty of words, sweetness of tune. In every class "Stardust" headed the list of older songs still popular. Its theme of thwarted love, the students decided, was general enough to have wide appeal.

They compared "Who Is Sylvia?" and "Come Live With Me and Be My Love" with their own popular songs. The class studied the characteristics of the age which these earlier songs embodied, then studied our age as reflected in song.

The teacher reports: "They developed a feeling of 'hail-fellow-well-met' for the Sixteenth Century. Next day they dug into Shakespeare's sonnets and were eager to get to the drama to see what it shows about the people and ideas of an age so rich in both."

### Nonreading Resources Provide Background

It is often of immense benefit in strengthening the reading power of students for an assignment not only to relate the new learning to their previous experience but also to provide them with background experience. You have probably noticed in your own experience as a

---

* Carolyn Parker, "Shakespeare in Swing Time," *Clearing House,* XIII (April, 1939), pp. 462–463.

reader how much easier it is to grasp the content of a selection if the subject matter is at least slightly familiar. The background information you acquire, for example, simply from watching a TV program, often helps you take hold of a selection about a subject otherwise unfamiliar and read that selection with greater ease, interest, involvement, comprehension, and speed.

Paradoxically, the use of nonreading resources often leads to better reading. Poor readers can get crucial background learnings through excursions, television, films, film strips, projected pictures, records and tape recordings, models, interviews, and talks by classroom visitors. Then, with their backgrounds strengthened, they can often "stretch" and handle readings that would otherwise have been too difficult. Of course, teachers can maximize the dividends for students from these nonverbal experiences through preliminary discussion, through pre-teaching crucial terms and concepts, through assigning questions to be held in mind during the experience and answered, and through follow-up.

### Nonreading Experiences Help with Vocabulary

Difficult key terms and concepts can often be handled more easily after students have met them through a nonverbal experience. An industrial arts teacher might strengthen his students for reading about mass production through the film, *A Car Is Born.** As the students view it, it is as if they are *on* an assembly line watching. They see the line, "like a giant river," absorbing 15,000 parts and giving birth to a precision machine which rolls off the line and is driven away. Now terms like *mass production, conveyor belt, quality control, division of labor, high output techniques,* and *specialization,* which might otherwise have been lifeless letters on the printed page, come alive with meaning.

### Nonreading Experiences Step Up Comprehension

Social studies teachers have used the film *The Twisted Cross*† to make the comprehension of difficult readings on Hitler's Germany possible. The students have front seats at dramatic events from the conquest of Austria to the death of Hitler; they hear voices and meet

* *A Car Is Born,* a film available on free loan (Dearborn, Michigan: Ford Film Library).
† *The Twisted Cross* (Champaign, Illinois: Visual Aids, University of Illinois, NBC, 1956).

people from this period of the past. Students who are less verbally oriented have a chance to get important background learnings from sound and pictures *before* they learn from words. After this experience poor readers can sometimes crack a difficult reading assignment, and capable readers can comprehend it better.*

Slides offer another means of bringing difficult reading matter more nearly within reach. When rigorous readings on population genetics confronted a class in biology, slides on blood typings helped some of the under par readers to work their way through the chapter. These slides were viewable again and again, as often as needed. Slides on the cell theory, on the cell and its parts, on the life cycle of a plant, and on photosynthesis have helped students grasp other difficult chapters.

### Filmstrips Offer Special Opportunities

Filmstrips offer exceptional opportunities for strengthening reading—provided their captions are read aloud. Through the caption the student is exposed to the stimulus of the printed word, an advantage not offered by films, television, or recordings. Here is a superb opportunity for synchronizing *hearing* a new word with *seeing* it—a coordination conducive to acquiring vocabulary. A filmstrip on *Air Masses and Weather Fronts* can serve as an example.† The student's recognition or understanding of an unfamiliar key term, such as *cyclone* or *anticyclone,* is made possible by the heard word as the caption is read aloud. He has the opportunity to form a visual image of the printed term *cyclone,* to "photograph" it with his mind's eye, and he will be more likely to understand it when he meets it in the readings he will soon be doing on the subject of weather. Good readers in the class can be called on to read the captions aloud. Captions that present difficulties or call for special emphasis can be read aloud by the teacher.

### Nonreading Experiences Stimulate Wide Reading

Nonreading experiences can be utilized to bring about more extensive reading. One class became interested in the problem: "How

---

* Margaret Fallers and Joel Surgal, University of Chicago Laboratory School social studies teachers. Remarks to Thomas, April, 1970.

† *Understanding Weather and Climates Series* (Chicago: Society for Visual Education, Inc., 1966).

can we help the friendly organizations of our community? How can they help us?" Seeing and doing preceded reading. There were excursions to the Red Cross, International House, the YMCA, and other organizations. The students collected quantities of pamphlet materials. Their living experiences made them more active, more involved, and more extensive readers.*

## Lead-Ins Strengthen Background

Of course the use of excursions, films, and filmstrips is not always practical as a means of strengthening the background of students for an assignment. Some teachers write a clear, easy to grasp lead-in to the selection assigned, ditto it, and hand it to the students. This lead-in is a preview that can close gaps in background, provide a thumbnail sketch of the content, intrigue the student with promise of what is to come, raise interesting questions, and give direction to the reading. When high school seniors are confronted with an abstruse, college-level treatise by Adam Smith on his *laissez-faire* economic doctrines, such a lead-in helps them grapple with—and grasp—the assignment.

Similarly, a social studies teacher helps her students step right into historical fiction.

> We use the reading of fiction to enrich a period. In order to be objective, textbook writers often drain all the life out of a period. Fiction writers put it back in. To less competent readers, the plots and characters of *Uncle Tom's Cabin* may seem as confusing as Tolstoy's. So I wrote an easy preview, making the two plots perfectly clear, introducing the student to each of the many characters, and intriguing him with promise of dramatic situations. With this introduction, some of those less capable can work their way through a book that would have been unreadable. Some teachers give such introductions orally.†

## COMPONENT 3—HELPING STUDENTS HAVE A PURPOSE

Suppose a student goes into an assignment with no real purpose. He may have been told only, "Read the next ten pages." What is he to do? There are many different purposes for reading. Is he to try to

---

* Alice Flickinger, University of Chicago Laboratory School social studies teacher. Remarks to Thomas, September, 1970.

† Flickinger. Remarks to Thomas, September, 1970.

remember the details? read just for the general impression? learn the author's viewpoint? weigh his arguments? search out certain relevant information? read for pure enjoyment? If he is told only to "read the next ten pages," he may run his eyes aimlessly over the pages, taking in little—his purpose only to get the assignment over with and close his book as quickly as possible.

Contrast his reading with that of a second student who has a real, immediate, vital, clear-cut purpose. Now the reading has sharp focus. The student weighs everything he reads in terms of his purpose, and as he does so his reading becomes an active thinking process rather than a passive covering of words.* He understands what he is to know and be able to do when he completes the reading, and as he closes his book he is *far* more likely to know and be able to do it.

### Purpose-Questions Give Direction

Among the various ways teachers can encourage their students to read purposefully are: 1) providing them with purpose-questions, and 2) helping them formulate their own purpose-questions.

Of course, these two are not dichotomous—purpose-questions for a given assignment will often include both teacher-given and student-formulated questions. Nor does the student necessarily advance as he progresses through school from all teacher-given to all self-formulated questions. With appropriate guidance students should formulate questions close to their concerns and then read to find the answers, from their earliest years of schooling. And during their higher education—even in graduate school, if they attend—few of their professors will wish to abdicate their own responsibility for guiding their students' reading by raising important questions. At every level, instructors are likely to recognize a dual responsibility: to provide purpose-questions centered around the needs and concerns of their students, and to help students formulate their own important purpose-questions. Gradually, however, students should become more and more independent of teacher-given purposes and should read more and more often for important purposes of their own.

The following guidelines are suggestive for preparing purpose-questions.

*Purpose-Questions Should Guide Students to Not-to-Be-Missed Learnings*    As you sit at your desk starting to plan a reading assignment you may wish to ask, "What are the learnings the student simply

* Hazel Pope Howland, Lawrence L. Jarvie, and Leo F. Smith, *How to Read in Science and Technology* (New York: Harper & Brothers, 1943), p. 7.

must take away from this reading?" And then, "What purpose-question(s) will guide him unerringly to these?"

*Purpose-Questions Should Lead to Learnings Close to the Needs and Concerns of Students* You may wish to ask not only "What do I consider crucial?" but also "What do my students want to know?"

A science teacher about to teach the storage battery, Rivlin observes, might limit his preparation to listing facts he considers basic.* Or he might concentrate on this question, "If I were a seventeen-year-old, what would I *want* to know about storage batteries?" He might reflect, "What contact have my students had with storage batteries? What difficulties? What experiences in using them?" His mind will doubtless run to the portable batteries of their transistor radios and record players, their flashlights, and their automobiles.

Chances are, Rivlin comments, the students will get as much factual information about storage batteries when the topic is presented from their point of view as they will from a more formal presentation. And they will gain more than mere knowledge if their interest in science is aroused and if they learn that the science classroom is a place to ask questions and try to answer them.

*Pivotal Questions Should Be Broad Enough* Pivotal questions should be inclusive enough to require a grasp of the essential content yet specific enough so that the reader knows clearly what he is after. When questions demand *only* directly stated details, the student may skim the assignment for bits and pieces of information and lose out on broad understandings.

A social studies teacher might ask this question: "Where would you have preferred to live in ancient Greece—in Athens or in Sparta? Why?"† This is clearly a broad coverage question. The student must read to compare the schools, social institutions, government, architecture, religion, ideals and values, and so on, of these two ancient cities and then make his choice between prosperous, culturally brilliant, democratic Athens and austere, self-disciplined, totalitarian Sparta.

*Minor Questions May Also Be Essential* Minor questions may be indispensable in order to enable the student to handle the major, pivotal questions. Higher-level thinking usually rests solidly on a foundation of facts—the student cannot build a second story without a first story. As an instructor plans the guiding questions for an assignment, he will often need to formulate sub-questions to help the student

* Rivlin, *Teaching Adolescents in Secondary School*, p. 192.

† Association of Teachers of Social Studies of the City of New York, *Handbook for Social Studies Teaching* (New York: Holt, Rinehart and Winston, Inc., 1967), p. 58.

"pull out" the underlying facts. The student will then be better equipped to answer pivotal questions that require him to make inferences or draw conclusions based on these facts.

*A Study Guide May Prove Extremely Helpful*   A printed study guide that provides the students with both pivotal and, often, minor questions can be a most effective device for improving reading comprehension. In a major study with 1456 social studies students, the effectiveness of approaching reading with questions versus approaching it without questions was explored. Providing preliminary questions brought *decided* gains in comprehension.*

A well-formulated question asked *before* students read a selection can help develop comprehension. If the same question is not asked until *after* the students have completed the reading [unless they return to the passage and analyze it], comprehension is tested but is not likely to be developed.†

For added insights about purposeful questioning, the reader may wish to consult the sources below. Many of the illustrative examples on the pages that follow have been drawn or adapted, with credit, from these sources.

Association of Teachers of Social Studies of the City of New York, Chap. 3, "The Art of Questioning," *Handbook for Social Studies Teaching* (New York: Holt, Rinehart and Winston, Inc., 1967), pp. 38.

Jacobson, Willard J., Robert N. King, Louise E. Killie, and Richard D. Konicek, *Broadening Worlds of Science* (New York: American Book Company, 1964).

Kenworthy, Leonard S., *Guide to Social Studies Teaching in Secondary Schools,* pp. 96–102, 119–121, 202–204, 217–220 (Belmont, California: Wadsworth Publishing Company, Inc., 1966).

Lewenstein, Morris R., *Teaching Social Studies in Junior and Senior High Schools* (Chicago: Rand McNally and Company, 1963).

Rivlin, Harry N., Chap. VII, "Using the Question as an Aid to Learning," *Teaching Adolescents in Secondary Schools* (New York: Appleton-Century-Crofts, Inc., 1948).

Sanders, Norris M., *Classroom Questions: What Kinds?* (New York: Harper & Row, Publishers, 1966).

* John N. Washburne, "The Use of Questions in Social Science Material," *Journal of Educational Psychology,* XX (May, 1929), pp. 321–359.

† Olive S. Niles, "Help Students Set a Purpose for Reading," *English High Lights,* XX (April-May, 1963), 2. (Chicago: Scott, Foresman and Company.)

The following ideas for devising interesting purpose-questions, along with the illustrative examples, may be suggestive to the creative teacher. There will be much overlap.

*Purpose-Questions Can Make a Striking Statement* A pivotal question can take the form of a provocative statement—one that catches attention, appeals to curiosity, or demands analysis. Sometimes there is a "believe-it-or-not" quality.

> Instead of "Read the next ten pages about Franklin D. Roosevelt," a teacher gives out two dittoed quotations. One praises him extravagantly. The other condemns him as an arch-villain of recent history. This statement sets the student's purpose for reading: "He was one of the most loved and most despised men in our history. Read to find out why and what you think of him."*

> An ancient Greek, one of the characters you have met in the *Odyssey,* steps out of the past and into your city today. Compare his life then and now, and write his reactions to his new "life style." Take your choice from among the characters you have met in the epic.†

> The first toy automobile costs $10,000. The next ten thousand sell for $1.00. Explain.‡

> Suppose tomorrow the earth suddenly stopped rotating on its axis. How would all of us be affected?§

Colorful phrasing can be used to stir the imagination of students. This is a perfectly clear and adequate question: "Why did Japan fear Russian expansion in Korea?" But this question gives the student a more vivid picture of the situation: "Why was Korea called a dagger pointing at the heart of Japan?"‖

Of course, effective questioning is more than pulling a novelty out of a bag of tricks, and motivation should be more than momentary. Ideally, purpose-questions should be a sustaining force throughout the reading.

*Purpose-Questions Can Set a Challenging Task* Students are unlikely to drift aimlessly through their reading when the assignment

---

* Adapted from Leonard S. Kenworthy, *Guide to Social Studies Teaching in Secondary Schools* (Belmont, California: Wadsworth Publishing Company, Inc.), p. 203.

† Emily Meyer, former University of Chicago Laboratory School English teacher. Remarks to Thomas, October, 1964.

‡ Association of Teachers of Social Studies of the City of New York, *Handbook for Social Studies Teaching,* p. 56.

§ Adapted from Association of Teachers of Social Studies of the City of New York, *Handbook for Social Studies Teaching,* p. 56.

‖ Adapted from Association of Teachers of Social Studies of the City of New York, *Handbook for Social Studies Teaching,* p. 42.

sets a task they find challenging. When students in a Spanish class were reading the epic *Araucana,* the teacher took on the class in a debate.

> For tomorrow you'll be reading how the conquistadores en-slaved the Incas and put to death their great chief Ata-hualpa. Which side was in the right? Tomorrow I'll take the side of the conquistadores. *You* come prepared to plead the case of the Incas. Look for evidence in your reading that the Incas were grievously wronged.

Now the students' reading became an active search for points to use in the debate rather than a passive translating of words."*

The student vaguely assigned to "look up medieval castles" may read with wandering attention because his goal is only to read the lesson. Contrast his performance with that of the student who is set this task: "Read to compare castle life with modern apartment living."†

Nominations to a Classroom Hall of Fame sometimes stimulate reading with real purpose.

> Select a living scientist to nominate for a Classroom Hall of Fame in biology. You must limit yourself to one. Prepare a strong campaign talk supporting your nomination. The class will select five scientists from among all those nominated.

Clashing quotations may set the stage for a challenging task.

> Social studies students are given conflicting quotations about the causes of the War of 1812. On a dittoed assignment sheet excerpts from Canadian history textbooks and U.S. history textbooks are juxtaposed. The students read to interpret dif-ferent viewpoints, to analyze source materials, to search out evidence, and finally to prepare their own well-supported statement on the causes of the War of 1812.‡

*Purpose-Questions Can Bring the Reading Close to Students*
According to a basic principle of learning, we learn best when we apply new knowledge to concrete situations close to ourselves. Ques-tions can be formulated to help students "relate to the reading matter," "identify with it," perceive its significance for their own lives, and read it with real purpose.

* Emma LaPorte, former Spanish teacher, New Trier High School, Winnetka, Illinois. Remarks to Thomas, May, 1970.

† Niles, *English High Lights,* XX, p. 2.

‡ Association of Teachers of Social Studies of the City of New York, *Handbook for Social Studies Teaching,* pp. 144–146.

The following question is perfectly clear and definite: "What future developments are predicted for automation?" But this one brings reading about automation closer to students: "What changes is automation likely to bring in the lives of students in this class—in *your* life—during the next quarter of a century?"

This question, too, is adequate: "Suggest some reasons that women have a greater life expectancy than men." This one, though, is more exciting: "According to life expectancy tables, you girls in the class—Sharon, Judy, Peggy—have the prospect of living about seven years longer than the boys. Can you find out some possible reasons?"

*Purpose-Questions "Personalize" a Problem.* Questions can lead students to see themselves *in* the problem situation.

Make a list of some of your own traits that you think are inherited, and list the members of your family who have the same traits. Make another list of characteristics you have acquired during your lifetime.*

> How can you as a teenager and a nonvoter take action against pollution?†

A classwide public opinion poll can bring instant involvement of every student in a problem-solving situation. The students examine some live controversial question or else they are confronted with sharply conflicting statements, and are then polled on their opinion.

> Should our nation increase its appropriation for underdeveloped nations?

After wide reading and discussion to arrive at an informed opinion, the students are polled again to determine how many have changed their views.‡

*Questions Can Lead Students to Play Roles* Role playing can help students to get inside the shoes and minds of other people—to feel as they feel or have felt, and to think as they think or have thought.§ Questions can encourage role playing.

> Pretend that you are a bystander who sees Monseigneur's carriage run over the child in *A Tale of Two Cities*. What do you think your feelings would be toward Monseigneur?

* Willard J. Jacobson, Robert N. King, Louise E. Killie, and Richard D. Konicek, *Broadening Worlds of Science* (New York: American Book Company, 1964), p. 208.

†Earl Bell, University of Chicago Laboratory School social studies teacher. Remarks to Thomas, April, 1970.

‡ Adapted from Association of Teachers of Social Studies of the City of New York, *Handbook for Social Studies Teaching*, pp. 37, 63.

§ Kenworthy, *Guide to Social Studies Teaching in Secondary Schools*, p. 119.

Assume the role of Galileo as you are interviewed by a classmate. The interviewer is likely to ask you about your pioneer use of the telescope, your discoveries while studying the skies, your use of the modern experimental method, your clash with Rome, your trial by the Inquisition, your enduring contribution to mankind.

Students dramatize the operation of the U. N. General Assembly. First, they study its operation and some of the issues facing it. Next, an agenda is chosen, and each student is assigned to play the part of the representative of a certain nation. The student researches this question: "How is your nation likely to react to these issues?" He tries to play his role accurately while taking part in the actual debate.*

*Purpose-Questions Can Create a "You-Are-There" Effect* Through questions the student can be encouraged to experience through his imagination what is far away and long ago.

If you could have foreseen the results of the French Revolution, would you have joined the crowd at the storming of the Bastille?†

Karl Marx wrote that during the heyday of the Industrial Revolution family ties were reduced to "a mere money relation." Was his observation sound? In what ways can *you* interact with your family today, in contrast to someone your age in, say, England in 1848?‡

Would you rather be a lord during the Middle Ages or yourself today?§

If you had been the Senator from your state after World War I, would you have voted to ratify the Treaty of Versailles?||

If you were living in Philadelphia in 1800, why might you want to move west?#

* Slightly adapted from Sanders, *Classroom Questions: What Kinds?* (New York: Harper & Row, Publishers, 1966), p. 83.

† Association of Teachers of Social Studies of the City of New York, *Handbook for Social Studies Teaching*, p. 54.

‡ Joel Surgal, University of Chicago Laboratory School social studies teacher. Remarks to Thomas, October, 1970.

§ Association of Teachers of Social Studies of the City of New York, *Handbook for Social Studies Teaching*, p. 53.

|| Association of Teachers of Social Studies of the City of New York, *Handbook for Social Studies Teaching*, p. 56.

# Kenworthy, *Guide to Social Studies Teaching in Secondary Schools*, p. 98.

## Students Should Formulate Their Own Purposes

We have discussed at some length teacher-formulated questions, for as has been noted, instructors will often need to guide the reading of students in important directions. But of course they will not wish to leave the student dependent on teacher-given questions. Being told what to look for in his reading is not the way a person learns during his adult years. Seeing questions that demand answers and then searching out solutions through reading is behavior that will prove useful to the student for the next fifty or more years of his life.

There is no timetable for advancing down the road to independence. Students should be involved in planning with their teacher and in asking questions as soon as and as much as possible—from their earliest years at school through their college years—gradually becoming more and more skillful at formulating important purposes of their own. They should also become adept at holding several purposes in mind simultaneously. Research on the learning process supports this move toward independence. According to studies, students learn best when they select problems of vital interest and importance to them, then probe for the answers themselves rather than being presented with "gift wrapped" answers.*

As a step toward independence, an instructor might pose a broad purpose-question for a class or group while encouraging the students to formulate other questions of their own.

Sometimes, after surveying the pages assigned, the students themselves set up an outline of what they want to look for while reading. This outline is duplicated and supplied to each class member as a study guide.

Students who have been assigned the reading of an important chapter and whose purpose is thorough mastery of its content should acquire the ability to preview the chapter, get a general view of what it's all about, then decide for themselves, "What should I look for when I go back and read this chapter carefully? What important questions will be answered?" Suggestions for helping students set their own purposes for reading a chapter are offered in "You Can Upgrade Students' Textbook Reading," the next section of this chapter.

## Setting the Stage for Student-Formulated Questions

The stage can be set for students to formulate their own purposes for reading by putting them into a situation that stirs interest

* Kenworthy, *Guide to Social Studies Teaching in Secondary Schools*, p. 217.

and provokes questions—some exciting observations, an experiment, an excursion, a fascinating travelogue, a filmstrip, an exhibit or a visitor in the classroom. The teacher might then ask, "What are some things you would like to learn about this (*scientific phenomenon . . . country . . . period . . . person*)?"

One instructor took some young science students out onto the school grounds to see a crabapple tree in bloom. Around the trunk close to the ground there was a conspicuous scar. The teacher asked, "What do you think caused that scar?"

The students thought this over. "A dog chewed it!" "Insects ate it!" "A wire was too tight!"

The instructor remarked, "I happen to know that that tree has roots of one variety and the trunk, branches, and leaves of another!"

The class had heard of grafting. Perhaps it was that! One student commented, "I've seen a tree with two different kinds of apples!"

The instructor added, "I've seen one with seven different kinds!"

The students were full of questions. "Why is grafting done?" "How?" "When?" "Does it always work?" "Can all plants be grafted?" Then with guidance they arrived at other questions. "Are there different kinds of grafting?" "How are these done?" "What determines the success or failure of grafting?"*

Questions like these can go onto the chalkboard and become a master list. The class has now developed its own study guide, which is dittoed and handed to each student.

In a class of advanced students, a science teacher dissected an earthworm, provoked many questions, refused to answer any, and turned her students into human question marks. The students asked, "What are those fibers?" "What is that white cord?" "Why is that organ a different color?" "What is that large swelling?" "Why is the front end darker?" "Where can we learn about this?" Impelled by their own purpose-questions, the students dug into the reading and covered references far beyond the assignment.†

## COMPONENT 4—HELPING STUDENTS ACCOMPLISH THEIR PURPOSE

It is not unusual for superior teachers to make assignments involving the components discussed thus far. They excite the interest of their students, bring the reading close to their experience, and help

* Illa Podendorf, former University of Chicago Laboratory School science teacher. Remarks to Thomas, November, 1970.

† Lestina Colby, former University of Chicago Laboratory School science teacher. Remarks to Thomas, October, 1965.

them read with purpose. Far less frequently, though, do an instructor's assignments include the fourth component—helping students know *how to read* the assignment.

### Haven't Students Already Acquired the Necessary Skills?

Most students have developed their reading procedures by trial and error, and the errors are many and costly. They may lack strategies for handling specialized patterns of writing that confront them in their courses. And they may need more effective general approaches. Some read the crucial content of a difficult expository chapter with the "once over lightly" approach suitable for a light novel. Then they close the book, having gained at best only a smattering of information. Others read a light novel as ploddingly as they would a crucial chapter. Many are not aware that the various parts of a passage may not all be of equal value for their present purpose. Somewhere along the way they have picked up the idea that it is a sin to scan or skim. Time-saving, productive reading techniques and approaches, tailored to the learning task at hand, are awaiting all these readers. But only if they are guided are they likely to discover them.

A teacher intent on bringing about reading success can do three things.

1. He can learn, often through observation, which skills his students already have.
2. He can examine the assignment to learn precisely what skills they must have in order to complete it.
3. He can tie in instruction in the skills in which they are deficient, thus removing the roadblocks.

This question is bound to come to mind: "How can an instructor find time for this?" Students' study can be extremely wasteful if unguided—and extremely unproductive. Instead of draining time, reading guidance stretches time. It removes obstacles to learning that would have blocked students day after day all through the year.

### When Can Reading Guidance Be Given?

Like other skills, reading skills are best learned in a functional setting, ideally in the very situation in which they will be used. Marked improvement in these skills should follow when this improvement is considered a worthwhile objective of classroom activities. Guidance in reading may be appropriate at the following times:

1. As the assignment is given, a few minutes can be spent discussing the best method of reading it. Brief pointers may be enough. If the students have time to start the assignment in class, they will have the added advantage of applying the suggestions—under the eye and with the help of their teacher—before the pointers grow cold.

2. Guided open-book practice can develop and strengthen reading techniques. Moments of need during the class hour may offer an opportune time. Sometimes only a brief while need be spent. "Let's turn to our textbooks and . . ." can be a frequent suggestion of teachers.*

3. It may be profitable to spend most of a class period in a how-to-read-it session, "walking" students through the model reading of a passage. Students read passages silently for specific purposes. Then they discuss and analyze. The subject matter content thus covered is likely to be thoroughly mastered, and in addition the students are likely to acquire effective techniques for their permanent use.

4. Sometimes, when the rest of the class is occupied with some other activity, the instructor may wish to work with a group in need of certain skills.

5. Help can be given to students during an individual conference or during a supervised study period as the teacher moves around the room.

6. Most promising for truly far-reaching results, many teachers are viewing assignments as an integral part of their students' school experience rather than as "overtime" work, and they plan these to cover longer periods of time. An entire class period—sometimes two or three periods—can then be spent on making the assignment. The time available makes possible an excellent sendoff on reading procedures—with extremely important benefits for students. The students work on these long-term assignments in class, in workshops, in laboratories, and in the library, under the watchful, helping eye of their instructor, who now has a chance to observe their blocks in reading and can go into action to remove them.

### What Students Are Likely to Need Reading Guidance?

Students have a special need for help on certain grade levels and in certain situations.

---

* Kenworthy, *Guide to Social Studies Teaching in Secondary Schools,* p. 104.

1. Students need a great deal of help during their junior high school years. Instruction offered at this time may enable them to succeed—and survive—during the school years that lie ahead.
2. The first year of high school is a crucial year for many students.
3. Students who are beginning a new course are especially receptive to help. If help is given during the first few weeks, many will be more successful in their course work all through the year.
4. A "how to use your textbook" session is appropriate just after students receive new textbooks.
5. There is a special need for help whenever the writing pattern of the assignment demands specialized techniques that the students may have had no opportunity to learn previously·
6. With slow learners there is a constant need to read and study under the supervision and with the assistance of the teacher.

## Meeting Observed Needs

The following pages offer ideas for developing two or three representative abilities and skills. They are intended merely to suggest possibilities. The concerned teacher will plan his own reading guidance to meet needs he sees in his students. The subject-area index at the front of this book and the general index can guide him to procedures others have found effective for teaching some of the specialized techniques called for in most school courses. Chapter 5, "Reading Skills for Problem Solving," offers him leads for giving students expertise for making investigations. He is offered leads to specific methods, adaptable for all levels, in *Reading, Grades 7, 8, and 9* (Curriculum Bulletin No. 11. New York: Board of Education of the City of New York, 1959); in Joseph C. Gainsburg's *Advanced Skills in Reading,* Books 1, 2, and 3, Teacher's Annotated Edition (New York: The Macmillan Company, 1967); and elsewhere.

## Rapid Reading for Background Information

The ability to read fairly rapidly for background information is called for in many subjects. The student who attacks all his reading with a slow, intensive approach will find himself spending impossible amounts of time. Broad coverage is especially essential in the social studies, for in this field depth of understanding demands extensive reading. The need for rapid coverage continues, and may even intensify, in adulthood. Much of the content of a person's professional reading, of popular magazines and newspapers, of many biographies, and of many novels, can and should be covered rapidly.

Some students have the impression that all their study demands concentration on details—that it is almost a sin to cover anything rapidly. They need guidance not only on how but also on when to do broad coverage reading.

Suppose the students' purpose is to get a general picture of what a tropical rain forest is like—its beauty, its lush vegetation, its dangers. The teacher might suggest, "Read this selection rapidly for a general impression—just to catch the feel of being in the forest, not to remember all the details."

Then he might ask, "How do you think you should do this type of reading?" With guidance, the students might suggest that they move right along, picking up main thoughts, learning all they can from the pictures, not slowing down to try to learn details, looking up unknown words only if these block their getting the gist—pressing on to learn the general drift.

The instructor might also call attention to the fact that previewing is a speed device—that through previewing one can often get an instant view of the general content. He might point out that introductory paragraphs often announce what is to come, that concluding paragraphs often wrap it up, and that topical headings (and sometimes topic sentences) helpfully yield the big points covered.

Before these pointers grow cold the students might read the selection in class. All year long this particular in-class practice might serve as a referent as the teacher suggests reading other selections "as we did the one about the rain forest."

Students who have always been "one pace plodders" are learning at last that different approaches to reading exist. Once they have acquired rapid reading techniques, just a word or two at the time the assignment is made should be enough to remind them to shift gears into this type of reading.

> Read this account of a southern plantation owner about the life of the Negro on his plantation. Then read *Up from Slavery* to see how a slave himself looked at those years. Read fairly rapidly—just to get the gist of these contrasting viewpoints.

> In reading this fast-moving adventure story your purpose is enjoyment. Fairly rapid reading is suitable for "The Most Dangerous Game."

Ultimately, students should be able to look over a selection, consider their purpose and what they already know about the subject, and then answer for themselves, "Is this something I can read rapidly, or should I read it slowly and carefully?"

If the assignment to be covered rapidly for background information is an informational book rather than a shorter selection, the reader may wish to share with students the pointers in "Can PQ4R Help You Read Supplementary Books?" later on in this chapter.

### High-Speed Scanning for Specific Information

Students may lack the extremely useful skill of scanning columns or pages for specific information. They sometimes plod doggedly down the page, line by line, when all they are after is a brief passage related to their problem. What a "drag" when they should be doing efficient reference reading! Specific suggestions for developing scanning techniques are offered later on (Chapter 4, "Developing Flexibility in Reading Rate").

After students have been introduced to scanning procedures, just a word from the instructor at the time the assignment is made will nudge them to apply their new techniques. A science teacher reminded the class when assigning the question, "Can we control our blushing?"

> Scan these pages quickly, looking for clues, until you *think* you've found your information. Then *slow way down* to see whether you've really located what you're after. If you have, settle down to read carefully.

Ordinarily, scanning is neither difficult nor time consuming to teach. Students quickly recognize its value and put it to work in reference reading in order to cut through masses of extraneous information.

### Close, Intensive Reading

Much of this book is devoted to helping students acquire techniques for the close, intensive reading frequently demanded of them in their school courses. The subject-area index and the general index will guide the reader to helps that may serve his needs. The section "You Can Upgrade Students' Textbook Reading," next in this chapter, offers helps for students in mastering the crucial content of a textbook chapter. Concerned teachers will draw on various sources and develop their own procedures.

Tips for close, intensive reading can sometimes be elicited from students, then combined with the expertise of the instructor to evolve the final guidelines. The instructor might ask the class, "Suppose you want to master the content of this passage thoroughly without a word of help or explanation from your teacher. How would you go about reading it?" With their attention focused on how they would read ideally, the students themselves often come up with some highly practical pointers.

Students will need first their instructor's how-to-do-it guidance and then his frequent when-to reminders.

> These three pages of science assigned you for tomorrow may be the equivalent of fifty pages of a novel for English. Read to trace the path of blood as it moves from your heart back to your heart, and try to remember its course.

> Do tomorrow's reading slowly and thoroughly—to learn the disagreements that almost wrecked the Constitutional Convention and how each one of these was settled.

### Approaches and Techniques Within an Assignment

Students will not necessarily select a single reading approach, then continue it without deviation until they have completed a passage. On the contrary, they will frequently need to shift their approach within the assignment. Their teacher's reminders will help them make this internal adjustment.

Students who have been assigned a chapter on the Civil War period might be advised to adjust their speed and method.

> You can read fairly rapidly these easy, interesting, story-type pages on Abe Lincoln's young manhood. But slow way down and read closely to learn and remember the provisions of the Thirteenth, Fourteenth, and Fifteenth Amendments in the same chapter.

Science students beginning a chapter on "Fish and Fishlike Vertebrates" might be reminded

> You can read this interesting narrative introduction about an invasion of lamprey eels into the Great Lakes fairly fast. Then reduce your speed for the closely packed body of the chapter. Speed up again for the easy paragraphs on sports fishing as a hobby.

### Independence in Selecting Reading Procedures

"Use this technique here . . . this one here . . . this one here" can be suggested to maturing readers from day to day. But as with setting a purpose, students should be led more and more to select for themselves the appropriate approach. Their life need is to be able to set their own purposes, then read in the appropriate manner to accomplish these purposes. A question like this is a step in the direction of independence.

> We have talked over the purpose of this assignment. How do you think you should read to accomplish this purpose?

Then on, even closer to independence:

> What do you think it is important to find out from this reading? What will be the best method of reading in order to find this out?

Students will need many experiences, under guidance, in setting their purposes and selecting their approach. The long-term goal is the development of the mature reader who is competent to survey the reading ahead, consider his purpose, judge the difficulty, and then decide on and use the approach to the passage—and the shifting of approaches within the passage—called for. The ideal of the "finished reader" who has reading competencies at his command for all his purposes is likely, however, to remain beyond complete attainment in secondary and even college classrooms. Bringing the ideal closer will be a continuing concern.

## YOU CAN UPGRADE STUDENTS' TEXTBOOK READING

> *Teachers ask, "How can I improve my students' reading of their textbooks when I've had no training or experience in teaching reading?" The PQ4R procedure, in which any teacher can instruct his students, incorporates some powerful study-reading procedures.*

Perhaps nowhere in all their years at school have students had help in developing an efficient approach to textbook reading. The waste of study hours, the unfulfilled potential, are appalling. Dividends can be tremendous if streamlined habits are developed, starting with the seventh grade at least, and proceeding through the college and university years.

A notebook section for students explaining how to use the PQ4R study procedure follows this introduction. The guidelines for students are intended to supplement something far more important—instruction in the application of PQR4 by the classroom teacher. Classroom teachers with no formal training in the teaching of reading have used such procedures to upgrade textbook reading. They have changed helter-skelter readers into more systematic readers. They have changed overly conscientious readers who tried to retain everything on the page into "differentiating" readers, better able to select out what is important to remember. They have transformed students who used to dream their way through the chapter into alert, participating readers.

A journalism teacher whose students were making a whip-through of their textbook reading sought the school's reading consultant. Together they served up PQ4R in attractive format, a handy booklet with its cover in school colors, and the consultant briefed the teacher in giving his classes reading guidance. The teacher reports: "Instead of blank stares, there are now excited, informed class discussions. The change in retention of important content has been dramatic. Several students have exclaimed, 'This thing really works!' I know this sounds too good to be true, but this is exactly what happened."*

PQ4R is a package of techniques that should be effective in improving the reading of chapter-length materials when the student's purpose is thorough understanding of the content. It should help him comprehend better, concentrate better, and retain better. The steps in the procedure are: Preview, Question, Read, Reflect, Recite, and Review. As explained in the opening pages of the students' guidelines, it is a variation of the SQ3R approach designed by Francis P. Robinson at Ohio State University and based on many years of experimentation with students. (The steps in Dr. Robinson's original approach are Survey, Question, Read, Recite, and Review.) In presenting PQ4R here, the writers have leaned heavily on his classic book, *Effective Study* (New York: Harper & Row, Publishers, 1961), on *Learning to Learn* by Donald E. P. Smith and others (New York: Harcourt, Brace and World, Inc., 1961), and on *How to Study* by Thomas F. Staton (Montgomery, Alabama: Box 6133, 1968). *How to Study* is an excel-

---

* Wayne Brasler. Remarks to Thomas, November, 1971.

lent little guide—inviting, clear, and readable—to put into the hands of students.

## PQ4R Upgrades Reading in Many Subjects

PQ4R is applicable to the reading of informational chapters in science, health, history, civics, contemporary problems, geography, sociology, economics, philosophy, journalism, homemaking, vocational education and industrial arts, business law, accounting, music appreciation, music history, music harmony, art appreciation, art history, and other courses—and in English when the chapters are expository. It is adaptable to expository passages in mathematics, to informational passages in a second language, and to articles in periodicals.

## PQ4R Meets a Special Need in English Classes

Many English teachers recognize proficiency in reading informational prose as one of the life needs of students. These instructors are aware that a student's success in almost every course at school is related to his ability to do expository reading. They want graduates to be well equipped to continue their educations through reading, to leave school proficient in grasping the content of informational books, of expository writing in popular periodicals, and in journals related to their trades and professions. They are likely to assign a high priority to instructing students in the reading of "practical" prose.

## Top Honor Students May Need PQ4R

Left to their own devices, what do students do when they open their book to study the chapter assigned for tomorrow? All too often they have no response other than plunging in and plodding through. They may "preview" the chapter by estimating its thickness between their thumb and forefinger! Then on they plod—from the first line on the first page to the last line on the last. Good, now they're through! Their only review technique is often a passive rereading.

Extreme cases? Studies of prospective Phi Beta Kappas at the University of Pennsylvania and of top honor students at Ohio State revealed the study methods of many to be quite inefficient. Their A's appeared to be the result of their superior scholastic aptitude—

*not* their superior study habits.* In another investigation junior high school students whose grades on their report cards were top ranking proved quite deficient in their approach to chapter length materials.†

### PQ4R Saves Time for Class and Teacher

A science teacher who instructs his students in PQ4R during the opening weeks of school was asked, "How can you manage to spare the time from science?" He answered, "I can't afford *not* to spare it. Ultimately it gives us more time. Students come better prepared all year."‡

### HOW TO TEACH PQ4R

Since old study habits are deeply ingrained in most students, practice under supervision is essential in order to build improved working techniques into their permanent habits. Simply reading printed guidelines or listening while the teacher talks about study methods is likely to fall short in effecting a permanent change in habits.§ But in a teaching followed by practice situation, skills can be brought closer to a top level of efficiency.

### Students Should Recognize a Personal Need

Obviously, for full advantage, "how to study" sessions should be offered early in the course, a time when students do not always recognize a personal need. To create a sense of need during the first few days, one science instructor simply assigns a representative section of a chapter for reading in class or at home—then, before there is any classwork on the content, he asks questions of the type students will be expected to answer all year. The shallowness of their reading

* D. G. Danskin and C. W. Burnett, "Study Techniques of Those Superior Students," *Personnel and Guidance Journal,* XXXI (December, 1952), pp. 181–186. R. C. Preston and E. N. Tufts, "The Reading Habits of Superior College Students," *Journal of Experimental Education,* XVI (March, 1948), pp. 196–202.

† Iver L. Moe and Frank Nania, "Reading Deficiencies Among Able Pupils," *Journal of Developmental Reading,* III (Autumn, 1959), pp. 11–26.

‡ Jerry Ferguson, University of Chicago Laboratory School science teacher. Remarks to Thomas, September, 1970.

§ K. E. Stordahl and C. M. Christenson, "The Effect of Study Techniques on Comprehension and Retention," *Journal of Educational Research,* XLIX (April, 1956), pp. 561–570.

is brought home to many students when they discover that they know far less than they need to about what they have read.* The stage is then set for a "how to read it" session.

## A Sendoff Demonstration

Early in the school year a chemistry teacher and a reading consultant planned a team sendoff for PQ4R. Using the chapter just assigned, the reading consultant suggested general procedures for previewing, formulating questions, reading to find the answers, and the like. After the consultant had explained each step the chemistry teacher demonstrated how he would apply that step in studying the chapter assigned. *Students are quickly turned off if they get the impression that PQ4R is slow and labored.* The chemistry teacher's run-through left the impression of an efficient, smoothly operating system of study.

## Success Can Sell PQ4R

Initial success experiences with PQ4R encourage students to continue using the method when studying on their own. One teacher deliberately plans striking "before and after" quiz results. To create a sense of need, he quizzes his students on their reading of an assigned passage *before* he introduces PQ4R. For some students the results are a disaster. He then demonstrates PQ4R procedures with another passage, guiding his students through a model reading. Finally he has them close their books and take a quiz on the material just covered. Most of the students are delighted to discover how well the new procedures have worked for them.

## Use PQ4R Flexibly

PQ4R is by no means a lock step system of study. Modifications are likely to be desirable from one subject to another, from one passage to another, and from one student to another. Individuals should be encouraged to make their own adaptations and to use the approach in the way that works best for them. As they approach each assigned chapter, they should ask such questions as "Did the instructor make any comments that would suggest a special way of

* Ferguson, Remarks to Thomas, September, 1970.

approaching this chapter?" "Is my purpose in reading it a thorough understanding or only a general impression?"

### Practice the Individual Steps

PQ4R consists of a number of proved study techniques packaged into a step by step approach. Instruction on the individual steps is often advisable before practice with the total approach is attempted. Possible ways to work with each separate step and then coordinate the steps into a smooth sequential operation are now offered.

### HOW TO PRACTICE THE PREVIEW STEP

(See pages 85–88 of the guide sheets for students.)

Ask a teacher, "Do your students preview the chapters you assign?" He will probably answer, "They just plunge in and read."

A study by Perry with 1500 freshmen at Harvard supports this observation. A chapter in social studies was assigned to the freshmen, who were directed to study the chapter as if they would have two hours to complete it. After 22 minutes, the students were interrupted and asked to make a brief statement telling what the chapter was all about. Only 150 out of 1500 had done any exploring beyond the page on which they were reading—and many of these had looked ahead only to estimate the length of the chapter! And only 15 could give a general view of where the chapter was going.*

### How-to-Do-Its from Students

A teacher might guide his students to make their own discoveries about the techniques and values of previewing: "How does an author help you to learn in just minutes what this chapter will contain? What are all the different means he uses to clue you in quickly on what you'll find in the chapter?" "Can you suggest a technique for previewing based on the use of the author's clues?" "What are some advantages of making an advance survey of each chapter?"

### Assignment Time Right for Preview Practice

One instructor selects a chapter ideally structured for students' preview practice. He suggests, "Let's practice the preview technique

* William G. Perry, Jr., "Students' Use and Misuse of Reading Skills: A Report to a Faculty," *Harvard Educational Review*, XXIX (Summer, 1959), pp. 193–200.

on the chapter assigned for tonight's reading. When you've finished, you should be able to answer these two questions: (1) What, in general, is the content of the chapter? and (2) What big points will be discussed? You may need about _____ minutes." (As students are first introduced to the preview technique, time allotments should be generous and flexible.)

As the students finish their examination of the chapter the instructor asks, "What did you find to be the general subject matter?" or "What broad problem(s) will be explored?" and then, "What aspects of the subject will be discussed? Can you possibly give them in order?" As the students name the big points they have gleaned from the major chapter division headings and the side headings, the teacher records these on the chalkboard, indenting to indicate levels of subordination and revealing to the class that in this well-structured chapter they have neatly discovered the author's "hidden" outline. The students perceive that they now have a map to guide them during their thorough reading.

Since many of the chapters students will need to preview are not so ideally structured as those a teacher might select during this instructional step, it is desirable later to practice with materials that present difficulties.

### "How Much Can You Learn in Just _____ Minutes?"

As students become adept in using their new preview techniques a time limit can be imposed to jolt some of them out of unnecessarily sluggish habits. "How much can you learn about the content of this chapter (or article) in just _____ minutes? Use your new preview techniques to hit the high spots of organized prose."

### Previewing—an Automatic First Step

As the next few chapters are assigned, students might quickly preview them in class, linking their background information and experience to the chapter, hitting the high spots of organized prose, getting a view of what lies ahead. Brief previews under guidance should be continued until previewing becomes an automatic first step in the study of every chapter.

### Practice on Everything

Students should be encouraged to practice widely and thus perfect their new techniques. "Preview *everything you read* (with the exception of fiction) before you do your more thorough reading. Preview chapters in your textbook for this class and other classes. Preview magazine and newspaper articles chosen for your personal reading. Make the Preview Step your lifetime habit. You're likely to do your reading *better and faster* for having previewed."

## HOW TO PRACTICE THE QUESTION STEP

(See pages 88–90 of the students' guide sheets.)

In a study with 1456 students the effectiveness of approaching reading with questions versus approaching it without questions was explored. The efficacy of four different placements of questions was also compared: (1) all questions just before the reading, (2) all questions just after the reading, (3) each question just before the paragraph(s) in which it was answered in the selection, and (4) each question just after the part of the selection in which it was answered. Two of these placements brought decided gains in comprehension: all questions just before the selection, and each question just before the part of the selection in which it was answered.*

Students should capitalize on their awareness of strategic question placement to increase their own comprehension. Where can they get their questions? They can formulate some of them simply by shifting the topical heading of each section into a question.

### In-Class Practice Turning Headings into Questions

Many students read headings passively as more or less non-meaningful phrases. However if a student tries to formulate a specific question from a heading, he is forced to focus on its meaning. He has made a desirable shift in mind set at the beginning, starting each section with an immediate questioning attitude, pausing to ask himself, "Why are we going into this?"†

If the author has provided specific headings which disclose the gist of the section that follows, it will be simple to recast them as questions. This should take just a few moments. (See examples in the students' notebook section.) During their first experience with the Question (Q) Step, students should work with headings that facilitate the shift to a question. They should move on, however, to

---

* Washburne, *Journal of Educational Psychology,* XX, pp. 321–329.

† Francis P. Robinson, *Effective Study* (New York: Harper & Row, Publishers, 1961), pp. 33–34.

headings that fall short of the ideal if their textbook includes them—vague, general, or very brief headings which do not reveal the specific content. A few minutes of the assignment time for several days would be well invested in converting some of the headings of the next day's assignment into questions.

### Depth Questions and Surface Questions

Donald E. P. Smith of the University of Michigan's Reading Service stresses the importance of asking depth questions in addition to surface questions. He gives an example from social studies. As students read the heading "Hitler's Rise to Power," they might think of the surface questions, "Who was Hitler? How did he rise to power? When?" It may, however, require a depth question to direct attention toward the more significant ideas of the author: "What generalizations for our own time can we make—in other words, are there certain conditions which in *any* society would threaten the democratic process?"* Students will need special guidance in moving beyond factual questions and probing "between the lines and beyond the lines" of their textbook.

### Practicing the Q Step

For added reinforcement of the Q Step, students might be asked to fill in a table (see Figure 3–1, next page) during their reading of an assigned chapter.†

### "What Questions Would Your Instructor Ask on This?"

One teacher projects a headed section of the assigned chapter on a screen, then suggests to the class, "Pretend you are the teacher. What question(s) would you ask the class on this section? Of course you want your question(s) to get at the important content." With help the students arrive at questions tailored to the content, and at depth as well as surface levels.

Next they are told, "Now you're no longer the teacher. You're *you,* the student. Now *really learn* the answers to your questions.

* Donald E. P. Smith and others, *Learning to Learn* (New York: Harcourt, Brace and World, Inc., 1961), p. 25.

† Ralph C. Preston and Morton Botel, *How to Study* (Chicago: Science Research Associates, 1956), p. 37.

| HEADING FROM YOUR TEXTBOOK | QUESTIONS WITH WHICH YOU APPROACHED YOUR READING OF THE SECTION |
|---|---|
| | |

*FIGURE 3–1. Q step table.*

Then close your book and write the answers." (Books are to be closed to discourage rote copying.)

"Now that's the way you should study—formulating questions, then reading to learn the answers."*

As the students perfect the Q Step they discover that their next tests and examinations hold fewer surprises. They now formulate questions so skillfully that they can often predict some of their test questions.

### "Won't I Overlook Important Content?"

Students may wonder, "If I read to find the answer to an overall question suggested by the topic heading, won't I overlook important content?" The following advice, which appears on the students' guide sheets, will need emphasis: Read to find the answer to your question *and other important content.* You'll need to continue questioning—to add questions and perhaps to adjust your questions *all the while* you're reading. Turn topic sentences into questions. Turn the heading of a series of steps or a list into questions as, "Just what are the steps in mitosis?" "Just what phyla are listed here?" Turn key concepts and terms into questions as, "Just what *is* a theory?"

Especially with questions that call for details, care must be

* Margaret Hillman, former director of St. Petersburg High School Reading Clinic. Remarks to Thomas, April, 1971.

taken lest students scan for the bits and pieces of the passage that answer the questions and bypass all the rest.

## HOW TO PRACTICE THE READ STEP

(See pages 90–92 of the students' guide sheets.)

Some students have no conception of what a rigorous passage demands. For years they have made a whip-through of demanding reading. A teacher might walk students through a model reading of a difficult passage. In the process, students—some of them for the first time—would experience digging into difficult sentences, reading and rereading a passage until they get a breakthrough, pausing to think something through—"Do I understand?" "What is the evidence for this?" "Can I make a generalization here?"

The reader will notice, in the students' notebook section, that an added R—for reflect—is built right into the Read Step. PQ4R is not intended to overstress the memory level of learning to the neglect of higher intellectual processes. Information that is worth remembering is a *foundation* for higher-level thought. As Sanders observes, "The memory category is indispensable on all levels of thinking. The more important and useful knowledge a student possesses, the better his chances for success in other categories of thought."*

## HOW TO PRACTICE THE RECITE STEP

(See pages 92–94 of the students' guide sheets.)

Students sometimes say, "I've read that chapter twice, but I still can't remember it." These students may have failed to firm their learning through self-recitation. They are likely to comprehend and retain better when they ask themselves as they complete each section of the chapter, "Just what have I read here?"

### The Steps Should Become a Smooth Operation

Guidance will be needed in coordinating the Question, Read, and Recite Steps into a smooth operation. Students are advised on their guide sheets to work through the chapter—carrying out the Question, Read, and Recite Steps in order—one headed section at a time. Guided practice—in which they actually perform these steps

* Sanders, *Classroom Questions: What Kinds?*, p. 27.

in sequence, converting the heading into a question, reading to find the answer, then self-reciting the essential information—is important in entrenching PQ4R.

### Making Notes and Marking Books

A number of quick, labor saving methods of making notes or marking the book (only if the student owns his book) are offered to students in their printed guidelines. Too often notemaking amounts to a labored and absentminded copying the book. Indeed, notemaking often *operates against learning*. Some students actually copy a sentence without ever having read it for its meaning, thinking, "I'll copy this now and learn it later"—if indeed they are thinking at all. Notemaking becomes merely a mechanical note*taking* of every sentence or so. Similarly, students underline without really reading the content.\*

One teacher holds a class session on "How to Make Important Points Flag You," projecting examples on a screen before the class. He prepares facsimiles of actual textbook pages as models of various marking or notemaking techniques: *selective* underlining, "mini notes" in the margin, marginal numerals, and others. He also shows on the screen model notes made in labor saving personal shorthand. He offers tips about the use of these techniques and discusses the pros and cons of each. Many students are intrigued by the prospect of developing their own personal shorthand, a shortcut suggested in the students' notebook section.

### HOW TO PRACTICE THE REVIEW STEP

(See pages 99–102 of the students' guide sheets.)

Having worked through the chapter section by section, questioning, reading, and reciting on the content, the student now returns —in the Review Step—to the total chapter.

Students who have no idea what thorough study involves may be inclined to leave out the Review Step, thinking, "All that for an assignment!" Demonstrating the deft review of a chapter should impress them with the fact that a skillful review—provided the preceding steps have been properly carried out—is not wearisome restudy but rather a relatively quick *overlearning* step that clinches retention. Of course the Review Step, too, should be an intensely active process, with the student looking away from the page and self-reciting and bringing every possible learning channel to bear.

---

\* Robinson, *Effective Study,* p. 38.

In one classroom large wall placards depicting "The Curve of Forgetting" (see students' notebook section) sound daily reminders to students to space out their reviews to their best advantage.

Instructors often lament, "Many students read their textbooks like a novel." Obviously, instruction on the various parts of the PQ4R process—previewing, questioning, self-reciting, involving multisensory channels, notemaking, spacing out reviews—discourages the impression that "he who runs may read" a textbook chapter.

## PQ4R for Supplementary Books

The steps discussed above and the guide sheets that follow deal specifically with the reading of single textbook chapters. There is also much value in students' learning how to apply PQ4R to supplementary books of an informational nature. Obviously, when the student is searching for information in a number of books he can't spend the amount of time he expends in the careful, intensive study of one textbook chapter. On later pages the reader will find a group of tips directed toward the student on how to adapt PQ4R to the reading of supplementary books.

## Practice with PQ4R Should Be Realistic

We have mentioned that not all textbook chapters are ideally written to facilitate study with PQ4R. Practice should be realistic. While the students' first experiences should be planned with chapters well structured for PQ4R, they should move on to passages that do not lend themselves ideally, and then on to material that confronts them with real difficulties.

## PQ4R Will Need Reinforcement

PQ4R should be reinforced as needed over the weeks and months that follow. A particular technique from the package of skills can be suggested at the time an assignment is made with which that technique will be especially helpful: "Your cover card will help you check this diagram to see if you've really grasped its parts and labels."

Students may need encouragement during a period of readjustment in which the newly adopted techniques seem difficult and awkward. Learning experts draw analogies with sports. A swimmer who changes his stroke to reduce water resistance is likely to feel clumsy at first, but ultimately he improves in speed and power and stream-lines his performance.

Of course, printed guide sheets for students are not a do-it-your-self kit—in themselves they are not likely to produce much of a change in habits. The ones that follow are intended as a supplement to the teacher's instruction, as a permanent reference for students, and as a constant reminder to practice PQ4R.

## Adopting Parts of PQ4R

A number of effective techniques have been clustered in PQ4R. If students adopt only the Preview Step and the practice of self-reci-tation, for example, they will have acquired two tools broadly ap-plicable in study. If they adopt the whole package, they will have acquired a most effective study method for the thorough mastery of a textbook chapter.

# STUDY BETTER AND FASTER WITH HIGHER-LEVEL STUDY SKILLS*

From time to time in class you'll be given tips to help you keep on top of your assignments. You can put these to work to get the maximum results from every moment you spend in studying.

### Capitalize on Scientific Learning

Psychologists at top universities have experimented for years to find out how students learn most easily and well. Certain principles of learning have become well established. Procedures that are based on such principles are called "higher-level study skills." Through these, you can learn more readily, remember longer, and conserve your study time. You'll want to cultivate techniques like these as you enter higher-level courses.

### Develop Higher-Level Skills

Of course effective study methods aren't inherent—they're acquired. *You can develop these skills.* Some students with extraordinary ability achieve little. Others with less ability achieve highly. What makes the difference? Often it's knowing how to study.

After all, teachers don't grade a student's intellect but the quality of work he does. It's important to make the most of capabilities. Higher-level study skills can help you do this.†

### Three Things to Do

You'll be introduced to higher-level study skills in class with your teacher and through a series of guide sheets. There are three things for you to do.

1. Make the most of tips from your instructor.
2. Study the guide sheets that follow, then file them in your notebook for reference.
3. And especially—without which there will be no value for you, now or ever—*practice* your higher-level study skills from here on.

* The term "higher-level study skills" belongs to Francis P. Robinson and is used in his *Effective Study* (New York: Harper & Row, Publishers, 1961).

† Ralph C. Preston and Morton Botel, *How to Study* (Chicago: Science Research Associates, 1956), p. 6.

## STUDY BETTER AND FASTER WITH HIGHER-LEVEL STUDY SKILLS

### Fair Exchange?

One learning expert comments, "You'll probably put forth more effort every hour you spend studying than you have in the past. Are you willing to do this—and finish the job with *more learned and more remembered* in the process? Scientific study procedures have enabled thousands of students to do that very thing: swap extra effort for better performance—and perhaps more free time. Fair exchange?"*

### STEP UP YOUR STUDYING WITH PQ4R

PQ4R is a package of study techniques. It can help you comprehend more difficult material, cut through what is less important and find main points, concentrate better, remember longer, and have a lifetime tool for better learning.

It is a variation of a study approach originated during a wartime crisis when a highly select group of young men had to be rushed through training courses. Although they had been selected for their high intelligence and top records at school, their study methods proved extremely inefficient. Dr. Francis Robinson, an authority on the psychology of learning, was called in. Drawing on the results of years of experiments with students, he designed scientific procedures to streamline their study. (The steps in Dr. Robinson's original approach are Survey, Question, Read, Recite, and Review, or SQ3R.)

The steps in PQ4R are **Preview, Question, Read, Reflect, Recite,** and **Review.** It should help you get solid results when your goal is thorough learning and retention of the content of a chapter.

Of course you'll want to vary any study system from one textbook to another and even from one passage to another. As you approach each reading assignment you'll want to ask yourself such questions as, "Did the teacher make any remarks that would suggest a special approach to this chapter?" "Is my purpose here a detailed understanding of the content or only a general impression?" You'll want to use the new method flexibly, adjust it to your needs and preferences, and add effective ways of your own.

You'll find on the pages that follow some powerful study techniques for mastering a textbook chapter.

* Thomas F. Staton, *How to Study* (Montgomery, Alabama: P.O. Box 6133, 1968), preface.

### A HIGHER-LEVEL APPROACH TO READING A CHAPTER

Suppose it's seven-thirty tonight. You've watched the news, had dinner, and now you're starting your assignment—the reading of a difficult chapter. How should you handle the job and learn and remember the maximum amount possible in the process?

No one should expect to comprehend difficult new material in a single reading, not the most gifted student nor even a scholar with special aptitude in the subject. So first of all you should plan to do more than a once over lightly reading.

### FIRST RUN-THROUGH

You would hardly plunge in blindly and try to cross rugged terrain if you could have in advance an accurate map of the region. When you plunge into a difficult chapter and "just read," you are trying to work your way through rugged territory without a map.

Spend a few minutes in an advance survey of the chapter to get a general view of what lies ahead.

### PREVIEW TO LOOK OVER THE TERRAIN

1. *Hit the "high spots" of well-organized informational writing.*
   (a) *Examine the title.*

   This in an instant should clue you in on the general content. Speculate, as you read it, about just what the chapter may have to offer.
   (b) *Read the introductory paragraph(s) thoroughly.*

   Here the author usually "announces" the general content, raises broad problems to be explored, conveniently briefs you on what's ahead. How does the content link up with what you've been studying?
   (c) *Now skim the body of the chapter.*

   As you do so, hit the headlines. What aspects of the general subject does the chapter zero in on?

   Sometimes the author flashes signals of his major thought-divisions in conspicuous headings. While textbooks vary, these headings are often centered and in large letters. You'll usually find no more than four or five of these within one chapter. Leaf through the chapter to locate these "announcements" to you from the author of the big chapter divisions under the title.

   Now take each of the big chapter divisions as a unit and look for signals of what it contains. You will often find side headings at the left side of the printed column clearly an-

*85

nouncing the sub-topics. These stand out; they are most frequently printed in a dark type called **boldface**. Perhaps there will be five or six of these sub-headings. Pause to reflect on each of these, and try to predict the content of the passage that follows it.*

THIS HEADING SIGNALS
A BIG CHAPTER DIVISION ———————➤

**2. Appearance of the United Nations Inspires Hope**

THESE BOLDFACE SIDEHEADINGS
SIGNAL SUB-TOPICS WITHIN
A CHAPTER DIVISION

*Birth of the United Nations Charter.* After preliminary conferences (i.e., Dumbarton Oaks and Yalta), delegates from fifty nations met at San Francisco in April, 1945, to draw up a Charter of the United Nations. Completed after eight weeks work, the Charter of the United Nations was ratified in July, 1945, by the Senate, 89 to 2. Other nations quickly joined, and the United Nations (UN) started operations in January, 1946, with Trygve Lie of Norway as the first Secretary-General. The organization voted to locate its permanent headquarters in New York City.

*Structure of the UN under the Charter.* According to the UN Charter there are six principal organs of the United Nations: the *General Assembly, the Security Council, the Economic and Social Council, the Trusteeship Council, the International Court of Justice,* and the *Secretariat.*

*FIGURE 3–2. Using headings. (Text material from Samuel Steinberg,* THE UNITED STATES, STORY OF A FREE PEOPLE. *Boston: Allyn and Bacon, Inc., 1963, pp. 587–588.)*

You may find that you have discovered the author's hidden outline—i.e., that his chapter division headings, and under them the side headings, fall into an outline. Of course, finding the hidden outline makes the chapter content easier to grasp. Now you have your map of the conspicuous features of the territory.

You may wish to examine the first and perhaps the last sentences of paragraphs. Topic sentences are often located here. In chapters that lack headings, topic sentences frequently announce aspects under the general subject.

Look over each graphic aid—photos, charts, graphs, art, etc. Each one is saying to you, "This is clearing up something important." It actually costs the publisher several times as much to use a graphic aid as it does to use ordinary print. He includes one, you may be sure, only to drive home something of special importance.

(d) *Read the concluding paragraph(s).*

In his last moments with you the author often wraps up important content—reviews the major principles and concepts ex-

* Gilbert C. Wrenn and Luella Cole, *Reading Rapidly and Well* (Stanford, California: Stanford University Press, 1954), p. 11.

plored in the chapter—drives home what he wants most of all to leave with his reader. By reading the summary or conclusion *first,* you may learn important content to look for when you go back to do your thorough reading.

(e) *You'll find exceptions!*

You'll find exceptions to much that's been said here. Introductions may fail to announce, and conclusions may fail to wrap up. Topic sentences aren't always first or last—or even present —in all paragraphs. You may need to preview flexibly—running your eyes over the pages, following one promising lead after another.

2. *Ask yourself, "What do I already know about this?"*

Summon up your background information—your own ideas and experiences on the subject. You'll grasp new learnings better if they click with something you already know.

3. *Questions should come to mind as you preview.*

Ask yourself constantly, "What can I expect to learn from this chapter? What should I look for when I go back and read it more carefully?"

If you own the book, try jotting in the margin questions you'll want to answer during your thorough reading.

If the book is not yours to mark, you might jot your questions on slips from a memo pad and place them between the related pages.

4. *Skillful previewing will not be instant.*

As with any skill development, you'll improve your survey techniques with practice.

5. *How long will it take?*

That varies with the student, his purpose, and the difficulty of the chapter for him. You should be able to work through a longer, more difficult chapter in ten or fifteen minutes. An easier chapter may take no more than five.

### Why Preview?

1. *You've taken the chill off the reading.*
   You have a general view of what it's all about and where it's going.

2. *Main points should now stand out.*
   If with no advance survey you just begin reading with the very first line and plod on through, you may find yourself lost among the details—you may have missed out on the main points completely.

3. *Details should now fall into place in relation to the whole.*
   Now you should retain them with less effort.

4. *Now you should intensify your concentration.*
   You'll be more alert when you know what to look for.

Don't conclude that previewing is time consuming. It's the first step in an approach which when practiced and perfected should enable you to pack 60 seconds of faster, firmer learning into every minute of study.

**QUESTION**

Now that you've previewed, you're ready for your in-depth reading of the chapter.

In this step, you work through the chapter mastering one manageable section at a time. A section marked off with a boldface side heading is likely to be a manageable amount for thorough study. Of course the length of the section you work with need not be rigid. A headed section has the advantage of being a fairly comprehensive thought unit. But if the headed section continues over several pages or is extremely difficult, you may wish to work with the content in smaller "bites."*

Carrying out the steps Question, Read, and Recite in order, you now read and master one section before going on to the next.

Read with a questioning mind set. This should help you crack the most difficult chapter. While you were previewing, you may have jotted down some questions. As you probe more deeply in your thorough reading, further questions should come to your mind. You constantly ask questions as you read along.

> More than one thousand college students took part in an experiment. Those who approached reading selections with *questions* showed decided gains in comprehension.† In another experiment students who approached reading selections with questions showed better *immediate retention* on tests just after their reading—and better *long-term retention* on tests two weeks later.‡

1. *Convert boldface headings into questions.*

   In his heavy black headings the author is shouting, "I'm presenting you with these headings as clear clues to major points. Shift them into questions and you'll be guided to the main ideas."

   Suppose a section has the boldface heading, **Results of the Scientific Process.** Quickly shift this into the question, *"What are* the results of the scientific process?" Suppose a section is headed, **The Differ-**

---

* Donald E. P. Smith and others, *Learning to Learn* (New York: Harcourt, Brace and World, Inc., 1961), p. 31.

† John N. Washburne, "The Use of Questions in Social Science Material," *Journal of Educational Psychology*, XX (May, 1929), pp. 321–359.

‡ Eleanor Holmes, "Reading Guided by Questions Versus Careful Reading and Rereading without Questions," *School Review*, XXXIX (May, 1931), pp. 361–371.

**ence Between a Physical and a Chemical Change.**
Change that heading into the question, *"What is* the
difference between a physical and a chemical
change?"

Some headings are quite general—**Systems of
Classification,** for example. You might formulate the
general question, "What are the important points here
about systems of classification?" Better still, skim the
content, then tailor a question to the information you
find there. You may discover that the section deals
with early and modern classification systems and formulate this question, "What systems of classification
have been devised?"

2. *You'll discover hidden questions.*
   You'll often find hidden questions in the topic or key sentences of paragraphs.

   There's one quickly apparent in the topic sentence,
   "Linnaeus used Latin as the language of plant classi-
   fication for several reasons." Rephrase it quickly:
   "What are the reasons why Linnaeus chose Latin?"
   There's a hidden question in this topic sentence, "Any
   system of classifying living things brings up problems."
   The question is obvious: "What problems are involved
   in systems of classification?"

3. *If boldface headings and topic sentences are missing or elu-
   sive, skim the content itself.*
   Glance through the content as you ask, "What question was
   the author trying to answer when he wrote this?" Zeroing in
   on the first few sentences of paragraphs will often suggest
   the question.

4. *Ask depth questions as well as surface questions.*
   Dr. Donald Smith of the University of Michigan's Reading
   Service points out that the questions suggested by a textbook heading may be surface questions—that you may need
   to ask deeper, more probing questions to penetrate to the
   really significant ideas of the author.*

   He gives an example from social studies. As you read
   the topic heading, **Hitler's Rise to Power,** you might think of
   the surface questions, "Who was Hitler? How did he rise to
   power? When?" It will, however, require a depth question
   to direct your attention toward the more significant ideas of
   the author: "What generalizations for our own time can we

---

* Smith and others, *Learning to Learn,* p. 25.

make—in other words, are there certain conditions which in any society would threaten the democratic process?"

5. *Be a human question mark!*
You may be wondering, "If I read to find the answer to an overall question suggested by the boldface heading, won't I overlook important content?" Take care not to skim for bits and pieces of the passage and bypass the rest. Read to find the answer to your question *and* other important content. You'll need to continue questioning, to add questions, and perhaps to adjust your questions all the while you're reading. Turn topic sentences into questions. Turn the headings of a series of steps or a list into questions—"Just what are the steps in mitosis?" "Just what phyla are listed here?" Turn key concepts and terms into questions—"Just what *is* a theory?"

*Why the Q Step?*

1. *Try it if you can't decide what's important.*
Since the author announces his important thought divisions in chapter division headings and boldface side headings, questions formulated from these headings should help you cut through what's less important to the main points.

2. *Try it if you can't concentrate.*
Now your reading becomes an active search for answers.

3. *Try it if you want a powerful tool for independent learning.*
As you perfect your skill in formulating your own questions, you become less dependent on teacher-given questions, and gain a lifetime tool for independent learning.

> A PASSAGE THAT WOULD HAVE BEEN A "STOPPER" FOR YOU MAY BE EASY TO GRASP IF APPROACHED WITH A QUESTION.

**READ—AND REFLECT**

The Read Step has an added R built right in—and this added R is *Reflect*.

| THINK |

Is reflective thinking built right into the way you operate in reading? Do you constantly read between and beyond the lines? Do you weigh and consider—explore implications—draw conclusions—speculate and wonder?

Reading and reflecting should be simultaneous and inseparable.

*90

After you've previewed you're ready for your close, intensive reading of the section of the chapter. You may be reading for a depth of comprehension never before demanded.

1. *Go in with a Question!*

   We have noted the plus values of approaching your reading with questions. A questioning mind set is a powerful aid to concentration. Holding questions in the forefront of your mind, you read searching intently instead of dreaming through the assignment.

   Now read to find the answer to your question and other important content.

2. *If full comprehension is important, read to "pull out" the meaning of each sentence.*

   New concepts are often built on full understanding of preceding ones. Keep at it until you get a breakthrough.

   When it's rough going, think over each sentence to be positive the meaning is clear to you. Try not to go on to the next sentence until you fully understand the one before.

   The meaning of very difficult parts will constantly escape you. Expect this! Successful students read difficult passages again and again. A passage that blocked you at first may come clear with a third or fourth reading.

3. *Reduce speed for dense passages.*

   Even your instructor, with his broad background and long experience in reading in his subject, finds that he must read difficult new material slowly. Reduce your own speed for passages that deliver a heavy load of ideas and information.

   Vary your approach and tempo as needed within a single section of a chapter. Within an otherwise fact-packed chapter in science you may, for example, come upon an interesting vignette of a great discovery in science or a short narrative sketch of the life story of a scientist. Speed up appropriately for this comparatively easy content.

4. *Complete stops are often called for.*

   In some reading situations a reading-straight-on pattern will be appropriate. You may wish to read in this way when you are covering light narrative material or when all you want to gain is a general impression of the content of a chapter. But in difficult materials, when your goal is comprehending fully, you will need to do stop-and-go reading. Part of the time you will read standing still! Thought time is needed in addition to reading time.

Read—then stop to ask: "Do I understand?" or "Can I give an example?" Stop to reflect: "What is the basic *why* of this?" "What outcome do I predict in view of this?" "Can I make a generalization here?" "How does this apply in the world outside of class?" Constantly question the written word: "What is the evidence that supports this?" Challenge the author. Stop to ask not just, "Why is this true?" but "Is it indeed true?"

Part of your reading time should be visualizing time. When the content lends itself, try to form a mental picture of what you've just read.

If an illustration is lacking, you may wish to draw one of your own. Making your own sketch helps you really *see*—brings what you've read into sharp focus.

5. *Graphic aids may give you instant insights.*

"Read" graphic material as thoroughly as you read words. Drawings, diagrams and the like save you reading time. A single diagram may make hundreds of words instantly clear.

Preview—Question—Read—Reflect—and now

**RECITE**

How can you "firm up" your learning? You can use the most powerful study technique known to psychologists. This is the technique of self-recitation.*

1. *Ask yourself, "Just what have I read?"*

In the Recite Step, ask yourself as you complete a section, "Just what have I read here?" Without looking at the print, check to see if you can recite to yourself the main points and the important sub-points. Put the ideas into actual words —*your own words.*

If you can't do this, that's your cue to reread appropriate parts. No need to reread it all. Skip the parts you can recall.

The Reading Study Center at Cornell University is nationally known for the solid gains it gets for college

* Walter Pauk, *How to Study in College* (Boston: Houghton Mifflin Company, 1962), p. 25.

students. These students are advised to keep the print out of sight at least 50% of the time they're studying, to look away from the book or cover it with their hand or with a card.

When college students at Cornell, in repeated experiments, spent *one minute* in recalling the content of a passage just read, they nearly doubled retention.*

2. *You may find a cover card convenient.*

A cover card is an index card of the size you find convenient, perhaps 5 x 8. Use it to conceal parts of your textbook (or notes) as you recite important content to yourself.

---

**A COVER CARD FOR FASTER, FIRMER LEARNING**

You may find a cover card a convenient device.

Use it to conceal parts of your textbook (or notebook) as you recite important content to yourself — not by rote but with full appreciation of the meaning. Expose just the boldface heading and/or perhaps the first sentence of each paragraph while you see if you can recall what the section or paragraph contains. Then lift the card and check. Expose an "official" term, cover the definition, then try to explain the meaning. Cover an important diagram while you see if you've grasped its message and perhaps its parts and labels.

Experts in the psychology of learning advise you to "keep the print out of sight perhaps 50% of the time you're studying." They are suggesting that you look away from your book (or notes) in self-recitation, and thus change half-learned to fully learned material.

Do you have trouble concentrating? Try a cover card. You can reread a passage and dream all the way through. The cover card *forces* you to concentrate as you struggle to recall what's underneath.

Self-recitation has been called the most powerful study technique known to psychologists.

---

*FIGURE 3–3. Cover card.*

3. *Turn on triple-strength learning.*

As you self-recite, you can turn on triple-strength learning. If you learn with your eyes alone, you're using just one-third of your sensory learning channels for mastering the printed page. Why not use all-out learning—visual plus auditory plus kinesthetic?

* Pauk, *How to Study in College,* p. 76.

Use your eyes in study, then add your ears and muscles:

See it!

Say it!

Hear it!

Draw it or write it!*

(a) Use your eyes as you *see* the printed words. You have now brought your visual memory into play.

(b) *Say* what you're learning, aloud or in a whisper. Now you've added kinesthetic (muscular) learning as you involve the muscles of your throat, lips, and tongue.

(c) Strengthen learning with your *ears* as you hear yourself say it. Now you've brought to bear your auditory memory.

(d) Add *kinesthetic learning* again as you make more jottings or draw a sketch. Here you've involved your motor memory.

"See it! Say it! Hear it! Draw or write it!" is a four-way reinforcement. The variety itself helps you recall. The change of pace—eyes, voice, ears, pencil—keeps you alert and increases absorption.

4. *You are not being urged to memorize—in fact, you are being urged* not *to memorize.*

Your textbooks may be condensations of broad fields of knowledge or distillations of centuries of experiment and observation and may well deserve your thoughtful study.

---

SELF-RECITATION IS ALL-OUT, ACTIVE STUDY. YOU'RE CHANGING HALF-LEARNED TO FULLY LEARNED MATERIAL.

---

### Make Important Points "Flag" You

You'll probably want to make the highlights *stand out in some way* so that you won't have to reread the entire chapter when you return to review important points later on.

1. *Select out what you want to remember.*

There are more than 500 facts and ideas crowded into some textbook chapters. You simply can't remember all of these.

* George J. Dudycha, *Learn More with Less Effort* (New York: Harper & Row, Publishers, 1957), p. 96.

The first step in retention is selecting out what is important to remember.

Facts given to illustrate a concept are usually less important than the concept itself. On the other hand, some facts and examples, once remembered, help you retain the concept.

2. *Delay marking or making notes until the end of a section.*

Having selected out the significant information, your next step is to mark the book or make notes.

Some students plunge into a chapter and mark or make notes immediately. They mark or copy whatever their eyes first glimpse on the page. It's probably best to delay marking or making notes until you've read to the end of a headed section. Why? Only then have you encountered all the ideas in the section, only then can you see their relationships, and only then can you judge their relative importance.

3. *The change of pace as you mark your book or make notes is a definite plus in study.*

The rapid succession with which ideas come crowding in one after another during reading tends to block your comprehension because of retroactive inhibition.* The break as you mark the book or make notes interrupts this rapid flow of ideas and provides "fixating" time for the ideas to make an impression.

4. *Take your choice of marking and note making methods.*

Techniques like those below—any one or a combination—will enable you to spot the high points immediately when you wish to review them later on. And you should collect a fringe benefit—pencil work has a "no-doze" effect.

a. If the books is yours to mark, the following marking methods—your preference—are likely to be useful.

(1) *Quick marginal lines.*

This is a high-speed marking method; much speedier than underlining, it's the quickest marking method of all. Draw a *solid* vertical line down the margin (just to the left of the column of print) next to a *major point* which you wish to stand out. Place your marginal line carefully to mark the exact extent of the part you've selected as important. Since your markings should show relative importance, use a *dotted* marginal line

* H. F. Spitzer, "Studies in Retention," *Journal of Educational Psychology,* XXX (December, 1939), pp. 641–656.

to mark an important *sub-point.* Using light pencil makes it possible for you to reconsider and perhaps revise your markings later.

(2) *Underline to show relative importance.*
You might underline main ideas with two lines and important details with one.

$$========= = \text{main idea}$$
$$——————— = \text{important detail}$$

Be selective. When you over-underline, none of the ideas flag you as outstanding, and the task of learning such a mass of detail looks overwhelming.

(3) *Use see-through color accents.*
Use color if you like—but use it sparingly. Because of the ease with which color accents can be applied, there's a tendency to become "color happy" and over-accent. You might accent main points with one color, sub-points with another.

(4) *Make marginal mini-notes, brief jottings of key words or cue phrases.*
Key words or phrases that call to mind main points can be jotted at the far edge of the left margin of your book. Key words that suggest sub-points can be jotted below these, set in a little.

When you review the passage later you can use these cue words to trigger your recall of the important points.

(5) *Use marginal numerals.*
As you read a paragraph or longer unit you might place numerals in the margin beside points to be remembered. You might use *a's* and *b's,* set under these, to indicate sub-points. For example, a paragraph which gives several different causes of an event in a series might lend itself to numerals placed in the margin.

(6) *Make asterisks.*
An asterisk (*) can guide your eye to an idea of supreme importance—the major idea of a chapter, for example, or an underlying principle or concept.

(7) *Use marginal question marks.*
A question mark in the margin can indicate a statement which you question or with which you disagree.

(8) *A check mark can remind you, "Check this out!"*
Use a check mark to indicate something you don't understand and plan to check with your instructor later.

(9) *"Capsulate" important content.*
A capsule summary of a concept, principle, or other crucial content can be jotted in the book itself, perhaps in the upper or lower margin. If you don't own the book, you can use a small slip of paper and place it between the related pages.

(10) *Where do* your *ideas come in?*
Of course, you'll want to make notes on your *own* observations, impressions, and conclusions. You might jot these in the margin, marking them with your initials or the word ME with a circle around it, or else place your own ideas in brackets.*

b. If the book is not yours to mark, the following note making methods are appropriate.

(1) *Make quick, labor saving notes (or an outline).*
A shorthand of your own will save you time. You can soon develop a personal "notehand" something like this:

| | | |
|---|---|---|
| about | = | abt |
| be | = | b |
| before | = | bf |
| no | = | n |
| are | = | r |
| point | = | pt |
| development | = | dev |
| observation | = | obsrv |
| environment | = | env |
| hypothesis | = | hypth |
| evolution | = | evol |

Note *taking* sometimes amounts to an absentminded copying the book. Don't take notes—*make* notes. Rephrase the content when possible.

How complete should your notes be? This varies with the person and the purpose. Enough for *you* to recall as much of the content as you need.

* Many of the ideas about marking a book were suggested by Pauk, *How to Study in College*, p. 46.

Again, it's probably best to delay making notes (or outlining) until you've read to the end of a section. Only then can you judge the relationships of the ideas and decide on their relative importance.

(2) *Memo slips can be useful.*

If the book is not yours to mark, you can easily jot your notes on a small memo pad and insert the slips between the related pages of the book.

When you've finished studying a chapter you'll want to remove the slips from your book. Otherwise your book will bulge with these inserts. Clip them together in order, label an envelope with the title of the chapter, and place these envelopes in order as "pockets" in your notebook.*

(3) *You can convert the Q Step into a quick, efficient way of making notes.*†

As you formulate questions during the Q Step, you might jot these on slips from a memo pad and keep them between the related pages of your textbook. As you come upon the answers during your thorough reading, jot them on the slips too.

(4) *The divided page is sometimes handy.*

Make a dividing line down a page in your notebook. In the *Question* column to the left, record the question you formulated during the Q Step. In the *Answer* column to the right, jot quick notes that call to mind the answer.‡

The divided page, you'll find, is handy when review time comes. The dividing line makes it possible to conceal the answers completely as you check your understandings later.

The divided page is convenient for recording important new terms and their meanings. Mark the end of each unit, perhaps with a double line. Now when you want to go back and check on the new words you've studied in a certain unit, you'll know exactly where to find them.

(5) *The divided notebook offers all the space you need.*

You may prefer the divided notebook to the divided page. Open your looseleaf notebook so that it lies flat

---

* Illa Podendorf, former science teacher at the University of Chicago Laboratory School. Remarks to Thomas, November, 1970.

† Horace Judson, *The Techniques of Reading* (New York: Harcourt, Brace and Company, 1954), p. 159.

‡ Preston and Botel, *How to Study,* p. 37.

on the desk before you. On the page that lies to the left, record the questions you formulated during the Q Step. Just across, in a corresponding position on the page to the right, jot notes that call to mind the answer. Check your memory later by folding the right-hand half of the notebook underneath so that the questions are exposed and the answers out of sight.

You may wish to leave extra space between your questions in the divided notebook for making class notes on related discussions and lectures.

(6) *What about your own brainstorming?*

What of your own reflections, your own interpretations, your own evaluations? If it's a case of inserting your own ideas right into notes you are making from other sources, you should enclose your own ideas inside of brackets. Or you might jot your own reflections on slips from a memo pad, mark them with your initials or with the word ME and place them between related pages of the chapter.

---

WHY MAKE JOTTINGS? NOW YOU'VE INVOLVED MOTOR MEMORY— IN MANY STUDENTS ONE OF THE STRONGEST LEARNING CHANNELS OF ALL. IF YOU WERE TO DO NOTHING MORE THAN RECORD YOUR NOTES, THEN LOSE THEM FOREVER, YOU WOULD STILL BE AHEAD. THE MUSCULAR ACT OF WRITING, IN AND OF ITSELF, WOULD HAVE STRENGTHENED YOUR LEARNING.

---

## REVIEW

Unless you learn for the future, a lot of hard work goes by the board. Several thousand high school students read a passage with no review. Within two weeks they had lost 80 per cent and retained only 20 per cent of what they had at first remembered. But when these same students carried out a review step just after their reading, the figures were reversed. They retained 80 per cent and lost just 20 per cent!*

ONE MORE TIME

1. *Regain the broad view of the chapter.*

You have just completed a close, intensive reading by applying Question, Read, Reflect, and Recite to sections of a chapter. You've been concentrating on sections—even bits and pieces, like the meaning of a single key term. As you've focused on each part you may have lost the broad chapter plan.

* Spitzer, *Journal of Educational Psychology*, XXX, pp. 641–656.

To regain the broad view, turn through the chapter in a final run-through. Try to recite its broad organization and to recall its big thought divisions. You've attended to the little pieces of the jigsaw. Now look once more at the total picture. Here you're focusing once more on what you learned in your preview.

2. *Then check on the important sub-points.*

Work through the chapter once again, checking your understanding of the content just below each boldface heading. Your cover card may be useful again. Reread parts you have forgotten.

3. *Once more, turn on triple-strength learning—eyes, ears, muscles.*

Use your *eyes* to reread selectively. *Say* things aloud and *hear* yourself. *Write* down cue phrases, little jottings of the key words in ideas you want to remember.

4. *Use the memory aid of overlearning.*

Learning for the future requires overlearning. A football player learns to take his man out in a run around left end. Then he goes over and over the play until he overlearns it. He does this so that there will be no forgetting or confusion. An actor memorizes his lines well enough to deliver them without error. Then he continues to go over them until they are automatic.*

Learning experts say, "Minimal learning is not enough. When you can say, 'I have learned this material,' you may need to spend perhaps one-fourth the original time overlearning it." In one study, students who overlearned a vocabulary lesson remembered *four times as much* after four weeks had passed.

5. *You can retain longer through spaced reviews.*

You can remember longer simply by the way you place your reviews. You can place your first review to minimize forgetting. Suppose you read an assignment today. When will forgetting take its greatest toll? If your forgetting is typical, the greatest loss will be within one day. Arrange your first review to check this drop. Place it from 12 to 24 hours after you study. Reinforce immediately, and you will remember *much* longer.

---

* Richard Kalish, *Making the Most of College* (Belmont, California: Wadsworth Publishing Company, Inc., 1959), p. 119.

A study expert* pointed out the "curve of forgetting" to military officers returning to academic study after being out of school for several years.†

The first student studied one hour on September 30, and six weeks later retained very little.

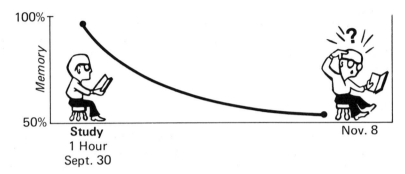

*FIGURE 3–4. Curve of forgetting. (Drawing reproduced by permission of Dr. Staton.)*

The second student studied only 30 minutes on September 30, but he spaced out reviews—15 minutes on October 1, and 10 minutes more on October 8. On November 8 it took this student just a 5-minute review to bring back what he wanted—with 100% mastery.

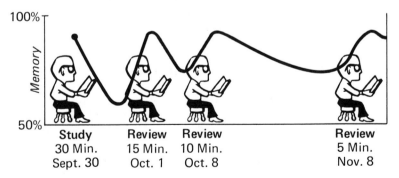

*FIGURE 3–5. Spaced review. (Reproduced by permission of Dr. Staton.)*

* Thomas F. Staton, a study expert, has contributed a number of the ideas used in several sections of this book.

† Staton, *How to Study,* pp. 58, 59. The drawing to illustrate the "Curve of Forgetting" is reproduced from page 59 with Dr. Staton's generous permission.

Both students studied just one hour, but the one who spaced out his review had far better retention.

### A Summing Up

In the Preview Step you're concerned with the entire chapter, surveying it for the total picture. Then you work through the chapter, one manageable section at a time, completing the Question, Read, Reflect, and Recite Steps in order, one right after another. In the Review Step you're concerned with the entire chapter again, as you regain the broad view.

### That Is PQ4R

Is it cumbersome? It was a method of fast, efficient study at Maxwell Air Base—and elsewhere—during a wartime crisis.

Will there be difficulties applying PQ4R? Poorly organized material is likely to present difficulties. But poorly written material makes strategies that facilitate reading even more essential.

What do we have in PQ4R? An approach to help you comprehend better, concentrate better, retain better, and have a powerful tool for more efficient learning—useful in reading *any* informational selection.

It's a cluster of techniques and skills. If you incorporate into your permanent habits just two or three of these techniques you should upgrade your study. If you adopt the whole package—or a close adaptation—you will have acquired a powerful study approach for the thorough mastery of a textbook chapter.

### CAN PQ4R HELP YOU READ SUPPLEMENTARY BOOKS?

Often your reading assignment is not a single textbook chapter. It may be an informational book or perhaps several books. Suppose your instructor has suggested, "Just read this rapidly for general background."

If you attack your extensive supplementary readings with the slow, intensive approach you use in studying your textbooks, you'll find yourself spending impossible amounts of time. PQ4R, adapted somewhat as follows, should help you *get what you're after faster* when you're reading supplementary books for general background.*

* In preparing this explanation, the writers have leaned on the insights of Francis P. Robinson, *Effective Study*, 1961, pp. 39–40.

***Consider why the assignment was made.*** Did your instructor make any comments about the *why* of this assignment? These may dictate a special approach. A teacher might suggest, "This book offers a point of view about the role of large corporations quite different from that in your textbook." Then you'll want to approach your reading with the question, "Just what *is* this different viewpoint?" Make the most of any suggestions from your instructor.

While your teacher's comments may suggest a special emphasis and way of approach, the following general suggestions— some or all of them—should prove useful.

***Preview the book.*** Provide yourself, first of all, with a "map" of the book. Through the preface, you can often discover the author's viewpoint. Through the table of contents, you can have at a glance a concise listing of the major topics which will be covered.

Skim the opening chapter. Sometimes this chapter takes the form of an introduction—a look ahead at what is coming in the book. Here the author may "tell you what he's going to tell you."

Skim the concluding chapter. This is sometimes a summary chapter—a look back. Here the author may "tell you what he's told you." The final chapter is often highly concentrated. It's the writer's *last opportunity* with you, his audience. So here he often wraps up the big ideas, drives home the points and conclusions he wants most of all to leave with you.

***Go in with a question.*** This time, you've been assigned an entire book as supplementary reading. You're probably not expected to read for minor details but for major points or "chapter points." Your teacher may have alerted you to important content to look for.

Converting *chapter titles* into questions may be an effective technique for guiding you to broad "chapter points." So will shifting into questions the conspicuous headings of *big* chapter divisions.

In Harry A. Overstreet's *The Mature Mind,* the first section of the book is headed "The Maturity Concept," and within that section the first chapter has the title "Psychological Foundations." A broad question with which to approach that chapter quickly comes to mind: *"What are* the psychological foundations of the maturity concept?" Chapter 2 is headed "Criteria of Maturity." Shift that into a question, *"What are* the criteria or standards for measuring maturity?" Chapter 3 is entitled "Two Old Theories and a New One." Convert that title into the question, "What are two old theories about maturity and what is the new theory?" Questions like these will guide you to the big ideas of chapters.

You'll probably want to jot down your questions as an aid in keeping them in mind.

*Read and reflect.* Working through the book one chapter at a time, you'll approach your reading with a broad "chapter question," "chapter division questions," and/or questions your teacher or the class has posed. Since you're reading just for major points, you can build up more speed on this type of reading.

You may want to give *certain spots within the chapter* your special attention. Beginnings and endings are often strategic spots within expository chapters. The introductory and concluding paragraphs are likely to give you an idea of the general chapter content. The beginnings of paragraphs frequently carry a heavy load of meaning. You'll often find topic sentences located here.

As always, reading and reflecting should be intermingled as you wonder about something—ask *why*—weigh a statement—argue with the author—and apply what you're reading to the world outside the classroom.

You'll probably want to make some quick notes on the answers to your questions.

*Recite.* In your in-depth reading of your textbook, you took small "bites"—perhaps you worked with a headed section, a fairly short section marked off with a boldface side heading. Since you're now reading just for main ideas, you can probably take larger "bites." The ends of chapters or of *long* chapter divisions are usually good places to stop for evaluation.*

Look away from the book or cover your notes while you try to recall the answer to your broad question(s). Reread—if you need to—to call something to mind.

*Review.* You've just worked through the book chapter by chapter. You may now need to call back to mind the book's total plan or broad view.

Turn through your notes, checking to see if you can answer each question with your notes covered. A run-through of the book as a whole should "firm up" your learning.

### Summing Up

1. Consider *why* you're reading.
2. Preview the book.
3. Approach with *broad* questions.
4. Read.
5. Recite.
6. Review.

* Robinson, *Effective Study*, p. 40.

## QUESTIONS TO DEVELOP COMPREHENSION SKILLS

*Comprehension is plural—a miscellany of different skills. Using the regular course materials, teachers in every classroom can foster the development of a full spectrum of skills for their subjects.*

Just what is comprehension? We sometimes hear the remark, "This student just isn't comprehending," as if comprehension were one general ability which a student either has or does not have.

But instead of being singular, comprehension is plural, an aggregate of many different skills. As Nila Banton Smith expressed it, "Comprehension is just a big, blanket term that covers a whole area of thought-getting processes in reading."*

Since we probably can help to develop comprehension more effectively if we understand a little of what it embraces, some of the component skills which seem apparent are listed below.†

1. Grasping directly stated details or facts.
2. Understanding main ideas.
3. Grasping the sequence of time, place, ideas, events, or steps.
4. Understanding and following directions.
5. Grasping implied meanings and drawing inferences.
6. Understanding character (emotional reactions, motives, personal traits) and setting.
7. Sensing relationships of time, place, cause and effect, events, and characters.
8. Anticipating outcomes.
9. Recognizing the author's tone, mood, and intent.

* Nila Banton Smith, *Reading Instruction for Today's Children* (Englewood Cliffs, New Jersey: Prentice-Hall, Inc., 1963), p. 257.

† The writers have based this list of sub-skills (with the exception of the added area of evaluation) on Helen K. Smith's enumeration of comprehension skills in Chapter IV, "Sequence in Comprehension" in *Sequential Development of Reading Abilities,* edited by Helen M. Robinson (Chicago: University of Chicago Press, 1960), pp. 51 ff. Other investigators who have explored the mental processes involved in comprehension have come up with somewhat different lists of sub-skills. For other analyses the reader may wish to consult Frederick B. Davis's "Research in Comprehension in Reading" in *Reading Research Quarterly,* III, No. 4 (1968), pp. 499–545, and Richard Rystrom's "Toward Defining Comprehension: A Second Report," in *Journal of Reading Behavior,* II, No. 2 (1970). Sanders's classification of classroom questions (based on Benjamin S. Bloom's categories of thinking) and his rich offering of clarifying examples is of related interest (Morris M. Sanders, *Classroom Questions: What Kinds?* New York: Harper & Row, Publishers, 1966).

10. Understanding and drawing comparisons and contrasts.
11. Drawing conclusions or making generalizations.
12. Making evaluations.

One of the authors confesses that during her years as an English teacher she regarded reading comprehension as esoteric—an indefinable something beyond her powers and requiring the training and experience of a reading specialist. She was not aware that she was already building comprehension in many ways from day to day in her classroom—and that she could do infinitely more. Classroom teachers who examine Smith's enumeration of sub-skills and the classifications of other investigators should appreciate more fully what they are already doing to achieve better comprehension. And they may respond, "But we can do more!" as the enumeration of sub-skills calls to mind specific needs they have observed in their students. They can then plot their strategy to add to their students' working stock of skills—and they will be sensitive to constant opportunities.

How can a classroom teacher encourage the development of the comprehension skills essential for reading competence in his subject? He can do so daily, using the regular course materials, by formulating questions intended to elicit the use of these skills—questions probing for information that won't yield itself without the use of the desired skill. Upon observing a deficiency in one of the aspects of comprehension, he can deliberately plan his question strategy to force the practice of the desired skill. At times the questions can be supplied as guides for students in advance of their reading. At other times questions can be raised in the course of class discussions.

## STUDENTS NEED ALL THE SKILLS

To grow toward maturity in reading, students need wide experience in using the full spectrum of comprehension skills. All too often, however, there is overemphasis in classrooms on the memory aspects—on just-plain-fact questions. When Helen K. Smith analyzed the questions asked by instructors on tests and examinations, she discovered a preponderance of questions requiring no more than factual information. She reported further that the questions teachers asked when assigning reading and making out examinations were strong determiners of the manner in which their students read.* If we are content, she observed, that students read merely to remember a body

* Helen K. Smith, *Responses for Good and Poor Readers When Asked to Read for Different Purposes* (doctoral dissertation abstract, University of Chicago, 1965), p. 14.

of factual information, then we will concentrate on factual questions: "Ask for details—get back details." If, on the other hand, we are committed to helping them handle ideas, cope with relationships, make critical evaluations, then we must compose our questions carefully with these higher purposes in mind.*

The comprehension skills enumerated above are in a sense a hierarchy, advancing as they do from *literal skills* (skills 1–4 are often literal), in which the student reads what is actually printed in the lines, to *beyond-the-literal* skills (skills 5–12), in which he reads "between and beyond the lines." Most higher-level thinking rests solidly upon a basis of factual information. Here again the student cannot build a second story without a first story. As the instructor plans guiding questions to accompany assigned reading, he may want to devise questions to help the student pull out the underlying facts. With these at his command, the student should then be better prepared to proceed to depth questions—ones that require him to grasp implications, draw conclusions, make generalizations, arrive at evaluations. Before the student can respond to the penetrating question, "What purely personal motives of Pericles can you infer from what he said in the Funeral Oration?" clearly he must have on call considerable factual information about Pericles and he must have grasped the literal content of the Funeral Oration.

Sanders views facts in this perspective: "For the most part, facts should serve as a means to an end rather than as ends in themselves. When a teacher approaches a new unit, he should ask himself: 'What are the most important generalizations that deserve to be emphasized? What facts are necessary to develop these generalizations?' "†

While well formulated questions encourage both breadth and depth of comprehension, skillful questioning alone is clearly not enough. Comprehension skills are "taught not caught." Guided openbook practice in which students analyze how to arrive at the answer to a question is a highly rewarding practice. "Let's turn to the passage and . . ." can be a frequent suggestion of teachers.‡

The rest of this section of the chapter consists of examples of questions classified according to the comprehension skill they foster and intended to encourage the development of specific skills of comprehension in various disciplines. Each question attempts to throw a searchlight on one aspect of comprehension. The reader will undoubtedly find these examples suggestive, will improve on some, and will generate a host of his own in keeping with the needs of his stu-

---

* Helen K. Smith. Lecture to class in methods of teaching secondary school reading, University of Chicago, 1960.

† Sanders, *Classroom Questions: What Kinds?*, p. 21.

‡ Kenworthy, *Guide to Social Studies Teaching in Secondary Schools*, p. 104.

dents and the materials they are reading. Many of the questions are not purely one type or another—there will be much overlap. Questions classified under one discipline may prove suggestive for another.

## QUESTIONS ENCOURAGING SPECIFIC COMPREHENSION SKILLS

### Grasping Directly Stated Details or Facts

#### All Reading Subjects

After introductory work with paragraphs, students practice with paragraphs in which the main idea sentence has various locations in the paragraph and is supported by clear-cut details. They are directed: Mark the sentence that gives the main idea, and number the details that support it.

Possibilities for introductory work with paragraphs will be found in "Finding the Key Thought" later on in this chapter. Highly practical ideas for working with the main idea and details of paragraphs are offered in Joseph C. Gainsburg's *Advanced Skills in Reading,* Books 1, 2, and 3, Teacher's Annotated Edition (New York: The Macmillan Company, 1967).

Students might analyze paragraphs with the aid of simple diagrams in keeping with the structure of each paragraph. They might be asked to record the main idea and the details of appropriate paragraphs on a framework like this:*

Students write the main thought here.

They jot down supporting details on these lines.

They note any minor details that support major details here.

* Ruth Strang, Lecture to class in methods of teaching secondary school reading, University of Chicago, summer of 1965.

In paragraphs in which the main idea is expressed at the beginning, students are asked to anticipate what lies ahead in the rest of the paragraph. They discover that the main idea sentence often provides a strong clue about what is to follow: supporting details, a clarifying example or two, an explanation or reasons, the details of a comparison or contrast, a series of steps in time order, the steps in a process. They experience being able to grasp the details with less effort once they foresee the trend of the paragraph.

They are asked, for example, to predict the contents of a paragraph starting with the topic sentence: "The Gregorian calendar is now used in almost every civilized country because of its great accuracy." From the moment they read the topic sentence with the phrase "because of its great accuracy," their minds are set to expect the reason or explanation for this great accuracy. They now know what to look for. Consequently they read the paragraph with greater understanding.*

### English

What details create a mood of melancholy in the opening paragraphs of "The Fall of the House of Usher?"

Would you like (a character in the story) for your friend? What has the author done or had the character do to make you like or dislike him?†

Illustrate this scene from the story. First, make quick jottings of details that the author has used to help you "see" the scene.

### Social Studies

Read this account of the life of John F. Kennedy. Notice how new paragraphs introduce new events in his life or important aspects of it. Make brief notes (just a word or two) that give the gist of the event or, if you own the book, jot a word or two in the margin.

### Science

What conditions are probably necessary for a tornado to form?

What are catalysts? What are their unusual properties?‡

---

* Joseph C. Gainsburg, *Advanced Reading Skills,* Book 2 (New York: The Macmillan Company, 1967), p. 232.

† Ruth Strang, Constance M. McCullough, and Arthur E. Traxler, *The Improvement of Reading* (New York: McGraw-Hill Book Company, Inc., 1961), adapted from p. 135.

‡ Biological Sciences Curriculum Study, *Biological Science: Molecules to Man,* Revised Edition (Boston: Houghton Mifflin Company, 1968), p. 145.

Can you find in this passage evidence that supports the author's statement that some present-day land areas were once covered by the ocean?

**Art**

Draw this character just as he is portrayed in this story. First, jot down the details the author uses to help you "see" him.

## Understanding the Main Idea

### All Reading Subjects

After introductory work, students are asked: "Can you find the main idea of this paragraph [or longer passage]? Look for the point the paragraph makes; the broadest, most significant message of the author; the idea he wants most of all to drive home and leave with you."

After being introduced to the paragraph patterns below (and others), students, upon meeting these types in expository materials, might be asked, "What pattern that we have studied does this paragraph follow?"

1. A paragraph whose main idea is supported—or proved to be true—by the details.

2. A paragraph whose main idea is explained or made clear by the details or by an illustrative example.

3. A paragraph in which the author leads you through a process of reasoning until you arrive at a conclusion that logically follows. In a paragraph of this type, the last sentence is often the general conclusion toward which a series of details, a line of argument, or a chain of reasoning has led.

### English

Read to find out why this selection has the title _____ _____?

What is a good title for this paragraph [or longer selection]? Be sure your title is a good wrap-up of what the paragraph contains and is broad enough to cover its content.

Write a telegram of ten words or less conveying the broadest, most significant information in this selection [or paragraph].

### Science

Read the procedures you will follow in this laboratory experiment. Give the purpose of the experiment in a sentence or two.

### Art

An art history class studying Twentieth Century art, including Marc Chagall's efforts to reinterpret Jewish and Hebrew folklore in terms of the Twentieth Century, had this assignment: "Within the next week, will all of you examine this book about Chagall and sum up in one sentence what he is trying to do?"*

## Grasping the Sequence of Ideas, Events, or Steps

### English

Briefly describe (a character) at the beginning of the story. Then describe him as he was when the story closed. List in order the people, things, and events that caused him to change during the story.†

### Social Studies

Read this selection about the territorial growth of the United States. Note the important events in order, associating them with their dates, and thinking how each event led up to the next one.‡

### Science

Trace an "excited electron" from the chlorophyll molecule in photosynthesis until it is added to oxygen during respiration.§

Jot down brief notes (a word or two) that call to mind each step in the life cycle of the gypsy moth [oxygen–carbon dioxide cycle, pasteurization process], or jot in the margin a word or two that sums up each step. Then look away and try to recall the steps. Are your steps in order?

Study the process of refining petroleum through the use of a fractionating tower. Shift your attention to the diagram whenever

* Robert Erickson, University of Chicago Laboratory School art teacher. Remarks to Thomas, May, 1971.

† Strang, McCullough, and Traxler, *The Improvement of Reading,* adapted from p. 135.

‡ Nila Banton Smith, *Be a Better Reader,* Book IV (Englewood Cliffs, New Jersey: Prentice-Hall, Inc., 1960), slightly adapted from p. 88.

§ Biological Sciences Curriculum Study, *Biological Science: Molecules to Man,* p. 211.

you are referred there. After reading a sentence explaining a step in the process, look at the diagram and try to picture the step as taking place. Continue to read, referring to the diagram after reading each step. Finally, try to express all the steps in your own words without looking at the diagram.*

### Mathematics

Read through this explanation of the derivation of a formula. See whether you can follow the reasoning that leads to its final form.†

## Understanding and Following Directions

### Science

What procedure do you follow to focus your microscope on an object?

### Mathematics

Study this explanation (for carrying out a certain process). Make brief jottings in your own words of the steps you'll take in reaching the solution. Then work a problem, carrying out this process step by step.

### Photography

Study these directions on the can for mixing a gallon of photo-developer. They must be followed 100% in order for you to have a usable product. To be sure you understand, write out in your own words a list of things to be done. Before mixing the developer, check your list with your teacher.‡

## Grasping Implied Meanings or Drawing Inferences

### English

Young Gareth took certain vows when he became a knight. What were these vows and what do they reveal to you about the values of his day?

What truth about the inner lives of all of us does Hawthorne suggest in "The Minister's Black Veil"?

* Smith, *Be a Better Reader,* Book V, adapted from p. 101.
† Strang, McCullough, and Traxler, *The Improvement of Reading,* p. 165.
‡ Erickson. Remarks to Thomas, May, 1971.

Figurative language often stirs your imagination and helps you see vivid pictures. Suggest through cartoons or humorous drawings the *literal* comparison being drawn in figurative expressions you'll meet in your reading for tomorrow. (Expressions like these suggest lively possibilities: His father *clipped his wings* . . . She *dropped her eyes* . . . He was *rooted to the spot* . . . The money *burned a hole in his pocket.*)

### Social Studies

What can you learn about the customs, values, and ideals of the Athenians from Pericles' Funeral Oration.*

### Science

From the characteristics of the bill of this bird, what do you infer about its eating habits?

## Understanding Character (Emotional Reactions, Motives, Personal Traits) and Setting

### English

What motive do you think prompted (a certain character's) action? Imagine what your reactions would be if you were in his situation.

Often a fiction writer tells you without telling you. Instead of revealing outright a character's innermost emotions, he challenges you to use your imagination. He provides hints through the character's actions, his conversation, the details of his appearance. Can you find in this passage a subtle revelation of what (a character's) true feelings toward (another character) are?

Often in a story we know full well what type of person a character is although the author has never once mentioned a personal trait. Instead he has revealed traits *indirectly* through the character's words and actions and through the reactions of others toward him. How much can you discover about (a character) in these few lines?

Sometimes the author, in the opening of a story, tells you outright where and when the action will occur. Other times he provides subtle clues, and you must *infer* the setting. In this story can you find such clues and identify the setting?

* Joel Surgal, University of Chicago Laboratory School social studies teacher. Remarks to Thomas, May, 1971.

Imagine yourself in Brutus' place when he heard Caesar say, "And you, too, Brutus!" How do you think he felt?

## Sensing Relationships of Time, Place, Cause and Effect, Events, and Characters

### Social Studies

You are living in the days of the Crusaders. Why will you go on a Crusade if you are (1) a parish priest, (2) a knight, (3) a scholar, (4) a king.*

History is the record of a chain of causes and effects. Read the passage to answer this question: "What causes led to the purchase of the Louisiana territory, and how did it in turn become a cause with its own effects on our national growth?"†

### Science

If you drop a needle carefully upon the surface of water, it will float. Can you explain why?

What will happen to the water line of a boat when it moves from salt water into fresh water? . . . Why does this happen?‡

## Anticipating Outcomes

### English

After the murder of Duncan, who will stand the strain of guilt better—Macbeth or Lady Macbeth?

You know this character—his disposition, his feelings, and his motives. What action do you anticipate?§

Authors often plant clues that lead the "sharp" reader to anticipate coming events. At the tournament what foreshadows a romance between Ivanhoe and Rowena?

### Social Studies

What changes is automation likely to bring in *your* life during the next quarter of a century ?

* Surgal, remarks to Thomas, May, 1971.

† Smith, *Be a Better Reader,* Book V, adapted from p. 66.

‡ Willard J. Jacobson, Robert N. King, Louise E. Killie, and Richard D. Konicek, *Broadening Worlds of Science* (New York: American Book Company, 1964), p. 317.

§ Strang, McCullough, and Traxler, *The Improvement of Reading,* p. 138.

### Science

What do you think man will use for energy when his coal and oil are exhausted?*

You know about this theory. What can we expect in a certain situation on the basis of it?

### Mathematics

When the proof of a theorem is on the page before you, complete with every step, try to resist the temptation to be a mere spectator. Use two index cards to conceal the proof supplied you by the authors. Cover the *Statements* with one card and the *Reasons* with the other. Read the statement of the theorem, examine the diagram, and search out what you're to prove and what's already given. With the first *Statement* concealed, ask yourself, "What will the author's first statement be?" Formulate your considered guess. Then lift your card and see if you predicted correctly. Next ask yourself, "What will the authors give as a reason?" Formulate your answer. Lift your card and check. Continue through the sequence of *Statements* and *Reasons,* lowering your card step by step.†

## Recognizing the Author's Tone, Mood, and Intent

### All Reading Subjects

It is well to ask, "What *is* the writer's purpose? Does he have a hidden motive for saying what he does? Does he want to win your support in behalf of some policy or practice to his advantage? Will your uncritical acceptance of his point of view result in his financial gain?" What might be the intent of the following writers: (1) the president of the National Association of Manufacturers writing about a proposed law to curb the activity of labor unions in politics; (2) the president of the United Automobile Workers writing about the same subject.‡

Read these two newspaper accounts that give sharply contrasting viewpoints of the same event. What is each writer's intent? Can you find emotionally charged words used by each to sway you to his viewpoint? Underline these words.

* Jacobson et al., *Broadening Worlds of Science,* p. 54.

† Paul Moulton, former University of Chicago Laboratory School mathematics teacher. Remarks to Thomas, May, 1968.

‡ Richard D. Altick, *Preface to Critical Reading* (New York: Holt, Rinehart and Winston, 1956), p. 181.

Is the writer an unbiased reporter, or do his own personal beliefs show through in this selection? If so, how? Is he trying to influence you to accept his viewpoint?

### English

Sometimes a writer says one thing, but the meaning he intends to convey is exactly the opposite. The ordinary meaning of the words he uses is the opposite of the thought within his mind. This writer is using *irony*. Can you find an example in the passage?

## Understanding and Drawing Comparisons and Contrasts

### English

For girls only: Whom would you prefer for a husband—King Arthur or Sir Lancelot? (or Cyrano or Christian)? Why?

For boys only: Whom would you prefer—Guinevere or Elaine (or Rebecca or Rowena)? Why?

### Social Studies

Where would you have preferred to live in ancient Greece—in Athens or in Sparta?*

### Science

Compare the telephone transmitter to the human ear, listing the similarities.†

## Drawing Conclusions; Making Generalizations

### All Reading Subjects

This sample question from social studies is easily adaptable to other subjects: A teacher supplied three examples of conflict of interest in passages to be studied by the class. He explained that the meaning of the concept could be determined from the three examples of the operation of the concept which he presented. After giving some time for studying the examples and composing the definitions, the teacher asked that some of them be read to the class. The one

---

* Association of Teachers of Social Studies of the City of New York, *Handbook for Social Studies Teaching*, p. 58.

† Jacobson et al., *Broadening Worlds of Science*, p. 361.

chosen by the class as the best was assigned to be remembered. The assignment for the following day was to find in the newspapers examples of the operation of conflict of interest or to make up plausible examples.*

Students might examine a well founded conclusion drawn by the writer, then search out the facts given in the passage to consider whether they warrant this conclusion. They might also examine a false conclusion and decide whether the data in the passage support it.

### Social Studies

A class might consider this question: "Why is our city located here rather than forty miles north or south? Who decides where to put a city?" They might study the early location of various cities, then generalize in answer to the question: "What determines the location of cities?"†

### Science

What general rule can you make concerning the effect of heat upon molecules?

What conclusion can you draw from the report of this experiment?

## Making Evaluations

### All Reading Subjects

After reading several descriptions of an event that is subject to controversy, such as a race riot, the teacher might ask, "Which report of this incident is most reliable?" Before the students undertake to answer such a question, they should set up standards for judging whether an observation statement is reliable.‡

### Social Studies

Would you favor having your political party engage in gerrymandering if it had the opportunity? Support your view.§

* Sanders, *Classroom Questions: What Kinds?*, p. 15.

† Alice Flickinger, former University of Chicago Laboratory School social studies teacher. Remarks to Thomas, November, 1970.

‡ Sanders, *Classroom Questions: What Kinds?* p. 25.

§ Sanders, *Classroom Questions: What Kinds?*, p. 5.

Were the great industrial figures of the late 19th Century "robber barons" or "industrial statesmen"?*

**Science**

Should we try to engineer man's heredity? If so, what kinds of people should we be engineering for? Should we be meddling at all?

## FINDING THE KEY THOUGHT

*An example of teaching procedures in helping students learn to work with a cluster of comprehension skills.*

As we have indicated, the art of questioning is a powerful tool in helping to develop comprehension skills. In addition it behooves the instructor to be aware of specific teaching strategies for specific comprehension skills. Too often we appear to follow the course of practice makes perfect—if a student can't recognize the main idea or key thought, give him more exercises until he can master the skill. For many students such a procedure succeeds only in causing further frustration and failure. We need to analyze an important aspect of comprehension and attempt to delineate the sub-skills needed to accomplish that type of comprehension. This section of the comprehension chapter attempts to do just that with one major comprehension aspect—key thought or main idea.

Finding or grasping the main idea or key thought is *not* an essential comprehension skill for all types of reading or for all purposes. Sometimes we overgeneralize and overemphasize its significance. For example, if we need to read to bake some cookies, there is no reason for searching out an overall main idea—it already exists in the mind of the reader; here, specific details in appropriate sequence with emphasis on how-to-do-it is the goal.

On the other hand, finding the key thought is often important, and many students from grade 7 through graduate school are sometimes unsure of themselves in this area. The following material is but very slightly adapted from H. Alan Robinson's original material.†

The concept of a cluster of skills grew out of the belief that students should not be asked to find the main idea before getting a

* Thomas A. Bailey, *The American Pageant Quiz Book* (Boston: D. C. Heath and Company, 1961), p. 106.
† H. Alan Robinson, "A Cluster of Skills: Especially for Junior High School," *The Reading Teacher*, XV (September, 1961), pp. 25–28.

great deal of practice in learning how to read for details. The ability to recognize and formulate main ideas calls for a decided degree of reading and thinking maturity. In the final analysis, in order to deal with main ideas or key thoughts, a student must be able to recognize important or key words in sentences, understand basic organizational patterns of written material, draw conclusions, and make inferences.

### Step One: Key Words in a Sentence

Hovious' technique of sending a telegram is used to establish the concept of key words as the most important words.* Students quickly observe that "Arrive Kennedy nine Wednesday evening" is a statement of the most important words in the sentence, "I shall arrive at the Kennedy International Airport in New York at nine o'clock on Wednesday evening." (Dependent upon background experience, some students may need to include *Airport* and/or *New York* as key words.)

Students should soon move from telegrams to looking at sentences taken from conversation. A typical sentence might be, "Please be very careful that you do not damage the brand new desks." When asked to underline the key words, most students will underline "do not damage" or "not damage" "brand new desks." Once proficiency is established at this level, and students are beginning to realize that they are finding the main ideas of sentences, much more practice should be initiated using sentences from content area materials. Some students who find it difficult to let go of details may need the individual attention of the instructor for a while. Other students might be given more complex sentences to figure out. During this step, however, all sentences should be isolated and not presented as parts of paragraphs.

### Step Two: Key Sentence in a Paragraph

In this step students first learn that they need to be concerned with fewer key words when sentences are treated together in a paragraph unit. They learn this through the experience of underlining key words in the sentences of short paragraphs. For example:

A school performs many services for the residents of a community. It offers instructional services for school-age children during the day and, often, courses for adults in the evening. It

* Carol Hovious, *Flying the Printways* (Boston: D. C. Heath, 1938), p. 163.

provides a meeting place for community organizations. It also serves as an active cultural center, as plays, concerts, and lectures are often scheduled.

In this paragraph the sentences are so closely linked that it is not necessary to keep repeating the subject when searching for key words in each sentence. Most students soon realize that they are primarily concerned with verbs and their objects once the subject is established.

The paragraphs presented in this step, at this point in time, should be well structured, containing definite key sentences mainly as first or last sentences. One or two of the paragraphs may contain key sentences placed in other parts of the paragraph.

Students are asked to list the key ideas (groups of key words) they have found in the paragraph. For example, this list might have been written about the paragraph on school services:

school performs many services

offers instructional services

provides meeting place

serves as cultural center

Students learn to add up the key ideas and decide whether or not one of them represents an overall idea. In the paragraph above, it happens to be contained in the first sentence. Here the overall or main idea is contained in a key sentence at the beginning.

Here is another example. The task is a little more difficult because some of the sentences in the paragraph contain two key ideas. Students learn to treat these ideas as separate units in their search for the key sentence.

Everyone saluted as the flag was slowly raised. A smartly dressed woman cracked a champagne bottle across the ship's prow and named it *Sea Hawk*. The order was given, and the *Sea Hawk* started down the ways. A new ship was launched.

Everyone saluted + flag raised + woman cracked bottle across ship's prow + named it + order given + started down ways = new ship launched. Obviously, the key sentence is the last sentence in the paragraph. Key idea + key idea + key idea = the overall or main idea contained in the key sentence.

Look at this example.

Animals have interesting habits. One of the habits of some animals is to use nature's medicines when they are ill. Deer may eat twigs and the very tender bark of trees. Cats and dogs may eat grass when they are not feeling up to par. Bears often eat different kinds of roots and berries.

Deer eat twigs and tender bark + cats and dogs eat grass + bears eat roots and berries = some animals use nature's medicine when ill. The first sentence in the paragraph serves only an introductory purpose. It may be introducing a series of paragraphs that will deal with interesting habits of animals. It is not, of course, the main idea of this particular paragraph. Hence in this case the key sentence is the second sentence in the paragraph. Some students need much assistance with this kind of directed teaching-practice to establish the fact that it is not necessarily *just* the broadest statement in a paragraph which expresses the main idea, but *the broadest, most significant* statement, very often a conclusion which the other key ideas support.

### Step Three: Main Thought in a Paragraph

After students have completed a great deal of successful guided practice in working with paragraphs containing key sentences in a variety of positions, they should be ready for this next step. At this time they might be presented with a paragraph very much like the one below.

We visited the seals frolicking in the water. Then we paid a visit to the colorful birds in the big new birdhouse. After that we stopped for a Coke and hot dog. Before going home we spent a lot of time watching the funny monkeys.

The students are again asked to find key ideas. Visited seals + paid visits to birds + stopped for Coke and hot dog + spent time watching monkeys = ? At this point numerous students will point out that there is no *stated* overall idea.

Students must now make inferences, for the author does not state the key thought in a sentence of the paragraph. The student must look at all key ideas and determine the main idea of the paragraph himself. In this easy paragraph most students, of course, will agree that the key thought is "we visited the zoo" or something similar. Further paragraphs should present more difficult material and should be intermingled with paragraphs that contain key sentences. The most important part of this step is having the student decide for himself whether the main idea is or is not stated by the author. We don't believe that students ever learn to make inferences well through deductive teaching techniques. They must be placed in the position of successful induction.

When students have mastered the basic ideas in this three-step cluster of skills using carefully structured materials, normal textbook material should provide application and reinforcement. Students soon become aware of the fact that paragraphs that are parts of chapters in books don't always stand by themselves. One main or key thought may be carried through a number of paragraphs without repetition in each paragraph. Often students will decide on the key thought by noting part of a main idea stated by the author and adding to it through their own reasoning. For instance:

> It is not only radio that has given them a great deal of help. Ballistics experts can tell whether or not a bullet was fired from a particular gun by examining the bullet under a microscope. Chemists help solve crimes by analyzing blood, dust, cloth, and other materials. Photographers, also, are used in helping police solve crimes. Often photographs, especially when enlarged, reveal clues that the human eye overlooked.

Obviously, in the paragraph above, the key thought is something like "various people and things help police solve crimes." Clues can be found in the paragraph, but the reader can also arrive at the key thought through reasoning and the context that preceded this paragraph. Certainly a preceding paragraph, or several, dealt with "radio as it helps police solve crimes."

The following worksheet is just an example of the kind of teaching-practice material that can be developed for working with the "key thought cluster." This particular worksheet was prepared for students who could proceed quickly through the concepts and for whom this lesson was by way of review and evaluation. It contains examples of the three steps in the key thought cluster. Instructors can develop a variety of worksheets—those with just examples of key sentences for step one, those just containing paragraphs where the key sentence is at the beginning of the paragraph, worksheets with the gamut of paragraph structures.

Most important of all, certainly as each new step is begun, is to provide a series of experiences that will make learning *successful*. The challenge of more difficult material is of tremendous significance *after* students feel that they have mastered the basic tools and can use them to explore ideas.

# WORKSHEET NUMBER I
## Skill: Finding the Key Thought

**Name** _____

**Class Period** _____     **Date** _____

### SENTENCES

1. Please be very careful that you do not damage the brand new desks.

2. Bob Johnson and Ann Magee were candidates for President of the Student Council.

3. If I were you, I should report to the office not later than 10 o'clock this morning.

4. The prize fight took place in Madison Square Garden on Wednesday, September 10.

5. The hurricane destroyed many of the farms and crops—such as wheat, corn, and rye.

### PARAGRAPHS

**A.** A school performs many services for the residents of a community. It offers instructional services for school-age children during the day and, often, courses for adults in the evening. It provides a meeting place for community organizations. It also serves as an active cultural center, as plays, concerts, and lectures are often scheduled.

**B.** Everyone saluted as the flag was slowly raised. A smartly-dressed woman cracked a champagne bottle across the ship's prow and named it *Sea Hawk*. The order was given, and the *Sea Hawk* started down the ways. A new ship was launched.

**C.** Animals have interesting habits. One of the habits of some animals is to use nature's medicines when they are ill. Deer may eat twigs and the very tender bark of trees. Cats and dogs may eat grass when they are not feeling up to par. Bears often eat different kinds of roots and berries.

**D.** We visited the seals frolicking in the water. Then we paid a visit to the colorful birds in the big new birdhouse. After that we stopped for a Coke and hot dog. Before going home we spent a lot of time watching the funny monkeys.

*123

## "GIVE HIM SOMETHING HE CAN READ!"

*In some classrooms there's a single book for everyone, and it's the survival of the fittest. Not so, though, in the classes of the teachers interviewed here.\**

"Give him something he can read!" The right book placed in the hands of the not-so-able reader may be a promising hope for his progress.

When, all through the school day, the poor reader is confronted with readings years beyond his reach, he simply cannot cope with these; he is deprived of the opportunity to practice, and may fall farther, even hopelessly, behind. But when he is guided to books suitable in difficulty, he has a fair chance to successfully complete his assigned readings. Hours of beneficial reading practice (along with real learning in the subject) may follow.

A handicapped reader has probably had hundreds of failure experiences. He goes to class day after day already defeated, full of insecurities, knowing in advance that he will probably not be able to read the pages assigned him. Fear may take over and add a serious emotional block to his other obstacles in reading. But readings on a level appropriate for this student can make it possible for him to have desperately needed success experiences. The lost reader is sometimes seriously contemplating dropping out of school. Reading matter that is "right" can help him take hold and renew his efforts. It can help make school a center for success for him instead of a place of failure.

Negative attitudes often lead to behavior problems and are difficult to change once formed. Such attitudes are less likely to develop if, from the first weeks of a new course, a teacher can get "manageable" materials into the hands of the student.

The self-confidence of a young person is a precious attribute and a generative force in much of his future achievement. But self-confidence can be devastated if day after day he is directed to perform impossible tasks. "It's heartbreaking," a school librarian comments, "to see a student take home heavy books at night and bring them back next day unread because they were years beyond

---

\* The following University of Chicago Laboratory School teachers answered interview questions: social studies—Edgar Bernstein, Margaret Fallers, Alice Flickinger, Philip Montag, and Joel Surgal; science—Jerry Ferguson and Murray Hozinsky; mathematics—Paul Moulton; library—Mary Biblo, Sylvia Marantz, and Winfred Poole; English—Emily Meyer. John Patrick, social studies, and Richard Smith, science —former Laboratory School teachers—also contributed comments.

him." Confidence is nurtured, however, when teachers and librarians make possible day to day reading successes.

A student's self-concept determines much of his behavior, including his reading behavior. A young person who views himself as an individual who cannot read tends to fulfill his own expectations. His concept of himself may be altered by experiences of success and approval in and through reading. He may do an about-face in his attitude toward his own learning potential.

## Appropriate Materials

It is a familiar cry that students should have materials appropriate for their reading achievement—that poor readers should have something they can cope with and that top readers should be challenged so that they can reach their full potential. But is it really practical to make these adjustments in the classroom? On the next few pages, teachers, librarians, and the reading consultant of the University of Chicago Laboratory School, in response to interview questions, share their efforts at adjusting materials, with the thought that their suggestions may help others find more effective methods or prompt them to share methods they have found effective.* The goal of adjusting materials throughout the school has not yet been attained in this school. There will be much for us to do tomorrow.

It should, of course, be added that merely providing suitable materials will not solve the problems of retarded readers. Instruction in reading skills in subject classrooms and through the school's reading services should complement adjustments in materials.

QUESTION    Is it practical to try to match the "reading reach" of students and their materials?

ANSWER    "I couldn't operate without it. It's hardly a matter of choice! I see Ron, who can read only around seventh-grade level seated beside Dave, who can read at the college level. Six-year spans, or more, within one classroom confront me daily."

QUESTION    How can you get some insights into what each student can and cannot read successfully?

ANSWER    A social studies teacher answers, "Early in the year I jot each student's reading test scores after his name in my record book. This is a first step in getting acquainted. Daily these scores give me a suggestion of the student's reading power and remind me to make adjustments. Sometimes I add a self-made test that checks

* Some of the teachers' comments appeared in an article, "A Social Studies Department Talks Back," by Ellen Lamar Thomas and Philip Montag, in *Journal of Reading*, IX (October, 1966), pp. 22–28.

the student's comprehension and speed when using actual course materials."

QUESTION    Can textbooks on varying difficulty-levels within a class help solve the problem of the reading range?

ANSWER    A teacher of United States history commented:* "At first we thought that having different textbooks would be unwieldy. Now we find them intensely practical. As our students start each unit, they are given guide sheets so that they can approach their reading with broad questions and problems. Although textbooks of varying difficulties are not strictly parallel in content, such broad topics as the discovery of the New World, life in the colonies, the making of the Constitution, the opening of the West, and the Industrial Revolution can be found in almost all the books.

"For our junior high school level American history course, we found four quality textbooks that span the reading levels within the classes. Moon and Cline's *Story of Our Land and People* (Holt, Rinehart and Winston, 1964) can be handled by most of our less competent readers. Bragdon and McCutchen's *History of a Free People* (Macmillan, 1967) challenges the best. For in-between readers there are Casner and Gabriel's *Story of the American Nation* (Harcourt, Brace and World, 1967) and West's *Story of Our Country*, revised by Gardner (Allyn and Bacon, 1963). We stock a number of copies of each of these in both the classroom and the school library.

"Making multilevel reference lists looked formidable to us— at first. Now we prepare them quickly and simply. We save time all year by using the initials of the authors' names to designate the books. These initials soon become familiar to the students. Casner and Gabriel's book is simply CG; West's is W.

"Here are some typical guiding questions. The students can find the answers in any of the books listed.

1. What disagreements almost wrecked the Constitutional Convention, and how was each one finally settled?

2. The government created by the Articles of Confederation might have been too weak to endure. How did the new Constitution correct the weaknesses of the Articles of Confederation?

3. What part did each of the following men play in the writing and ratification of the Constitution: Washington, Franklin, Madison, Hamilton, Jay?

"This easily prepared reference list accompanies these questions.

| Pp. 209–224 in MC | [Students of sixth-grade reading level and up could handle this one.] |

* John Patrick, former University of Chicago Laboratory School social studies teacher. Remarks to Thomas, October, 1964.

| Pp. 146–167 in W and | [These are suitable for readers |
|---|---|
| Pp. 169–179 in CG | of seventh- and eighth-grade |
| | reading levels and up.] |
| Pp. 93–102 in BM | [This would challenge a reader |
| | on eleventh- or twelfth-grade |
| | level.] |

"How is each student guided to a book he can handle successfully? Of course, no notation of the difficulty of a book appears on the student's reading list. But when each student comes into class the first few days he finds on his desk a text that I have carefully selected for him on the basis of his reading achievement as suggested by his reading scores and my observation. Chances are he will have success with this book and will search it out and use it for future assignments."

[*Note:* Teachers of some public school classes would need easier materials than those referred to here, since those mentioned are appropriate for the population of the Laboratory School. Some publishers offer parallel textbooks appropriate for use within a single classroom. Two tenth-grade world history textbooks which are similar in content and organization are *Man's Story,* on tenth-grade reading level, and *Living World History,* on eighth-grade reading level, by T. Walter Wallbank and Arnold Fletcher (Scott, Foresman, 1964).]

The social studies department chairman regards the use of multilevel textbooks as a force which helps counteract a partisan interpretation of history: "Students who day after day turn to a single textbook may come to view it as the source of a divinely revealed point of view. Using several textbooks within a class invites a comparison of the interpretations of different historians."

An experienced teacher, however, expressed the view that the use of several textbooks within one class may create problems: "Some teachers find it difficult to handle a class using multilevel textbooks. There may be confusion for both teacher and students. These teachers miss the security, the stabilizing values, the unifying values of using a single textbook. It may be preferable for these teachers to select a textbook most of the class can read and then challenge the top readers and provide for the poorest through a wide range of supplementary readings."

In some school situations teachers cannot influence one way or another the choice of textbooks they will be working with from day to day. New teachers coming into a school simply "inherit" a textbook. The realistic question, then, becomes how to use this textbook to best advantage.

QUESTION   Do you have any suggestions for counteracting the disadvantages of a single textbook?

ANSWER   A biology teacher answers, "Although a single textbook may be prescribed for all the students in a class, they need not necessarily feel locked into this one book. We keep a number of easier-to-read textbooks on a reserve shelf in the school library. The student who is thrown by the explanation of mitosis in his more advanced textbook, *Modern Cell Biology,* by William D. McElroy and Carl P. Swanson (Prentice-Hall, Inc., 1968), may be able to grasp the simpler explanation in *High School Biology,* BSCS Green Version (Chicago: Rand McNally and Company, 1963). Now, having acquired some background understandings of the terms and processes, perhaps he can extend himself and digest the corresponding passage in his own textbook. If not, he is still ahead in what he has learned about mitosis from the easier book."

The reading consultant adds: "It is often desirable for the student to arrange his readings in this easy-to-difficult sequence—to select a relatively easy source in order to get his background orientation to the topic. Broadening background information is a major factor in increasing power of comprehension. Once the student has strengthened his background, he may be able to stretch and handle more difficult reading."

QUESTION   Is it practical to span the reading levels of students through their supplementary readings?

ANSWER   A science teacher whose classes were soon to study reptiles said to himself, "Surely, with all the books on reptiles, there should be something everyone can read about this exciting subject." Then he began to search out the materials. "I turned through the card catalogue, then assembled a reserve shelf of promising books. The guide sheet opposite was provided for each student. Of course, no notation of the reading difficulty of a book appeared on the student's book list."*

The reading consultant adds: "Reading lists can lure readers with attractive paperbacks, slim and trim enough to invite the hand of a reluctant reader. Some of the teen-tested titles listed in *Hooked on Books* by Daniel L. Fader and Morton H. Shaevitz (New York: Berkley Publishing Corporation, 1966) might be considered. Short pamphlets, perhaps from the library's vertical file, may offer quick rewards to poor readers—a sense of accomplishment as they easily reach the last page. Easy-to-grasp booklets with a disarming comic book format are available on certain subjects from industrial firms like General Motors and General Electric. Popular magazines and newspapers offer live content related to every subject on the students' schedules. A clipping-file, growing from year to year, can become a rich classroom resource."

A science teacher comments: "I find long term problem solving units an opportunity to keep a sharp eye for the student who is overwhelmed by a book and to guide him to one that *he* can overwhelm. The students often study the background of a problem

* Richard Smith, former University of Chicago Laboratory School biology teacher. Remarks to Thomas, January, 1965.

**GUIDING QUESTIONS FOR THE STUDY OF REPTILES**

THESE
BROAD
QUESTIONS
ARE
ANSWERABLE
IF THE STUDENT
CONSULTS
ONE OR MORE
OF THE BOOKS
LISTED.

1. List some characteristics which distinguish reptiles from other verte-brates.

2. What four groups of venomous snakes are found in North America?

3. What arguments can you give for the conservation of snakes, especially the nonpoisonous species?

4. Describe the methods used by various snakes in capturing their prey.

5. What are the benefits of many snakes and lizards to man?

6. What characteristics distinguish snakes from lizards?

7. Where do most reptiles make their homes?

8. What do they eat?

9. Which reptiles are good pets?

10. What reptiles live in my part of the United States?

THIS IS ON
JUNIOR
HIGH
SCHOOL
READING
LEVEL.

**REFERENCES**

THIS IS RIGHT
FOR A
STUDENT
WITH
HIGH SCHOOL
READING
ABILITY.

Carr - - - - - - - - - - - - - - - - - - - *Reptiles*

Danforth - - - - - - - - - - - - - - - - *What You Should Know About Snakes*

Ditmars - - - - - - - - - - - - - - - - *Fieldbook of North American Snakes*

Ditmars - - - - - - - - - - - - - - - - *Reptiles of the World*

A STUDENT
WITH
GRADE 4–5
READING
ABILITY
COULD HANDLE
THIS ONE.

Ditmars - - - - - - - - - - - - - - - - *Reptiles of North America*

Hecht - - - - - - - - - - - - - - - - - - *All About Snakes*

Hylander - - - - - - - - - - - - - - - *Animals in Armor*

Otto and Towle - - - - - - - - - - *Modern Biology,* Chapter 37, "The Reptiles"

A STUDENT
WITH
GRADE 4–6
READING
ABILITY
COULD
HANDLE
THIS ONE.

Parker - - - - - - - - - - - - - - - - - *Reptiles and Animals of Yesterday*

Pope - - - - - - - - - - - - - - - - - - *The Reptile World*

Schmidt and Davis - - - - - - - - *Fieldbook of Snakes of North America and Canada*

Storer and Usinger - - - - - - - - *General Biology,* Chapter 33, "Class Reptilia"

THIS IS
FOR
STUDENTS
WITH
COLLEGE-
LEVEL
READING
ABILITY.

Zim - - - - - - - - - - - - - - - - - - - *Reptiles and Amphibians, A Guide to Familiar American Species*

*FIGURE 3–6. Through this reading list a science teacher provides some-thing everyone in his class can read. He meets the needs of his poorest readers and challenges the best.*

together, then they divide it into sub-topics and do individual and group research, using a great diversity of reading and nonreading resources. Under my eye and with my help, they 'research' their sub-topics in the classroom and in the school library. I have appropriate books in mind and ready to offer the less able readers."

QUESTION   Suppose a core of readings seems desirable for commonality of experience and almost everyone in the class can handle these. What can be done for a very few handicapped readers?

ANSWER   A social studies teacher suggests, "In our unit on the early colonial period in Africa, we have a core of readings all of which are beyond the poorest readers. I make certain that there 'happens to be' a need for special investigations of related topics. These topics are right in difficulty and interest for the handicapped readers, who are guided in conference to references they can handle. They share their findings with the others in the class. Through class discussions, slides, and the opaque projector, the 'special investigators' get some of the information they missed through not completing the assigned readings. They do not feel that they are second class citizens. Instead, they seem to like being exempt from the regular assignment in order to pursue a bit of original 'research.' Particularly good readers, too, can be used as 'specialists.' Knowing they are to serve as resource person for the class, they often read far beyond my expectations in order to make themselves the 'teacher of the moment.' "

QUESTION   What about books to be read for enjoyment?

ANSWER   An English teacher sees a special opportunity: "English teachers have an extremely wide selection of books from which to choose. Our list of novels includes a gradation of difficulty levels, almost chromatic, from *A Bell for Adano,* within the reach of our least able readers, to *Giants in the Earth,* a challenge to the best. Our lists of suggested vacation books span all the levels."

QUESTION   What about school librarians as a help in matching materials?

ANSWER   A librarian contrasts how *not to* and *how to* enlist the librarian: "Librarians are asking—no, they are *begging*—to work with teachers to plan for the benefit of students. The students cannot possibly lose, and the possibilities of gain are limitless.

"First let me give you an example of how *not* to give an assignment. I will use a recent, actual example.

"A question or problem is passed out to students. A list of sources to help solve this problem is also distributed. The teacher has . . . checked to see whether the students in his class are all equipped to read at least some of these sources—or has he? One thing is sure—he has not checked to see whether any of these sources are in our library. We don't even know what he and his class are up to. I think you know what happens next. The first few students through the library doors grab off the shelves whatever books we do have on the list, regardless of whether these are the best books for them. The rest of the students find nothing, and are frustrated and discouraged before they begin, or are forced to go all over the town looking.

"Other fine books on the subject, which we may have waiting to be cataloged, will never be used. Books already on our shelves but not on the list may be searched out by the brighter or more persistent students or may not be found at all. And, of course, all our efforts to learn the reading abilities and interests of the students so that we can help each to find the materials on his level cannot be used. By the time some student passes the assignment on to a librarian, it is usually too late to do much.

"But let's leave this dismal picture—it is one that I have viewed, with variations, too many times—and move to a brighter and more productive one. Let me paint for you the bright, encouraging picture of the kinds of projects we feel are productive and successful, partly at least because the librarian and the teacher worked together.

"The first step, planning the assignment, is usually done in the teacher's mind. But once the assignment begins to take shape, he is already thinking in terms of materials, and this point is where we like to start our part of the job. Teacher and librarian, working with the class's reading profile in mind, can begin to discuss what the students can profitably use to solve the problem the teacher will pose. If students help with part or all of the planning, the questions remain the same—Will we need to make a special search for easier-to-read materials to have enough for the slower readers? How about some filmstrips or slides for the less verbally oriented students?* [How librarians can have quick access to the reading levels of individuals and can use class reading profiles to advantage is discussed in Chapter 12.]

"Now that the materials are being made ready, it is time for a decision on how to give the assignment so that each student can find the materials best suited for his solving of the problem. Sometimes we have found it wise to bring the materials into the classroom where the teacher and/or the librarian can work with the students individually to guide them to their best sources. Sometimes, instead of or in addition to this, the librarian will prepare a bibliography with annotations, not only of what the materials cover but also with such key words as *readable, popular treatment, scholarly,* and *highly technical* to help the student find books on his reading level in that subject.† Often a special collection is assembled in the library for this particular assignment. Then when the students rush through the library doors, they find a well and suitably stocked reserve shelf.

"Our ideal assignment concludes with a joint evaluation by teacher and librarian (and usually students, who are—in our school —quite free with their opinions). Here is where we discover that

---

* Slightly adapted from Sylvia Marantz, "A Hot Issue for a Cool Librarian," in *Fusing Reading Skills and Content,* edited by H. Alan Robinson and Ellen Lamar Thomas (Newark, Delaware: International Reading Association, 1969), pp. 123–124.

† Marantz, *Fusing Reading Skills and Content,* p. 124.

we need more copies of a book which so many found just right; or that a few poor readers never did find anything they could use to solve the problem, a condition indicating a need for easier-to-read books or perhaps a different kind of problem if there are similar poor readers next time. . . ."*

The possibilities just mentioned—the increase in students' potential for succeeding in their assignments as a result of the librarian's services—suggest the desirability of a school's having more than one librarian. If services like these are not available in a school, it may be that the librarian is serving an overload of students.

QUESTION   Aren't poor readers extremely sensitive about their handicap? How can they be guided to easier materials in such a way that they don't appear different from the others?

ANSWER   Here are some observations of teachers and librarians:
"Poor readers are nearly all sensitive. Guidance to easier materials must be done quietly, constructively, and understandingly. We may do more harm than good if they feel exposed as poor readers."

"Of course, a book should not offend through a juvenile appearance, and there should be no notation of its difficulty."

"Some students do not seem to need much guidance. When given a list of readings and freedom of choice, they select books suitable in difficulty."

Quiet guidance can often be offered with positive comments about the book. It is not necessary to specify that the book is easy. Thus, "All these books are excellent. This one has some good points that may be useful to you. Why not look it over and see if you like it?" Or, "How about trying this one? It really covers that assignment. I think you'll find all the answers you need right here."

Readers may need to be warned away from too rigorous books with "You may want to read this as background before you read this." Or, "Maybe that one's a little too difficult. I know students in college who could not read that book." And, "You can take this one now if you wish, but you'll enjoy it much more in a year or two."

One teacher who notices that a student has checked out a book that is too difficult has another one quietly ready next day.

A frank discussion may be desirable with certain students: "You have a reading problem. We are trying to meet it by starting with less difficult materials and then advancing. Many people have this problem. You have the ability to become a good reader."

A realistic teacher cautions, "No teacher should be discouraged when the ideal of individual guidance of students is always beyond reach. In large classes and in the press of things, the individual word of guidance to a student is often impossible."

---

* Marantz, *Fusing Reading Skills and Content*, pp. 124–125.

QUESTION  Isn't there danger of providing poor readers with easy materials and then leaving them there so that they never stretch their reading ability?

ANSWER  The reading consultant observed, "At first, materials for a retarded reader should be selected to guarantee success. Relatively easy materials help to overcome a failure mind set. Books a year or two below the student's reading level may be appropriate at first. However, we should not overlook the importance of keen interest in empowering a student to stretch and read material seemingly beyond him. If we can find a topic vital to a student, he may be able to handle surprisingly difficult reading. Of course, it is desirable to challenge students with more difficult readings as rapidly as possible. The ideal is a sequence of increasingly difficult reading experiences with the student held to all he can do. Teachers will experience deep satisfaction when, as time passes, they see some of their poor readers advance to more difficult materials."

QUESTION  In summing up, then, it *is* possible for a teacher to provide materials for students reading on a wide range of levels?

ANSWER  "Let no one give teachers the impression that doing this is easy. Years of searching go into this! Two of our teachers spent two summers searching for appropriate materials. Experience is essential for teachers to develop a feel for the difficulty of materials. The right reading for the right reader is an ideal to work toward, a little at a time. No teacher should be discouraged when attainment of the ideal all at once is not possible."

QUESTION  Of course, readings matched to students can make them more comfortable and help them acquire subject matter learnings. But how can appropriate readings help build reading power?

ANSWER  The reading consultant answered, "The world of words has never been the world of the poor reader. When a teacher guides him to a book right for him in difficulty and interest, he may, for the first time, spend many hours in the world of printed words. As he reads, he may be practicing basic skills of word attack, silently figuring out words he does not recognize. He meets new words repeatedly in similar and different settings, often with a little increment of meaning at each encounter, and gradually incorporates them into his vocabulary. His reading practice tends to strengthen his comprehension. Speed is developed at the easy end of the reading spectrum. As students read easy, interesting material for pleasure and information, many of them increase their speed. Fast moving, narrative-style biographies and exciting novels, including historical novels and science fiction, may be effective speed builders."

Staggering sums are required to reclaim students who leave the doors of schools without reading power and without earning power. The efforts of teachers to renew the hope and confidence of young people and to make progress possible through individualizing reading materials is an investment in *prevention*.

## BIBLIOGRAPHY

Association of Teachers of Social Studies of the City of New York, *Handbook for Social Studies Teaching,* Chapter 3, "The Art of Questioning." New York: Holt, Rinehart and Winston, Inc., 1967, pp. 38 ff.

Davis, Frederick B., "Research in Comprehension in Reading," *Reading Research Quarterly,* III, No. 4 (1968), pp. 499–545.

Dudycha, George J., *Learn More With Less Effort.* New York: Harper & Row, Publishers, 1957.

Herber, Harold L., *Teaching Reading in Content Areas.* Englewood Cliffs, New Jersey: Prentice-Hall, Inc., 1970.

Herber, Harold L. and P. L. Sanders, eds., *Research in Reading in the Content Areas: First Year Report.* Syracuse, New York: Reading and Language Arts Center, 1969.

Kalish, Richard, *Making the Most of College.* Belmont, California: Wadsworth Publishing Company, Inc., 1959.

Kenworthy, Leonard S., *Guide to Social Studies Teaching in Secondary Schools.* Belmont, California: Wadsworth Publishing Company, Inc., 1966.

Lewenstein, Morris R., *Teaching Social Studies in Junior and Senior High Schools.* Chicago: Rand McNally and Company, 1963.

Pauk, Walter, *How to Study in College.* Boston: Houghton Mifflin Company, 1962.

Preston, Ralph C. and Morton Botel, *How to Study.* Chicago: Science Research Associates, 1956.

Rivlin, Harry N., *Teaching Adolescents in Secondary Schools,* Chapter VII, "Using the Question as an Aid to Learning." New York: Appleton-Century-Crofts, Inc., 1961, pp. 203 ff.

Robinson, Francis P., *Effective Study.* New York: Harper & Row, Publishers, 1961.

Rothkôpf, E. Z., "Learning from Written Instructive Materials: An Exploration of the Control of Inspection Behavior by Test-Like Events," *American Educational Research Journal,* III, No. 4 (1966), pp. 241–249.

Rystrom, Richard, "Toward Defining Comprehension: a Second Report," *Journal of Reading Behavior,* II, No. 2 (1970), pp. 144–157.

Sanders, Norris M., *Classroom Questions: What Kinds?* New York: Harper & Row, Publishers, 1966.

Smith, Donald E. P. and others, *Learning to Learn.* New York: Harcourt, Brace and World, Inc., 1961.

Staton, Thomas B., *How to Learn Faster and Better.* Montgomery, Alabama: Box 6133, 1958.

Staton, Thomas B., *How to Study.* Montgomery, Alabama: Box 6133, 1968.

Weaver, Wendell W. and Albert J. Kingston, "Questioning in Content Reading," *Journal of Reading,* II, No. 2 (1967), pp. 140–143.

Weintraub, Samuel, "The Question as an Aid in Reading," *The Reading Teacher,* XXII, No. 8 (1969), pp. 751–755.

# 4

# DEVELOPING FLEXIBILITY
# IN READING RATE

This chapter presents a rationale concerning rates of reading together with practical insights for developing rate adjustment through the day to day work of classes. You will find specific how-to-do-it suggestions for helping students acquire and use a full range of reading rates.

These are times when speed reading programs often appear to be promoted as panaceas for the ills of retarded readers, and when fantastic speeds are encouraged in inappropriate situations. Perhaps the rationale and suggestions presented here will help as a source of support for school administrators and instructors who are under pressure to alter basically sound programs, and for parents and students who are making a selection from among a number of possible reading improvement programs.

We, therefore, again offer a set of questions followed by answers which we trust will provide some sound and practical solutions.

1. What is a sound rationale concerning rates of reading?
2. How can you acquire insights about student attainments and needs in rate adjustment?
3. What is an appropriate sequence for developing rate adjustment?
4. How do you drive home the concept of flexibility of rate of reading?

5. How can you help students acquire appropriate rates of reading?

6. How can you help students reach the goal of independence in adjustment?

# DEVELOPING FLEXIBILITY IN READING RATE
## Rationale

### General Beliefs About Reading Rates

1. The efficient reader demonstrates flexibility, adjusting his rate according to the reading task at hand.

2. While speed in many situations is highly desirable, constant speed is not a characteristic of a highly skilled, purposeful reader.

3. It is desirable for each student to acquire reading rates along a continuum from slow and careful to very rapid reading, to develop techniques of scanning and skimming, and to learn to identify the situations for which each is appropriate.

4. As teachers work with the approaches suitable for reading about the causes of World War II, for following the steps in an experiment, for reading dense analytical passages in mathematics, or for understanding the universality of an essay by Emerson, they are building training in rate adjustment into the daily work of their classes.

5. Students will need much guidance in using the appropriate approach—at first. They should move in the direction of independence as they learn to select the approach with less guidance from their instructors. The long-range goal is independence, with the student proficient in selecting for himself the suitable approach.

6. It is possible and highly desirable to increase the speed of many students on certain types of reading matter and in certain reading situations.

7. Students whose habits are overly conscientious when the situation does not demand close reading should be encouraged and assisted to increase their reading rates appropriately.

8. Students within a single class may differ markedly in the speed attainable. Rate of thinking and, hence, rate of comprehension appear to be factors which influence the speed an individual may achieve.* Nothing is accomplished when the student covers the pages

* Guy T. Buswell, "Relationship Between Rate of Thinking and Rate of Reading," *School Review,* 59 (September, 1951), pp. 339–346.

faster than he can assimilate the ideas. Personal tempo may play a role.* Some students who are below average in rates of reading may already be reading well up to their capacities, even straining beyond. Some who are above average may be far below their potentials.†

9. A number of students need help in acquiring a close, careful, reflective approach to reading. Teachers often observe that some students tend to read rapidly and superficially in inappropriate situations. Standardized test scores frequently confirm this observation. And, indeed, there is a danger in overemphasizing rapid reading with today's young people, who belong to the most propagandized generation in history. The maturing student reader must often "pierce to the basic truth or falseness of any piece of writing . . ."‡ by reading it with searching questions—weighing authority, detecting weak links in a chain of reasoning. The problems of today's bewildered and bewildering world call very often for deeply reflective reading.

10. Master teachers of literature deepen awareness of writing as a form of art. Encouraging students to read the great books at excessive speeds might be compared to training them to run through an art gallery and boast, "I ran past Van Gogh's *The Starry Night* in five seconds."

11. Many students who read slowly do so because rate flexibility is blocked by deficiencies in basic skills. Inadequacies in word analysis may be the roadblock. Precision instruction by a patient instructor may be required to release this brake on flexibility of rate. Or when vocabulary is meager, reading may be an obstacle course. A student can hardly profit from covering a page rapidly if he does not know the meanings of the words on the page. Instruction in skills of comprehension may be necessary before speed can be increased. Until the student has the sub-structure of essential skills, pressuring him to build faster rates of reading may be futile and probably harmful.

12. When interfering factors are no longer present, increased flexibility in rates of reading often follows without special training. On the other hand, directed guidance through classroom instruction and practice is in order and often highly desirable.

* June Frary Mitchell, "Prediction of Increase in Silent Reading Rate," *Clinical Studies in Reading II.* Supplementary Educational Monographs, No. 77 (Chicago: University of Chicago Press, 1953), pp. 89–93.

† John J. DeBoer and Martha Dallman, *The Teaching of Reading* (New York: Holt, Rinehart and Winston, 1964), p. 181.

‡ Richard D. Altick, *Preface to Critical Reading* (New York: Holt, Rinehart and Winston, 1963), p. 172.

## Characteristics of the Ideal Graduate

The ideal product of the reading program evidences the following understandings and abilities with respect to rates of reading:

1. The student has acquired the concept of rate adjustment.

2. He has acquired reading rates along a continuum from slow and careful to rapid reading, and he has developed techniques of scanning and skimming.

3. He demonstrates the ability to identify the reading situation for which each approach is appropriate.

4. He has built rate adjustment into his permanent habits, shifting in view of three considerations: the difficulty of the material for him, his purpose at the moment, and his familiarity with the subject matter at hand.

## ATTAINMENTS AND NEEDS IN RATE ADJUSTMENT

Diagnostic insights are an important first step in helping students acquire and use a full range of reading rates. Sub-scores on rate from standardized survey tests offer useful insights. Observation, students self-appraisals, and teacher made tests are desirable supplements.

## Standardized Tests

A great many schools have the results of standardized reading tests available. Many tests have rate-of-reading sections. Should such results not be available or should you wish to supplement the results with another standardized test, the test below should be helpful. It is easily administered and scored.

> *Cooperative Reading Test;* Cooperative Test Division, Educational Testing Service; Lower Level intended for grades 9–12; Upper Level intended for superior students in grades 11 and 12 and for college freshmen and sophomores; two forms.
>
>> The Cooperative Reading Test offers subscores in vocabulary, level (power) of comprehension, and speed of comprehension. The score on level of comprehension is based on the number of answers correct. The score on speed of comprehension is

a function of both the number correct and the number completed. The content of this test is primarily fairly difficult study material. The speed score gives you some indication of the speed with which the student can handle reading matter of this type.

Of course a low speed score combined with a high comprehension score suggests the need for the student to increase his rate of reading study-type material. A high speed score combined with a low comprehension score suggests the need to adjust speed downward for closer, more reflective reading.

### Standardized Test Scores Leave Unanswered Questions

Most standardized tests yield a single rate of reading score based on the student's performance with only the type of material represented by the test items. We may be left completely in the dark about the following:

Is the student aware of the need for rate adjustment?

Can the student scan a mass of material for specific information?

Can he skim a passage for the general drift?

Can he speed up appropriately for *easy* informational material?

Can he attain high speeds on easy, fast-moving fiction?

Is the student able to shift to slow rates when demanded by the type of study material?

### Classroom Observation

Observation from day to day often provides clues for identifying students whose needs are urgent:

Does the student consistently finish in-class reading tasks among the last in the group?

When all he is seeking from a passage is a single bit of information, does he start at the beginning and read ploddingly line by line?

Does he fail to adjust his rate in other situations?

Does he do his work thoroughly and well but fail to finish on tests over course content as well as on standardized tests?

Does he shy away from long recreational books because they take too long to finish?

Does the student speed through in-depth study assignments in math, science, or other subjects with minimal comprehension?

**Teacher-Made Tests**

Teachers can use informal tests to get at the specific needs of individuals. It is possible to make brief tests to explore whether each student has the following rates in his "collection":

1. A thorough reading approach for study materials
2. A rapid rate for easy fiction
3. A skimming rate
4. A scanning rate

A graph comparing all four rates might be used as an eloquent message to students. A student who performed all four reading tasks at much the same rate can see clearly that he is in special need of rate adjustment.

Rewarding gains should follow when students are encouraged to set their own specific goals, then move toward them under their own momentum. The interpretation of diagnostic findings should leave the student with clearly defined aims in mind: "I need to read study material more slowly to get the thought of the passage," or "I need to read fiction faster and yet get the amount of comprehension I want," or "I need to speed up my scanning since my purpose is just to find a specific detail."

## DEVELOPING RATE ADJUSTMENT

Instructors concerned with encouraging the use of a full repertory of reading rates may find the following sequence useful. In many instances the steps may come out of sequence or, indeed, be concurrent.

1. A first step is acquiring insights into the attainments and needs of the students.
2. The concept of rate adjustment should be introduced and driven home.
3. Appropriate guidance in acquiring the full range of rates should be provided.
4. Much teacher guidance in identifying the approach suitable for different reading situations is necessary—at first. Day to day assignments offer abundant opportunities.
5. Students should identify the suitable approach for an assignment with gradually decreasing guidance from the instructor.

6. The long-range goal is independence—with the student proficient in selecting for himself the appropriate approach.

## DRIVING HOME THE CONCEPT OF RATE ADJUSTMENT

It cannot be assumed that students in high school or college have already acquired the concept of rate adjustment. With seemingly fantastic reading speeds in the national spotlight, it is not surprising that some students view speed as the be-all and end-all. In science, where reading rates must usually be slow, some teachers report that many students read the text and other materials as though they were reading a novel. At the other extreme, an overconscientious student may think, "It's a sin to skim or skip," and he may read a Perry Mason mystery at a very slow pace.

### Opportunities in Course Materials

Abundant opportunities for introducing and reinforcing the concept of rate adjustment present themselves from day to day as instructors work with subject area materials. Teachers encourage rate adjustment as they lead students to search the context for clues that illuminate the meaning of a difficult new word, to scrutinize the word for familiar parts, and to reach for the dictionary whenever essential. They are helping to build rate adjustment into students' lifetime habits when they work with the reading approaches suitable for a lyric poem, a historical document, obscure passages in an essay, a scientific treatise, a fast-paced short story, a theorem in geometry, a sewing pattern, the directions for a shop project.

### A Lively Exercise Introduces the Concept

The following exercise, "Can You Adjust Your Reading Rate to the Task at Hand?" has proved highly effective in introducing the concept of rate adjustment. The teacher elicits from or shares with students the insights on the first few pages of the exercise. The students then complete the practice exercise, sizing up various reading tasks and making a deliberate choice of approach. Lively discussion of their decisions follows. Students are aware that there is not always a "right" answer, that reading rates are highly individual and suited to particular purposes.

## CAN YOU ADJUST YOUR READING RATE TO THE TASK AT HAND?

If someone asked you, "What is your speed in reading?" you would know that he does NOT know much about reading.

You should have not a single rate but *several different rates.* Reading everything fast is a sign of a poor reader. The good reader develops *flexibility* instead of constant speed.

For your reference:

    I. Shift from one rate and method to another in view of these considerations:

      A. Your *purpose*

        *Why* are you reading this material?

          —to get just the gist of an easy selection?

          OR

          —to learn, point by point, a specific process or a detailed sequence?

          OR

          —to find one particular point in a selection you've already read?

          OR

          —to entertain yourself with light, easy reading?

      B. The *difficulty* of the material for you

          —Is the selection easy for you?

          OR

          —Is it rough going?

      C. Your own personal *familiarity* with the subject matter

        We all read FASTER in FAMILIAR TERRITORY.

          —Do you already have broad background on the topic?

          OR

          —Is it "new terrain"?

    II. You should have in *your "collection"* of rates the following *approaches:*

| APPROACH | HOW FAST | WHEN TO USE |
|---|---|---|
| Very Rapid Skimming (sometimes called *scanning*) not a true reading rate; just glancing until you find what you want | *Maybe* 1500 or more words per minute (rate is an individual matter) | —when glancing down columns to find a single piece of information |
| Slower *skimming* approach (previewing or overviewing) not a true reading rate; just getting the gist of the article—hitting the high points | *Maybe* 1000 words per minute | —to get the general content of an article, "what it's all about" |
| *Actual* Reading Rates | | |
|    1. **Very rapid** | *Maybe* 400–600 words per minute | —for light, easy, fast-moving fiction (entertainment reading) |

## CAN YOU ADJUST YOUR READING RATE TO THE TASK AT HAND?

| APPROACH | HOW FAST | WHEN TO USE |
|---|---|---|
| 2. **Rapid** | *Maybe* 350–400 words per minute | —for fairly easy materials<br>—when you want only the more important facts, ideas |
| 3. **Average** | *Perhaps* 250–350 words per minute | —for magazine articles such as *Scientific American;* some chapters in social studies; some travel books; some novels like *My Antonia* or *Cry the Beloved Country.* |
| 4. **Slow and careful** | From 250 words per minute— all the way down to a *slow* 50 words per minute or *even slower* | —for difficult concepts and vocabulary<br>—for thorough reading of technical material<br>—for retaining every detail<br>—for weighing the truth of difficult reading (Here *"thought time"* is needed in addition to reading time.) |

## INTERNAL RATE ADJUSTMENT

You may need to *shift* from one rate (and approach) to another *within a single chapter* of a textbook or within an article.
Example: Chapter on "Fish and Fishlike Vertebrates" in *Modern Biology:*

| | PURPOSE | APPROACH |
|---|---|---|
| A. Beginning of chapter (happens to be an easy, interesting, narrative opening) | —to get introduced to the contents of chapter | Fairly fast |
| B. A section in the middle (steps in a specific process) | —to retain the details of the step-by-step process of digestion in the fish | Slow and careful |
| C. End of chapter (easy paragraphs, sports fishing as a hobby) | —to get the high points about sports fishing | Fairly rapid |

There are *other factors* which influence rate. The *speed attainable is not the same* for each person.

# CAN YOU ADJUST YOUR READING RATE TO THE TASK AT HAND?

A. Temperament—Some people, by nature, are just plain FAST in almost everything and, of course, some are just plain SLOW!

B. Intelligence

. . . so, do not work for *indiscriminate speed* in reading; rather, work for *flexibility of rate!*

*Adjust your approach to the demands of different types of reading tasks!*

**PRACTICE SHEET—WHAT APPROACH WILL YOU TAKE?**

Remember: Your purpose
Difficulty of the material for you
Personal familiarity with material

### Deliberate Choice of Approach

1. Very Rapid Skimming (scanning)
2. Slower Skimming
3. Actual Reading
   a. very rapid reading
   b. rapid reading
   c. average reading
   d. slow and careful reading

Suppose you are to read the materials described below for the purposes as stated.

Consider the pointers as listed above, then select your approach. Of course, practice in setting your approach by examining the actual material you're to read is essential, and your course will provide such practice soon. This practice exercise is just to alert you to the considerations which should control your reading rates.

| TYPE AND DIFFICULTY OF READING MATERIAL | YOUR PURPOSE IN READING IT | ESTIMATE THE SPEED AND APPROACH FOR YOU |
|---|---|---|
| 1. The chapter on Reconstruction after the Civil War in a social studies textbook. | Your instructor has announced that thorough understanding and retention are expected. There is to be a test on the details. | |

# CAN YOU ADJUST YOUR READING RATE TO THE TASK AT HAND?

| TYPE AND DIFFICULTY OF READING MATERIAL | YOUR PURPOSE IN READING IT | ESTIMATE THE SPEED AND APPROACH FOR YOU |
|---|---|---|
| 2. A light, fast-moving Perry Mason story, *The Case of the Borrowed Brunette* | You are reading only to pass time pleasantly. | |
| 3. A chapter on "The Chemical Basis of Life" in a science textbook | You want to retain the main ideas and all the important details in this chapter. | |
| 4. Your science teacher has assigned the problem: "What are the factors which influence the climate of any area of the earth's surface?" | You want to look through various books to locate the parts that offer material which you will read carefully later. | |
| 5. A health insurance policy that you are considering for yourself | You want to understand the exact extent of the coverage provided under the terms of the policy. | |
| 6. An interesting detective story in a magazine | Your only purpose is entertainment | |
| 7. A *Reader's Digest* article | You would like to find out the general content before deciding whether you want to read the article. | |
| 8. An encyclopedia article on the life of President Franklin D. Roosevelt | You want to learn what college President Roosevelt attended. | |
| 9. The various essays on friendship by Emerson, Aristotle, and Bacon. The rhetorical patterns are complex. Some of the concepts are abstract and difficult to comprehend. | You are reading for ideas that will guide your own thoughts and actions in your relationships with your own friends. | |

*145

# CAN YOU ADJUST YOUR READING RATE TO THE TASK AT HAND?

| TYPE AND DIFFICULTY OF READING MATERIAL | YOUR PURPOSE IN READING IT | ESTIMATE THE SPEED AND APPROACH FOR YOU |
|---|---|---|
| 10. The chapter on colonial life in a social studies textbook | Your teacher has explained that you are to get an overall picture of what it was like to live in colonial times. You are expected to gain from your reading just a general impression, not specific facts. | |
| 11. A feature article, "The Latin Pot Comes to the Boil," discussing unrest in Latin America, in the magazine section of the Sunday newspaper. | You want to broaden your general information | |
| 12. The section of Plato's *Symposium* dealing with Platonic love. Concepts are abstract and difficult to grasp. "Thought time" is required. | You would like to understand fully what Plato means by Platonic love. | |
| 13. News stories of local interest in your daily paper | You wish to keep informed about what is happening in your city. | |
| 14. A Shakespearean sonnet that "defines" enduring love | You want to grasp Shakespeare's ideas about the experience of a love that lasts. As you read, you will be comparing Shakespeare's experiences with experiences of your own. | |
| 15. A chapter in a social studies textbook containing easy, interesting material on Abe Lincoln's young manhood and also more difficult material on the provisions of the Thirteenth, Fourteenth, and Fifteenth Amendments. | You want just a general impression of Abe Lincoln's young manhood. On the other hand, you want long term retention of the provisions of the three amendments. | |

## INTERNAL RATE ADJUSTMENT

The frequent need for *internal* rate adjustment, for shifts of rate within a single reading task, should be brought home to students. A placard with the following "speed signals" was displayed in one class as a constant reminder.

**Reduce Speed Signals**

1. Unfamiliar terms.
2. Difficult sentence or paragraph structure.
3. Difficult concepts.
4. Detailed technical materials—especially those on which you have scant background.
5. Difficult and detailed directions.
6. Material on which you want detailed retention.
7. Material with a diagram, requiring constant shifting from text to diagram.
8. Material you wish to weigh carefully.
9. Material that requires "visualizing time."
10. Artistic writing which invites your lingering.

**Increase Speed Signals**

1. Simple materials with few ideas new to you.
2. Examples and illustrations unnecessary for understanding.
3. Detailed explanation and elaboration which you do not need.
4. Ideas which are restatements of previous ones.
5. Material from which you want only the more important ideas and facts.*

Student groups might formulate and display on a placard their own speed signals, adapted to the materials of the course at hand. It is also helpful for internal rate adjustment to have students read a common selection within which varying rates are appropriate, and then discuss the selection. They should indicate where and why the variations in rate were needed as they discuss the material with their classmates.†

---

* These lists of signals are adapted from pages iv–70 of *Developing Reading Competence* by John K. Wilcox and others (Denver, Colorado: Communication Foundation Ltd., 1961).

† DeBoer and Dallman, *The Teaching of Reading*, p. 183.

## ACQUIRING APPROPRIATE READING RATES

We have discussed developing the awareness that the expert reader has rates at his command that move along a continuum from slow to very rapid, as well as techniques of scanning and skimming, and that he varies his approach according to the reading situation. Though developing this awareness is clearly an important step, it is not to be assumed that students will *acquire* this complete set of rates or bring them to peak efficiency without further instruction.

### SCANNING

#### Developing Techniques of Scanning

Teachers and librarians often note students plodding line by line down a long column or page when all they actually want is a single bit of information. These students are surprised to learn that the date of an event, for example, can be located without reading every word— that, with practice, they can search out a given fact or figure from 15,000 or 20,000 words in a minute or two!* Countless opportunities to help students acquire or perfect scanning techniques arise in the day to day work of courses as students need to scan for answers to live questions—a fact they need for a certain assignment, a statement that will prove or disprove a point, a quotation they wish to locate. Their scanning techniques will prove invaluable while they are doing research for a discussion, a report, or a paper.

How can students acquire highly efficient techniques of scanning for particular information? A progression through increasingly difficult levels of scanning appears to be desirable.

*Level 1*   Scanning for a bit of information that stands out easily—the date of a historic discovery in science, or the university with which a noted author was affiliated.

*Level 2*   Scanning for an answer that is worded like the question.

*Level 3*   Scanning for an answer that is worded differently from the question.

* George D. Spache and Paul C. Berg, *The Art of Efficient Reading* (New York: The Macmillan Company, 1966), pp. 53–54.

Spache and Spache* identified three steps in the process of scanning:

1. The student should fix in mind exactly what he is searching for. When possible, he should fix in mind the form in which the information is likely to appear.
2. He should glance swiftly down the page or column expecting the information to stand out from the rest of the page.
3. He should verify that he has indeed found the sought-for information [or else reject it] by reading carefully.

Alerting students to conspicuous signposts of the author can markedly increase their speed in scanning. These include chapter titles, headings of chapter divisions, side headings close to the margin, and boldface or italic section headings. These signposts suggest whether the section at hand may yield the student what he is seeking or whether he can speed on past that section. Within a section, topic or concluding sentences sometimes suggest whether a certain paragraph is a promising or an unpromising hunting ground. By noting the author's signals the students can often rapidly bypass whole sections or chapters. Use of the index is another shortcut in scanning.

## Scanning Using Classroom Materials

An instructor might share insights like the following, or elicit them from students, when a long unit on the planet Mars, for example, confronts students with the necessity for frequent scanning. The students scan for the answers to questions stated in their assignment, using the regular materials of the unit.

He might suggest, "You will often need to use a text or reference book to search out a single fact, the answer to a single question, or one aspect of your topic. High speed scanning can *save you time* in study. You can learn to crack the printed page, moving your eyes down the page swiftly to the heart of what you want.

"First, fix in mind exactly what you're looking for. Hold this in the forefront of your mind. Flash your eyes down the page for this information *only*.

"Suppose you're looking on a page for the date of *Mariner IV's* space probe of Mars. How should you move your eyes in scanning? Perhaps there is no one best way. Some top speed scanners suggest a

* George D. Spache and Evelyn B. Spache, *Reading in the Elementary School* (Boston: Allyn and Bacon, Inc., 1969), p. 281.

vertical sweep right down the middle of the page or column. Others prefer a zigzag pattern every five or six lines. Still others suggest that a regular pattern may make you think of your eyes instead of the meaning and that it may be preferable just to "float" down the page in a relaxed way without a definite pattern. Running your index finger down the page ahead of your eyes may help your concentration. You might try these different techniques and see which works best for you.

"Once you've found lines in the passage that may yield what you're seeking, stop scanning instantly. Shift gears into careful reading as you weigh whether you've really found what you're after."

### First Level of Scanning

"For your assignment on Mars you are concerned with the question, 'On what date did *Mariner IV* flash the first photographs of Mars back to Earth?'

"There are three levels of scanning. Level One is easy and very rapid. Here you're looking for one particular item—a proper name, a number, or a word or phrase—that stands out easily. In the part of the passage that answers this question, what is likely to stand out? [Possibilities appear to be the numerals in the date itself, the words *"Mariner IV,"* or the word *photographs.*]

"You'll sweep down the page—alert every second for the date and the target words—rejecting everything else! When you think you may have found your information, shift to careful reading in order to make sure.

"Start to scan when I give the signal. When you've located the information, look up."

The instructor observes which students finish quickly and which ones are plugging along down the page, obviously deficient in scanning. Those who scanned most successfully tell the class how they arrived at the answer first.

### Second Level of Scanning

"Level Two of scanning is still easy and rapid. Here you're scanning for an answer worded like your question. Try it with this question: 'What is the temperature range in summer at the Martian equator?' In what form is the answer likely to appear? What may flag you? [The students suggest the words *temperature, summer,* and *equator.* Someone also suggests the degree symbol °, *F* for fahrenheit, or *C* for centigrade.]

"Those are your targets. Good scanners concentrate—their attention is unwavering. Take the attitude of expecting what you want to stand out from the rest. Find what you think to be the answer. Then slow way down! Check to make certain you've found it, then look up!"

Higher rates will come with practice. It is desirable for students to perfect their techniques with Levels One and Two before advancing to Level Three.

### Third Level of Scanning

"Level Three is considerably more difficult. You'll need Level Three to answer a question such as, 'What climate are the first Earth-men likely to find near the Martian equator?'

"Now the answer is worded differently from the question. The word *climate* may not appear on the pages at all. But climate involves a number of sub-topics. What words are you likely to find as signals that you're close to information about the climate? [Individuals may suggest *temperature, seasons, rainfall, humidity, winds.*]

"You can really see why Level Three of scanning is the most exacting. You are scanning for any idea related to climate. You must have a mind set for ideas rather than for key words. Your scanning rate will now be much slower. [The group now locates and shares such answers as "average temperature—32° F," "seasons similiar to Earth's but longer," "no rainfall." The top scanners in the group share their success secrets.]

"Obviously, when you're on your own you will not always know which of the three levels of scanning will be called for. Today we clued you in, in advance. In practice, take a moment before you begin scanning to reflect on the possible 'formats' your answers are likely to take."

Students should expect their rate on Level Three to be considerably slower than on Levels One and Two.

## Classroom Opportunities for Practice

*Sharpen Up Your Scanning* As opportunities arise in class from day to day, students are reminded that here is a chance to sharpen up their new techniques of scanning. The occasion might be verifying a statement, finding a quotation, supporting a line of argument, locating a new word in context.

*Chapter Titles Are Signals* Students scan the chapter titles in the table of contents to find one that appears to offer help with a special problem.

*The Index—a Speed Device* Students practice using the index to learn the page location for an item, then scan the page to find the information. They may compete to locate it first.

*Which Source Is Promising?* Students who need information for a current assignment are supplied with a number of possible resource materials. They are encouraged to use their new scanning techniques to decide, within a few minutes, which of the sources promises to be useful. A time limit might be imposed.

*Key or Topic Sentences Are Signals* Students practice using key or topic sentences as an aid in scanning. They scan a selection for the key or topic sentence that signals the desired information, then scan within the paragraph to find the information.

## SKIMMING

### Getting the Gist of Informational Writing

A skill extremely useful in study and personal reading is skimming for the general drift of a passage. Teachers observe that students do not just grow into this skill, that much is to be gained from demonstration, instruction, and practice.

After observing the need for proficiency in skimming for the drift of a passage, a teacher might select from the course materials a chapter or selection that lends itself almost ideally to developing this technique. The introductory paragraph(s) announce the content, boldface or italic headings announce important thought divisions, topic sentences carry key ideas, and the conclusion is a general summing up.

For days in advance the instructor might advertise the coming lessons on high-speed skimming, catching the interest of students. Then when the day arrives he says, "Today you'll be learning how to do high-speed skimming. It will be convenient to make a distinction between *preview* skimming (a rapid coverage to learn the general content before reading), and *overview* skimming (a quick coverage to get the drift when no second reading is intended). Though the purposes differ, the techniques involved are much the same. Both preview and overview skimming should save time for you in both study and personal reading.

"President John F. Kennedy is said to have 'read' three books a day and to have whipped through newspaper and magazine materials at extremely high rates. He pointed out that at these rates he was overview skimming—hitting the high spots. He knew where the strategic spots were located—those likely to yield the general content. He was familiar with the structure of well organized factual writing, and he turned this knowledge into speed. (President Kennedy followed his rapid survey with a more careful reading when appropriate.)

"Once you've learned, as he did, to get the gist very quickly, you'll want to preview-skim almost everything you read—chapters assigned in your textbooks, newspaper and magazine content, almost everything but fiction.

"How do you skim for the drift of a selection? First, you examine the title. This is often a concise label of the content. Examine the sub-title if there is one. With magazine and newspaper feature articles, you'll sometimes find a little blurb about the content. This is often gist-packed and should be read carefully.

"Next, read the introduction carefully, a paragraph or two or three to see if you can get the gist. Here the author often announces the content—tells you what he's going to tell you—conveniently briefs you on what's ahead.

"Be sure to hit the headings within the selection. Do you see any in this passage? [Students note the italicized sub-headings that mark off sections of the selection.] These signal thought divisions and announce or suggest the content of each coming section.

"Where within each paragraph will you look for key ideas? [Students suggest the first, and, less frequently, the last sentence.] First and last sentences often carry a heavy load of meaning. Words in italics or boldface also flag you down for important content.

" 'Read' the diagrams and pictures—often worth many words.

"Last, read the concluding paragraph or two. What do you think a writer might do in his conclusion? It's his last chance with the reader. He often wraps up or summarizes the big ideas—drives home what he wants most of all to leave with you.

*"You'll find exceptions to all that's been said.* Introductions may fail to announce, and conclusions may fail to wrap up. Topic or key sentences may not always be first or last—or even present at all—in paragraphs. Your skimming techniques cannot be rigid. A flexible floating down the page or through a paragraph following one promising lead or another is often desirable.

"When you're finished, take your preview test. You may be surprised and delighted at how much you've learned from just a preview."

Students now skim the selection (untimed during the learning stage), then take a preview test of five or ten short-answer questions all of which are readily answerable if they have examined the strategic spots. Good scores help sell the worth of the new technique. Since speed rather than perfectionist attention to detail is being encouraged, 80% is considered a commendable score. The instructor deliberately plans an encouraging success experience.

The class is asked, "What possible uses do you think you might make of skimming?" With some guidance, students arrive at these uses:

1. You'll study better and faster if you preview-skim chapters you're going to study at school before your thorough reading.
2. Skim to learn how the author has organized the material.
3. Skim chapters and articles when all you want is a general impression.
4. Skim a chapter or article to decide whether you want to read it at all.
5. Skim to see whether, in view of your purpose, the entire selection or just parts should be read. What a saving of time to bypass irrelevant parts!
6. Skim to see if a passage or a book is relevant to a research problem.
7. Skim when you wish to learn only the writer's opinion or point of view on a given question.
8. Review-skim.

Students discuss: "Are there possible dangers in skimming? What cautions would you add?" (They might suggest: It is important not to substitute hitting the high spots when you want in-depth comprehension of the entire selection. A complete reading is often necessary to clarify concepts or learn how the writer supports his points. Content which you wish to weigh carefully or artistic expression which you wish to savor does not lend itself to light skimming.)

*The point that selections are not always perfectly structured for skimming should be strongly emphasized.* Students should move on from well-structured material to prose that does not lend itself ideally to skimming, then on to material that confronts them with real difficulties.

### High-Speed Skimming for Top Executives

One instructor sparks enthusiasm with this selling point: "You've just learned a technique corporation executives often learn in speed courses. Top executives at General Electric have been trained to skim first—then use a slower rate when needed—to get through the load of reading matter on their desks. They have learned, many of them, to skim their daily correspondence and the reports they receive, before reading carefully. They find that much of the load requires no more than skimming. Communications that *do* require a second reading are covered more rapidly and efficiently because they were skimmed first.

"Skim all printed matter—except fiction—before you do anything else. Skim your daily paper and your weekly news magazine. You'll be surprised how soon you can get so much from deft skimming that much of your reading, like that of the top executives, will require only this."

## Skimming a Book

Students sometimes ask, "How can you skim an informational book?" The following procedure should give the reader a quick grasp of the general content. After this sampling he may conclude that the overview is all he wants. If not, he will read the book more efficiently for having previewed.

1. Examine the title, and the sub-title if there is one. These are often the author's labels of the content.

2. Read the publisher's blurb on the jacket. This is dense with information—gist-packed.

3. Examine prefatory material. Here you will often find a statement of the purpose and scope of the book.

4. The table of contents may be closely packed with major topics. When read continuously the chapter titles may offer a concise summary of the book's content.

5. Skimming a book is in many respects an expansion of skimming a short selection. The opening chapter corresponds to the opening paragraphs of a short selection. It is often somewhat general and announces the general content.

6. As the student leafs through subsequent chapters he will discover that introductory and concluding paragraphs are often "strategic spots."

7. The concluding chapter is frequently highly concentrated. It is the writer's last chance with the reader. Here he often wraps up his big ideas—drives home what he wants most of all to leave with his reader.

*The reader will find exceptions to these guidelines.* There is no intent to prescribe rigid procedures.

### Activities for Skimming Practice

*What Can You Learn in One Minute?*   Using an unexplored textbook chapter or magazine article, students are set this task: "How much can you learn about the content of this chapter (or article) in just one minute? Use your skimming techniques to hit the high spots of well organized prose."

*Do You Want to Read This?*   Using a magazine, students are given this task: "Skim this article, using your new techniques, to see whether you want to read it at all. What a time saver in personal reading to make this quick appraisal, then reject an uninviting selection!" (Students should be prepared to offer reasons for rejection or acceptance.)

*What's His Point of View?*   Using the editorial page, students practice skimming editorials solely to learn the writer's opinion or point of view. They discuss this question: "Suppose you wish to learn the stand of the writer of this editorial on _____ (some critical local, national, or international issue). That's all you want—just to learn the editorial viewpoint. Where do you think you might zero in as you do this type of skimming?" (The group may suggest examining the editorial's conclusion. Here the writer may stress the point he wants most to leave with the reader. The introduction, too, may reveal the viewpoint.)

The same type of activity might also be conducted with contemporary and "classical" essays.

*Can You Skim a News Story?*   Students are led to observe that straight news stories require a different technique of skimming. Here the headlines, the sub-heads, and the lead yield the quintessence. The lead is dense with the answers to key questions: the five *w's* and sometimes *h*—who? what? when? where? why? how? The content of the rest of the news story tapers off in importance. Against a time limit, students skim the headlines, the sub-heads, and the lead for the gist of front page stories.

## RAPID AND MODERATELY RAPID READING

Students like Bill D—— urgently need their teachers' guidance in acquiring rapid rates of reading. His parents reported to an English teacher, "He studies until twelve and one each night—and most of the weekend, too. His grades are good, but he sacrifices relaxation and friendship. His interests are math and science. He's done so much slow reading in these fields that now he reads the lightest novel, even the comics, slowly."

Students who, like Bill, have an absorbing interest in science and/or math, students who concentrate on nonfiction to the neglect of fiction, and students who are overconscientious are likely to be slow readers.

How can an instructor help the Bills in his classes attain higher rates of reading? He can (1) encourage practice with highly interesting material read for less exacting purposes, (2) give assignments that call for the general impression, (3) provide timed practice exercises, and (4) use instruments to force more rapid reading.

## Practice with Highly Interesting Material

Much practice with easy, highly interesting material, read for less exacting purposes, is a natural, effective means of increasing rates. The material should be a grade or two lower than the student's instructional level and should present no vocabulary or comprehension blocks. The student should be pulled along by intense interest.

Browsing sessions offer classroom teachers an opportunity to influence book selections. Exciting, fast-moving fiction and narrative-style biographies, rather than books like *War and Peace,* are appropriate for students who need to increase their rates. Librarians, too, can guide students to fast-moving books which match their interests.

Having a student graph his rates of reading easy material, so that he observes his day to day improvement, should spur him on to greater efforts. Many students respond well to the "Alarm Clock Graph" and the "Ten-Page Graph," later in this chapter.

## Reading for the General Impression

Making assignments that call for the general impression—cutting down, for the time being, the number of demands for detailed information, should be of special value to readers in need of speed. Directing attention to the role played by introductions and conclusions, topical headings, topic sentences, and to the technique (when appropriate) of hitting the meaning-carrying words and slighting those less important should help these students get a quick grasp of important content.

Tests on the content of a selection should be keyed to reading purposes. Exhorting speed on a selection and then quizzing students on the details is unfair. The type of question that encourages rapid reading calls for a general reaction to the passage. Noting details, unless they are very obvious, calls for a slower rate of reading.

The reader will find helps for students on how to do rapid reading for general background in "Turn On Reading Power Through Assignments" in Chapter 3.

### Timed Practice Exercises

Timed practices are suitable for students whose word recognition, vocabulary, and comprehension are already adequate. Deficiencies in any of these areas should be remedied before time pressures are imposed.

Groups or individuals read short selections under time pressure, then answer comprehension questions. Under pressure, students often discard unnecessarily sluggish habits. Selections intended for rapid reading should include few unfamiliar words.

Asking for rapid identification of the main ideas of paragraphs, without intent to note details, might go hand in hand with the study of paragraph patterns in writing. After students have made an intensive study of paragraphs of cause and effect, comparison and contrast, problem and solution, and the like, the main ideas should stand out and be more quickly graspable.

Whatever the exercise, from the first the students should have concrete evidence of progress. By starting with easy material the instructor should deliberately plan encouraging success experiences. Graphing improvement spurs continued effort.

### READING PACERS

While pacers produced by different manufacturers vary, with all pacers a cover, a bar, or a beam of light moves down the page, pressuring the student to increase his rate. A dial controls the speed of the descending occluder or light beam.

Pacer training is motivational for most students and profitable for many as long as word recognition, vocabulary, and comprehension skills are already adequate. If not, until such inhibiting factors are removed, forcing such training may be extremely harmful. In one reading laboratory a young man was in tears about his performance on the pacer. He was being forced to "read" faster and faster when he did not know the meanings of the words on the page.

When no blocks are present, remediation in the area of rates of reading is rapid as compared with vocabulary and comprehension.

Reading clinicians comment, "Pure rate cases are the easiest and show the most rapid improvement of all remedial problems." They caution though, "When a severe emotional problem is present, imposing an added pressure through rate training is usually inadvisable."

## CONTROLLED READING TECHNIQUES

In addition to the functions of the pacer, controlled reading devices force specific left-to-right eye movements. Such techniques are used in connection with films or filmstrips. Probably the most popular of these techniques is the filmstrip approach used in the Controlled Reader (for four to fifteen students) or the Controlled Reader Jr. (for one to three students) produced by EDL-McGraw-Hill. Taylor and Frackenpohl* caution that students should be grouped for such training on the basis of reading achievement levels and rate of reading with comprehension.

### Rapid Reading Activities Without Instruments

*Easy Fiction Speedway*   Here's an adaptation of an idea that Spache and Berg suggested for readers who dally over easy fiction: "If a light novel of 200 pages would ordinarily take you five hours to read, set a four-hour time limit. That's about 25 pages every half hour. Mark every twenty-fifth page through the book with a paper clip, to drive toward. Check yourself at these points to see if you're up to schedule. If you find yourself lagging, attempt to catch up the next 25 pages. On your next book, try to top your performance by setting an even shorter time limit."†

*What Can You Gain in an Hour?*   Strang made this suggestion for conscientious students overly careful in reading light fiction: "Assume that you have just an hour to spend in reading a light popular book which you have heard mentioned frequently and are eager to read. See how much you can get from this short contact." Students report in class what they have gleaned. They often surprise themselves.

With dreamers who need to call back wandering thoughts, she adapted this idea to appropriate sections of textbooks: "See how much you can gain from this section in ten minutes."‡

---

* Stanford E. Taylor and Helen Frackenpohl, *Controlled Reading,* Teacher's Guide (Huntington, New York: Educational Developmental Laboratories, Inc., 1968), p. 38.

† Spache and Berg, *The Art of Efficient Reading,* p. 91.

‡ Ruth Strang. Class lecture in the teaching of secondary school reading, University of Chicago, summer, 1965.

*Supersonic Reading*    Strang also told about one instructor who held "supersonic" speed sessions—two each week, each only ten minutes long. Students read easy, interesting, fast-moving fiction for one minute, then counted the words read and recorded the count on a file card. During each succeeding timing they tried to break their records of the minute before. Even these short sessions proved helpful when reinforced with much fiction reading outside of class. The average increase was 200 words per minute.*

*Alarm Clock Graph*    Students are advised: "The reading material best suited for developing your speed is probably easy, interesting, fast-moving fiction read for enjoyment. One secret is forcing yourself beyond your usual rate. Soon the increased rate should become a comfortable rate for you."

Unless the next book a student reads corresponds in words per page and in difficulty, he will need to start a new graph.

*Ten-Page Graph*    The student notes his starting time, beginning on an even minute, then reads ten pages of his fiction book and records his time on the graph. He then reads ten more pages, trying to cut down his time. He may wish to count ahead ten pages and mark the "finish line" with a paper clip to drive toward. Daily practice is desirable.

Busy students may prefer the "Ten-Page Graph" to the "Alarm Clock Graph," for though it may be difficult to set aside a full hour, they can often manage the time required to read ten pages.

* Strang. Class lecture, summer, 1965.

## ALARM CLOCK GRAPH
## (For Home Practice)

Reading material best suited for speed practice is easy, interesting fiction read for pleasure. Set aside an hour (or half hour) each day if possible for rate practice at home. Set your alarm clock to ring at the end of an hour (or half hour), count the number of pages read, chart the results below, then try each day to better the record of the day before.

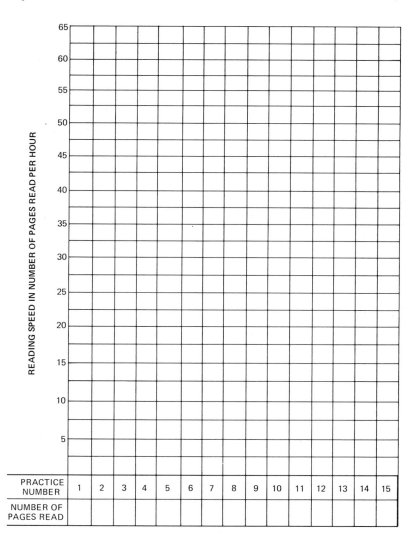

| PRACTICE NUMBER | 1 | 2 | 3 | 4 | 5 | 6 | 7 | 8 | 9 | 10 | 11 | 12 | 13 | 14 | 15 |
|---|---|---|---|---|---|---|---|---|---|---|---|---|---|---|---|
| NUMBER OF PAGES READ | | | | | | | | | | | | | | | |

# TEN-PAGE GRAPH

The reading material best suited for developing your speed of reading is easy, interesting, fast-moving fiction read for pleasure. Read ten pages of your book. Record the time this takes. Then read ten more pages trying to improve the first record and *pushing* yourself to read faster than seems comfortable for you. One secret of increasing your reading speed is *forcing* yourself beyond your usual rate. Soon the new increased rate should become comfortable for you.

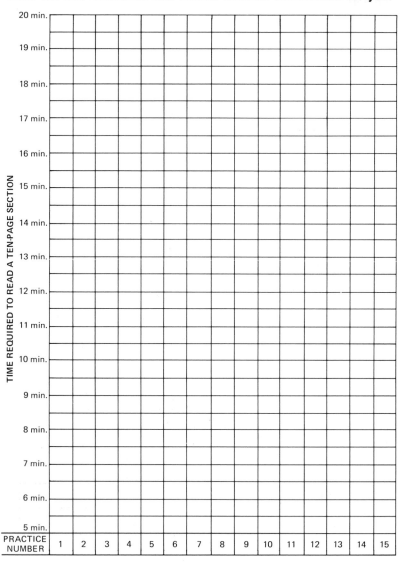

TIME REQUIRED TO READ A TEN-PAGE SECTION

| | 20 min. | 19 min. | 18 min. | 17 min. | 16 min. | 15 min. | 14 min. | 13 min. | 12 min. | 11 min. | 10 min. | 9 min. | 8 min. | 7 min. | 6 min. | 5 min. |

| PRACTICE NUMBER | 1 | 2 | 3 | 4 | 5 | 6 | 7 | 8 | 9 | 10 | 11 | 12 | 13 | 14 | 15 |

*Push-Card Pacer* Some students may find it helpful to improvise a reading pacer with an ordinary 4 x 6 card, using it somewhat as follows:

1. The student places the card *above* the line to be read. He then moves it down the page, forcing himself to keep ahead. Or he may prefer to place the card just *below* the line to be read, exposing the reading matter line by line and "chasing" the card down the page.

2. He pushes the card down the page more rapidly than he thinks he can comprehend. He may be surprised at the speed attainable without loss of comprehension.

3. This suggestion is given: "You now have a lifetime 'portable reading pacer.' If you really want to pick up speed, use it with easy newspaper and magazine content and light, fast-moving books."

Some students find the push-card distracting and respond negatively. Others quickly become accustomed to it.

*Two-Readings Procedure* Judson suggested a series of speed practice sessions using materials from day to day reading. The reader pushes strenuously just fifteen minutes at a stretch, no more than once a day and no less than three times a week.*

1. Preview the selection quickly.
2. Then do a first reading, using a push-card if you like, dangerously beyond your comfortable rate. Recite to yourself what you have learned.
3. Then read the selection again, more slowly, to discover what you missed on your first reading.
4. Do not hesitate to push yourself dangerously on your first reading. You can always pick up on the second reading anything you missed.
5. With practice you will miss less and less on your first reading until finally, on many occasions, only one reading will be necessary.

## SLOW, CAREFUL READING

As teachers work with the approaches suitable for reading the propositions underlying a theory in science, the precise parts of a mathematical equation, a Shakespearean sonnet, or the directions in typewriting, they are encouraging habits of close, intensive reading.

* Horace Judson, *The Techniques of Reading* (New York: Harcourt, Brace and World, 1963), pp. 82–83.

Much of this book is devoted to helping students develop the thorough reading constantly demanded in school courses. The subject-area index in Chapter 1 will guide subject teachers to strategies others have found effective. Procedures for helping students do thorough reading of an informational chapter are offered in "You Can Upgrade Students' Textbook Reading" in Chapter 3.

## INDEPENDENCE IN RATE ADJUSTMENT

We have mentioned steps (often concurrent) for building rate adjustment into students' permanent habits:

1. Diagnosing attainments and needs
2. Introducing the concept of rate adjustment
3. Developing the full range of rates
4. Guiding students in selecting the suitable approach
5. Eliciting the suitable approach from students—with less instructor guidance
6. Achieving independence in using the appropriate approach

We have considered in detail steps 1, 2, and 3. Now let us move on to the ultimate objective—guiding students to full independence in the use of suitable approaches.

Rate adjustment is likely to come for the majority of students only with guided practice in actual course materials. It is here, in their day to day assignments, that they can experience reading rates "in action."

One of the foremost causes of ineffective rate of reading, McKim stressed, is the absence of clear purpose. And, conversely, she listed as the first and fundamental step toward rate adjustment *insuring that students know the purposes for which they are reading and discussing with the group how they will read to achieve these purposes.*\* Ways and means of accomplishing this are considered in detail in "Turn on Reading Power Through Assignments" in Chapter 3. An instructor might profitably suggest the following at the time a reading assignment is made.

> "In reading this fast-moving short story, the purpose is enjoyment. What rate do you think is appropriate for 'The Most Dangerous Game'?"

\* Margaret G. McKim, *Guiding Growth in Reading* (New York: The Macmillan Company, 1963), p. 341.

"All you need is a general impression of this chapter. How will you read for the general content?"

"There are many books for you on the library table. How could you skim so as to find those that will be most helpful to your group?"*

"We have talked over the purpose of this assignment. How do you think you should read to accomplish this purpose?"

"What do you think it's important to find out from this reading? What will be the best method of reading in order to find this out?"

Ultimately, students should be able to deliberate and decide for themselves the appropriate approach for the material and purpose at hand.

No teacher should be discouraged when the majority of students move slowly and gradually toward rate adjustment. Training to achieve it must be a continuing instructional concern through the school years. Such training is given not only directly as discussed in this chapter but through many indirect ways—vocabulary instruction, help with comprehension, stress on purpose, work with the structure of prose and with patterns of writing, and the improvement of study habits. Strang cited as one of the most important insights gained in her long and distinguished career: "Generally effective instruction in reading is a means of improving speed. A good reading program will have speed as a byproduct."†

But the direct teaching of rate adjustment as a concomitant of purposeful reading is a decided plus factor. Instructors who work actively with rate adjustment are helping students acquire a strategy that conditions to a large degree their success in high school and college, efficient informational reading in adulthood, and lifelong enjoyment in personal reading. Rate adjustment is one of the hallmarks of the mature reader.

* McKim, *Guiding Growth in Reading,* p. 341.
† Strang. Class lecture, summer, 1965.

## 5

# READING SKILLS
# FOR PROBLEM SOLVING
# AND TOPIC DEVELOPMENT

With knowledge exploding in almost every field, the answers of today can—and may—become obsolete tomorrow. For the 1970's, the student must have resources for searching out the current answers. Teachers whose subjects call for such reading tasks are concerned that students gain the expertise they need for making investigations.

This chapter offers for your consideration a number of helps for students as they face investigative tasks. And it alerts the teacher to the many and complex skills students must have in order to attack problems through reading.

We hope you will find the following questions suggestive, and the answers we offer pragmatic, as you consider ways to strengthen students for their problem solving tasks.*

1. Does the student know how to narrow the problem to manageable proportions and to state it precisely?
2. Does the student know how to set up reading targets?
3. Can he locate books and other sources of the desired information?

* The interest of Laboratory School teachers and their insights into students' needs were a contribution to this chapter. In science, these teachers include: Department Chairman Ernest Poll, Jerry Ferguson, Murray Hozinsky, Judith Keane, Barbara Wehr, and also A. J. Ferrantino and Hiroshi Kanno, formerly of the school. In social studies, they include Earl Bell and former Laboratory School teacher, Gerald Marker. Ernest Poll was generous with time and help when asked a multitude of questions by the writers.

4. Can the student use a book's table of contents and index as aids in locating the sought-for information?

5. Can the student scan a passage for information that bears upon his problem?

6. Does he discriminate between what is relevant to his problem and what is irrelevant?

7. Does the student evaluate what he reads—selecting or rejecting after a critical appraisal?

8. Can the student make notes efficiently from a number of scattered sources?

9. Can the student bring the information he has collected into an orderly presentation of his own?

10. Does the student keep an open mind for later evidence that may modify his solution to the problem?

## URGENT NEED FOR PROBLEM SOLVING SKILLS FOR THE 1970's

Man has acquired more knowledge in the last twenty-five years than in the preceding thousand years. With human knowledge growing and changing at this fantastic pace, the advanced information of today may appear primitive tomorrow. Today the successful student must have on call resources for searching out the current information. Among these resources is a complete collection of reading skills for solving a problem or investigating a topic.

We can no longer regard a single textbook as containing a course in science or social studies. Many courses are now centered around problem solving. Indeed, the student's success in almost all his subjects and on all levels is becoming more and more dependent on his ability to search out answers independently.

### Haven't Students Already Acquired These Skills?

Haven't students in secondary schools and colleges already developed the reading skills they need for making an investigation? Instruction in these skills is not often given in depth as part of the elementary school program in fundamentals of reading. Nor is it generally offered in secondary school English or reading courses. Indeed, the responsibility for these skills is a no man's land. The result? Students are often assigned problems that involve complex skills of reference reading, then left to explore these problems largely unassisted.

## Isn't a Compelling Interest in the Problem Enough?

If the teacher can arouse the student's curiosity—create a compelling purpose for reading—involve him in his very own thing, isn't that enough? Certainly it would be difficult to overstress the drive generated when the student is caught up with interest in a problem of immense significance to him. But are students led, simply by virtue of the task set, to develop the most rapid, the most labor saving, the most effective problem solving techniques? Left to their own devices, poor students often develop deficiencies that disable them as they try to attack most of their school subjects, and capable students have at their command only those skills which they have picked up haphazardly along the way.

When students already possessed with interest in an exciting problem have the added advantage of their teacher's guidance in the most effective techniques, an ideal situation is created. The immediate need motivates the student to learn the facilitating skill. He is likely to react, "That's a real short cut!" His satisfaction leads to his continued use of the skill and to its reinforcement.

## How Can You Take Time from Your Regular Class Work?

One science teacher whose course is problem oriented accompanies his students to the school library, where he guides them in the skills they need for problem solving. If he is asked, "How can you find the time?" he answers, "I can't afford not to find it. The problem solving jobs are at the heart of the study of science. During a school year my classes spend thousands of 'student hours' in problem solving. I want these hours well spent, so I take down the obstacle course. I *spend* the time—to *regain* it later as students search out information more rapidly and intelligently and with considerably less supervision."*

A teacher intent on building reading skills for problem solving can do three things:

1. He can learn which skills his students already have.
2. He can analyze the assignment to learn precisely which skills they must have in order to complete it.
3. He can tie in instruction in the skills in which they are deficient, thus removing the roadblocks.

* Murray Hozinsky, University of Chicago Laboratory School science teacher. Remarks to Thomas, May, 1970.

The teacher who develops reading skills for problem solving is helping to prevent discouragement and frustration and to sustain his students' interest in study and in school. He is preparing them for tasks demanded in almost every subject and on every level. And he is developing skills essential for solving *life* problems after their courses at school are over. Can the school afford to leave these vital skills of reading—these basic tools of learning—these imperatives for the 1970's—to the student's fumbling efforts to develop them himself?

## WHAT IS REQUIRED OF THE STUDENT?

Scholarly adults to whom the use of reading tools has become second nature may not be fully aware of the weighty demands that solving a problem or developing a topic imposes upon the student. But how does the task appear to the student? If his problem or topic is complex, he may need to narrow it to manageable proportions, then analyze it into its component aspects before he can begin his search for material. He may have to find his way among thousands of books and periodicals. It may be important to consult specialized sources of whose existence he is unaware. Once he has a promising book in hand, he must select what is relevant to his problem and reject what is irrelevant. He must know how to make notes efficiently on widely scattered information. Finally, he must organize all this information— bring all the bits and pieces into a unified, orderly presentation of his own.

The rest of this section will call attention to some of the specific and often sequential steps essential for the broad problem solving tasks just mentioned. For a heightened awareness of all that is involved, the writers are indebted to *Reading, Grades 7, 8, 9, A Teacher's Guide to Curriculum Planning* (Curriculum Bulletin No. 11. New York: Board of Education of the City of New York, 1957). The reader in search of a comprehensive list of skills combined with practical how-to-do-it suggestions may wish to consult this ageless bulletin.

### Many Skills Can Be Taught in Minutes

The following skills and strategies need not, by sheer weight of numbers, seem overwhelming. They should be approached with the question, "Which of these skills do my students need in order to complete this particular assignment?" Many reference skills can be taught with just a few brief pointers. In just minutes, students can be introduced to such useful reference aids as the encyclopedia's most recent yearbook or its priceless index volume. In a short period of time students can learn to use the *Reader's Guide to Periodical Literature*—and have this tool at their command through *years* of reference reading. Many of the skills and understandings enumerated here are accompanied by instructional suggestions. In the case of others, selected references are offered to the reader.

Students' day to day reports, their talks to the class, their research papers, their projects that combine laboratory investigation with reading to find out what others have discovered—all stand to improve as students become accomplished users of the tools of reference reading.

## CAN THE STUDENT NARROW THE PROBLEM AND STATE IT PRECISELY?

Let us suppose that a class or a group expressed interest in making a study of the planet Mars. The teacher suggested, "You could spend *lifetimes* studying Mars. What do you want to find out about Mars? Are you interested in its distance? its motion? a recent space probe? a future space probe? the mysterious canals?"

It appeared, after a discussion, that the interest of the students centered around the topic, "What will the first Earthmen find on Mars?" The teacher pointed out that Mars is a vast expanse from icy polar caps to equatorial "deserts." The students concluded that further limitation was in order. They decided to assume that the first Earthmen would make their landing somewhere in the equatorial regions of Mars. The topic they finally decided on was "What are the first Earthmen likely to find on Mars if they land near the equator?"

"You'll find a tie-in," the teacher added, "between limiting your topic, as you have just done, and skillful reference reading. By narrowing your subject, you've put on 'reading blinders.' Your blinders will help you focus on what is related and shut out what is unrelated. For example, you'll reject as unrelated—at least to your specific problem—passages about the surface features of Mars *away from the equator,* the change of seasons away from the equator, and about perils to Earthmen in the Martian polar areas. You'll examine thoroughly passages about the mysterious blue-green areas of Mars to check whether these extend to the equator."

## CAN THE STUDENT SET UP READING TARGETS?

### A Complex Problem or Topic Requires Breakdown

Obviously a simple problem or topic requires little analysis before the student begins his search for information. The student may be looking for the answer to a single question, for instance, "What is the usual direction of travel of a tornado?" A complex problem, however, requires breakdown into its component aspects. When the problem is broad, preparing in advance a framework of questions—setting up, insofar as possible, specific reading targets—will greatly facilitate locating the information.

### A Class Sets Up Reading Targets

We have imagined a class or a group selecting as a major project the problem, "What are the first Earthmen likely to find on Mars if they land near the equator?" (For purposes of illustration, a complex problem has been selected. Many of the problems students explore will involve far fewer aspects.)

The instructor suggests, "You've selected your broad problem. Now try to think of everything you'd like to learn about it. Break it down into sub-topics. These will become your reading targets—the specific information you'll search for during your investigation. Now what *are* some of the things you want to find out?"

As the students offer suggestions, someone writes them on the board.

WHAT THE FIRST EARTHMEN ARE LIKELY TO FIND ON MARS
NEAR THE EQUATOR

*Your Reading Targets*
1. How will the terrain appear?
2. Are they likely to observe signs of life? plants? animals?
3. How will the sky appear?
4. Will they find water? bodies of water?
5. What will the temperature be?
6. Will they find any canals?
7. Will they find any plants?
8. What are the perils to man's survival? What life support systems will they need?
9. What about the climate? Does it rain?

10. What will the pull of gravity be? its effect on walking?
11. Does Mars have a moon?
12. What kind of soil?
13. What about the atmosphere? Can they breathe?
14. What about the seasons?

Obviously, here is an outpouring of major and minor topics in chaotic order. The teacher suggests, "Will it be any easier to read for the answers if we group together topics that are related?" The students consider the *why* of this—the convenience of approaching their reading with grouped together questions when related bits of information are found close together in a certain section of a book. With guidance, the class perceives that their broad problem falls into several major subdivisions: SURFACE FEATURES—ATMOSPHERE—CLIMATE—POSSIBILITY OF LIFE—PERILS TO SURVIVAL—and others. These main topics go up on the chalkboard, with plenty of space to insert sub-topics later.

WHAT THE FIRST EARTHMEN ARE LIKELY TO FIND ON MARS
NEAR THE EQUATOR

*Your Reading Targets*
   I. Surface features
  II. Atmosphere
 III. Weather
  IV. Features of sky
   V. Force of gravity
  VI. Life forms (if any)
 VII. Perils to human survival

The class is now helped to perceive how the sub-topics in which they expressed interest drop into slots under the main topics. As they sort and arrange these, they refine some and add others.

WHAT THE FIRST EARTHMEN ARE LIKELY TO FIND ON MARS
NEAR THE EQUATOR

*Your Reading Targets*
   I. Surface features
      A. Terrain
      B. Materials
      C. Canals (if any)

II. Atmosphere
    A. Composition
    B. Pressure
III. Weather
    A. Seasonal variation
    B. Daily variation
IV. Features of sky
    A. Appearance of solar system and stars
    B. Appearance of moon(s)
V. Force of gravity
    A. Comparison with Earth
    B. Effect on weight
    C. Effect on movement
VI. Life forms (if any)
    A. Plant life
    B. Animal life
VII. Perils to human survival
    A. Specific problems, i.e., oxygen
    B. Life support systems needed

"Of course this list of target information," the teacher comments, "is incomplete and tentative. You'll modify it as you do your reading. You'll run across important sub-topics you haven't thought of. You may find a discussion of possible hot springs on Mars and decide to add the sub-topic "hot spots" under the heading SURFACE FEATURES. You may find yourself reading about the shortage of water vapor and decide to add the sub-topic humidity under the main topic ATMOSPHERE. You may decide to drop out one of your topics or sub-topics. You'll be *constantly* revising your target outline as you do your research reading."

**Simple Problems or Topics Require Simpler Reading Targets**

As has been noted, a simple problem or topic calls for little analysis before the student begins his reference reading. He may be searching for the answer to a single question, "What are the signs of an approaching tornado?" and his report, oral or written, may be quite brief.

Many problems explored by students involve far fewer aspects than the one on Mars. A class was interested in investigating the supply of water they use each day. At the suggestion, "Try to think of everything you'd like to find out about it," the students brought up these questions:

Where does it come from?

How pure is it?

How much does it take to supply us?

Is there enough?

How is it purified?

How is it brought to our homes?

Is there enough for the future?

The teacher continued, "Can you sort out these topics? Bring together the ones that are related? Arrange them in logical order?" The class worked out this simple framework:

OUR WATER SUPPLY

*Your Reading Targets*
 I. Where the water supply comes from
 II. How it is brought to our homes
 III. How it is purified
 IV. How pure it is
 V. How adequate the supply is
  A. How much our community needs
  B. Whether the supply is sufficient for now
  C. Whether it is sufficient for the future

## Target Outlines Take Shape During Reading

With many investigations the student will have no idea how he will organize his information until he is well into his reading. Sometimes his target outline will not shape up until he has almost finished his reading.

A social studies class became interested in how they, although nonvoters, could take action against air pollution.* Class members, divided into five committees, set out to gather facts. Each committee approached the reading with one of the broad questions below:

What federal, state, and city laws to control pollution are now on the books?

Which industries must take preventive measures?

What procedures has the government taken in the past to control air pollution?

* Earl Bell, University of Chicago Laboratory School social studies teacher. Remarks to Thomas, May, 1970.

What are the scientific reasons for air pollution?

What scientific measures are used to estimate the degree of pollution?

It was during the process of reading that many of the sub-topics to be included in each committee's report emerged.

## Why Reading Targets?

Students might think about and discuss the why of reading targets. With guidance, they will arrive at some of the plus values below.

---

### WHY SET UP READING TARGETS?

1. You'll find reading targets a speed device. You'll get what you're after faster. The key words in your topics and sub-topics will now serve as clue words for locating your information. These will speed you to appropriate books and chapters and, within a chapter, to the target information.

2. Some students stop searching before they have fully explored a problem—discovering too late that they have omitted crucial information. Clearly, your target plan, with its thoughtful advance listing of topics, will do much to insure complete coverage.

3. Some students include in their reports information that is unrelated, that is off target. Your target plan is an advance lineup of really relevant topics. It's easy to be lured by catchy but unimportant content. When you set up specific targets you will not be sidetracked by what is dramatic and spectacular yet really insignificant in relation to your problem.

4. Now you'll approach your reading with a mind full of questions. A questioning mind set should greatly increase both your reading comprehension and your retention of the information.

5. Your reading targets should step up your concentration. You'll be more alert when your reading is an active search for answers.

---

## CAN THE STUDENT LOCATE BOOKS AND OTHER SOURCES?

Whenever an individual either during his years in school or thereafter, wants to attack a problem by means of reading, one of the first tasks he faces is that of locating relevant information. Locational skills, as Gainsburg observed, are better taught than caught. Without teacher help, students often wander like lost souls among the thousands of books and periodicals in the library. With teacher help they can be equipped with the basic tools, the keys, that open up for lifelong use the endless resources that await them there.*

The following check list of questions is intended to sharpen awareness of the many locational skills involved in problem solving. In preparing the sections on the card catalog and the *Reader's Guide,* the writers have drawn some helpful suggestions from Martin Rossoff's *Using Your High School Library,* an excellent guidebook for students (New York: The H. W. Wilson Company, 1964).

The reader may wish to consult the following sources of instructional methods†:

Boyd, Jessie, and others. *Books, Libraries and You* (New York: Scribner, 1967)

Buttle, Faye J. *Steps to Beginning Research* (Provo, Utah: Extension Publications, Division of Continuing Education, Brigham Young University, 1967)

Cleary, Florence D. *Discovering Books and Libraries: A Handbook for Upper Elementary and High School Grades* (New York: H. W. Wilson, 1966)

Kranyik, Robert. *How to Teach Study Skills* (Englewood Cliffs, N.J.: Prentice-Hall, 1963)

Rossoff, Martin. *The Library in High School Teaching* (New York: H. W. Wilson, 1964)

Rossoff, Martin. *Using Your High School Library* (New York: H. W. Wilson, 1961)

Shankmann, Florence V. *How to Teach Reference and Research Skills* (Englewood Cliffs, N.J.: Prentice-Hall, 1963)

### Moments of Need Are Often Enough

Teaching locational skills need not place a heavy drain on time. Many of these skills can be taught in just minutes at the time students need them. The school librarian can be a strong ally, available to visit classes or work with groups in the library. Again a check list of skills need not, by virtue of its length, seem overwhelming if approached with the question, "Which of these skills does the student need *right now* in order to complete his coming assignment?"

---

* *Reading, Grades 7, 8, 9, A Teacher's Guide to Curriculum Planning,* Curriculum Bulletin No. 11 (New York City: Board of Education of the City of New York, 1957), p. 40.

† List compiled with the assistance of Sara Fenwick, Associate Professor, Graduate Library School, University of Chicago.

### A CHECK LIST OF LOCATIONAL SKILLS FOR PROBLEM SOLVING OR TOPIC DEVELOPMENT

_____ 1. Is the student generally oriented to the library?

       _____ a. Does he know its floor plan—charging desk, card catalog, information (or vertical) file, magazines and newspapers, microfilm, microfiche, films, tapes, recordings, pictures, and the like?

       _____ b. Does he know where reference books, fiction, non-fiction, bibliographies, and special collections are placed on the shelves?

_____ 2. Can the student use the card catalog to learn what materials the library has to offer on his particular subject and where he can locate these?

       _____ a. When confronted with what might be a bewildering array of wooden trays, does he find his way by means of their alphabetical labels?

       _____ b. Is he aware that although he may not know of a single piece of material or book on his subject or of a single author who has written about it, the subject card will guide him to materials that bear upon his problem?

              _____ (1) Does he realize that knowing the subject under which to look is not always obvious—that he will wish to ask himself thoughtfully, *"Just what key word* will lead me to the information I'm after?"

              _____ (2) Does he know that he may need to cast about in his mind for every possible related topic? If, for instance, his topic is "What Are the First Earthmen Likely to Find on Mars?" he may find it rewarding to look not only under Mars but also in other catalog drawers under such subject headings as Solar System and even Astronautics?

              _____ (3) Is he aware that his specific subject may require search under a *broader* classification—that if again his subject is Mars, he may turn up rewarding sources by consulting the subject card Planets?

              _____ (4) Does he follow the recommended sequence of first thinking of the most precise subject heading, then working his way to broader or more inclusive subject headings? Would he proceed, if necessary, from Mars to Planets to Solar System to Astronomy?

———— (5) Is he aware that he may find a valuable added resource in the cross reference or "see also" card? He may find one of these placed in the card catalog just following the last card under Mars. This cross reference card is saying, "You've looked through all the cards under Mars. If you still need material, why not try the additional subject headings below?"

```
Mars

    see also


Astronomy
Mariner IV
Planet
Solar System
Space Exploration
```

*FIGURE 5–1. Cross reference card.*

———— (6) Does he realize that often there is no sure way of knowing which key word will lead him to the information he is after? An expert offers this suggestion: "Locating the appropriate key word is a matter of trial and error. If you don't find what you're looking for under one subject, try another. Keep trying every possibility until you have exhausted them all."*

———— (7) Does he understand that determining the key word is crucial in investigating a topic? Does he persist until he gets a breakthrough?

———— c. As he goes along, does he compile a "working bibliography"? When a book looks promising, does he make a 3 x 5 bibliography card? Does he save a great deal of time later by taking down all the essential information *at once?* (See Figure 5–2, next page.)

———— (1) Are the items he takes down on the card *the same* and *in the same order* as those

* Martin Rossoff, *Using Your High School Library* (New York: The H. W. Wilson Company, 1964), p. 22.

he will need for his final bibliography? Will he compile his final bibliography with speed and ease because he has made out these cards with care?

\_\_\_\_\_ (2) Does he accurately record the call number—the "address" where he can find the book on the shelf?

\_\_\_\_\_ d. For quick access to a particular card he wants while doing his research, does he arrange the cards in a pack alphabetically by the last name of the author?

\_\_\_\_\_ 3. Does he know the broad classifications of the Dewey Decimal or Library of Congress systems? Can he use the call number to locate a book quickly from among the thousands on the shelves?

\_\_\_\_\_ 4. Can he use the encyclopedia to full advantage?

\_\_\_\_\_ a. Does he appreciate the encyclopedia as a possible starting point, sometimes the ideal starting point in making an investigation? Is he aware that it may offer a quick overview of his subject—that he can base his more detailed study on this helpful orientation? Does he know that once he has strengthened his background through this general introduction, he may be able to advance to more difficult, more techcal material and comprehend reading matter which would otherwise have been beyond him?

\_\_\_\_\_ b. Can he draw quickly and efficiently from the vast fund of human knowledge stored up in an encyclopedia? Does he value the index as a guide to "easy finding"? Does he often turn to the index first?

\_\_\_\_\_ (1) Is he aware that the information he is

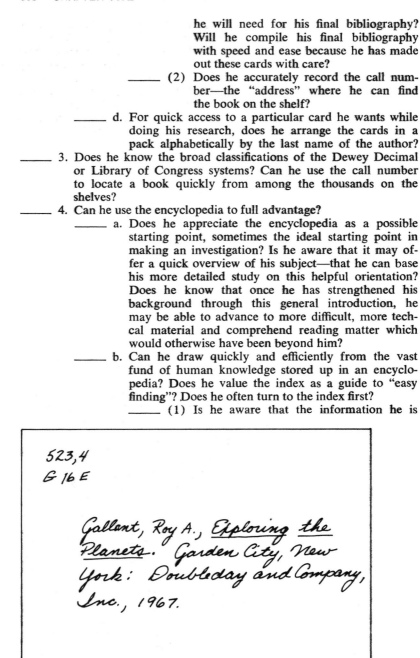

*FIGURE 5–2. Sample bibliography card for a book.*

seeking may be scattered here and there among thousands of articles and that the index is the *only sure way* to locate this scattered information?

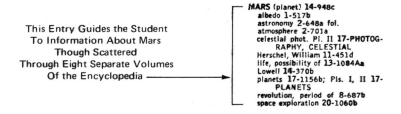

This Entry Guides the Student
To Information About Mars
Though Scattered
Through Eight Separate Volumes
Of the Encyclopedia ⟶

MARS (planet) 14-948c
albedo 1-517b
astronomy 2-648a fol.
atmosphere 2-701a
celestial phot. Pl. II 17-PHOTOG-
RAPHY, CELESTIAL
Herschel, William 11-451d
life, possibility of 13-1084Aa
Lowell 14-370b
planets 17-1156b; Pls. I, II 17-
PLANETS
revolution, period of 8-687b
space exploration 20-1060b

*FIGURE 5–3. Index entry on Mars. (Reprinted by permission from the* ENCYCLOPAEDIA BRITANNICA, *Index Volume. Chicago: Encyclopaedia Britannica, Inc., 1969, p. 360.)*

_____ (2) Does he realize that, if he overlooks the index, crucial information on his topic may be lost to him? Suppose he needs the astonishing evidence about Mars that *Mariner IV* brought to light. If he looks for *Mariner IV* in the "M" volume, these findings will elude him—he will find no article on that subject. If, however, he looks in the index under *Mariner IV,* he will find references to scattered articles with crucial information.

If He Fails to Consult This Entry,
The Student May not Find
*Mariner IV's* Startling Revelations
About Mars

Mariner (satellite)
space exploration 20-1046a fol.;
fig. 10 20-1049
Mars 14-948c
Van Allen radiation belts 22-875d

*FIGURE 5–4. Index entry on Mariner IV. (Reprinted by permission from the* ENCYCLOPAEDIA BRITANNICA, *Index Volume. Chicago: Encyclopaedia Britannica, Inc., 1969, p. 358.)*

_____ (3) Does he know where to look for the index, this "key to maximum usefulness" of his encyclopedia—usually not in the last pages of each volume but in a separate volume? Has he ever actually held an index volume in his hand and availed himself of its direction?

_____ (4) Since the arrangement of an index entry and the symbols used may differ from one encyclopedia to another, does he consult the simple, clear directions that precede each index?

_____ (5) Can he correctly interpret a "see" cross reference? Does he understand that a "see" reference directs him not to an encyclopedia article with that name but to *another subject heading in the index* where the information he desires may be found?

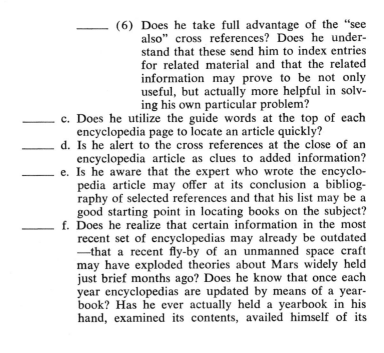

FIGURE 5–5. A *"see" reference. (Reprinted by permission from* THE HARPER ENCYCLOPEDIA OF SCIENCE, *Vol. 2. New York: Harper & Row, Publishers, 1967, p. 1343).*

_____ (6) Does he take full advantage of the "see also" cross references? Does he understand that these send him to index entries for related material and that the related information may prove to be not only useful, but actually more helpful in solving his own particular problem?

_____ c. Does he utilize the guide words at the top of each encyclopedia page to locate an article quickly?

_____ d. Is he alert to the cross references at the close of an encyclopedia article as clues to added information?

_____ e. Is he aware that the expert who wrote the encyclopedia article may offer at its conclusion a bibliography of selected references and that his list may be a good starting point in locating books on the subject?

_____ f. Does he realize that certain information in the most recent set of encyclopedias may already be outdated —that a recent fly-by of an unmanned space craft may have exploded theories about Mars widely held just brief months ago? Does he know that once each year encyclopedias are updated by means of a yearbook? Has he ever actually held a yearbook in his hand, examined its contents, availed himself of its

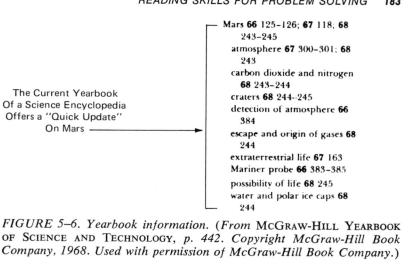

The Current Yearbook
Of a Science Encyclopedia
Offers a "Quick Update"
On Mars ⟶

Mars **66** 125–126; **67** 118; **68** 243–245

atmosphere **67** 300–301; **68** 243

carbon dioxide and nitrogen **68** 243–244

craters **68** 244–245

detection of atmosphere **66** 384

escape and origin of gases **68** 244

extraterrestrial life **67** 163

Mariner probe **66** 383–385

possibility of life **68** 245

water and polar ice caps **68** 244

*FIGURE 5–6. Yearbook information. (From* McGraw-Hill Yearbook of Science and Technology, *p. 442. Copyright McGraw-Hill Book Company, 1968. Used with permission of McGraw-Hill Book Company.)*

index to update his information on some current topic?

_____ g. Does he know of the existence of encyclopedias in specialized fields, for example, *International Encyclopedia of the Social Sciences* and *The McGraw-Hill Encyclopedia of Science and Technology?* When appropriate, does he consult these for more detailed, more technical information?

_____ 5. Does he know which of his needs in reference reading will be served by other general library tools—almanacs, atlases, gazetteers, *Who's Who,* dictionaries, biographical dictionaries, and others?

_____ 6. Does he avail himself of valuable source materials in specialized fields—science, social studies, music, and others—whenever he needs these to complete an investigation?

Encyclopedias of specialized knowledge (Example: *International Encyclopedia of the Social Sciences*)

Dictionaries of terms in specialized fields (Example: *Harvard Dictionary of Music*)

Biographical dictionaries (Examples: *American Men of Science, World Who's Who in Science*)

Trade books on specialized topics

Scholarly research papers and abstracts of scholarly papers

_____ 7. In an age when knowledge is changing and increasing at a furious pace, is he alert for ways to search out the latest information?

_____ a. Does he realize that publishing an ordinary book may take from six months to a year, a reference book even longer, and that consequently books cannot offer him the most recent information? Does he view periodicals—issued more frequently—as a promising source of up-to-the-minute information? Has he discovered that the *Reader's Guide to Periodical Literature* will help him locate information on his subject from among *thousands* of magazine and newspaper articles?

_____ (1) Does he appreciate the *recency* of the latest *Reader's Guide?* Is he aware that through the green paperback supplements he is offered a guide to periodicals which is updated as often as twice each month?

_____ (2) Is he aware that the crucial problem in finding articles related to his problem is determining the subject heading under which these will be listed—that the heading Mars may lead him to rewarding articles—also the heading Space Flight to Mars?

_____ (3) Is he aware that the specific information he is seeking may require search under a broader subject—that to locate certain information about a Mars probe he may need to look under the more inclusive term, Space Probe?

_____ (4) Can he read an entry in the *Reader's Guide* correctly and completely, interpreting all the abbreviations and all the numerals (volume, date, page number)?

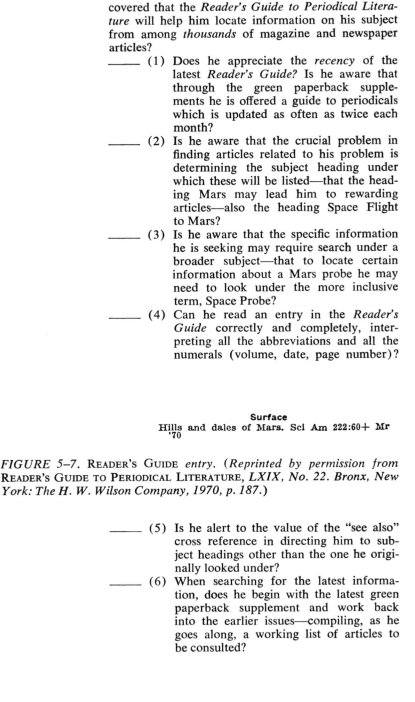

**Surface**
Hills and dales of Mars. Sci Am 222:60+ Mr
'70

FIGURE 5–7. READER'S GUIDE *entry. (Reprinted by permission from* READER'S GUIDE TO PERIODICAL LITERATURE, *LXIX, No. 22. Bronx, New York: The H. W. Wilson Company, 1970, p. 187.)*

_____ (5) Is he alert to the value of the "see also" cross reference in directing him to subject headings other than the one he originally looked under?

_____ (6) When searching for the latest information, does he begin with the latest green paperback supplement and work back into the earlier issues—compiling, as he goes along, a working list of articles to be consulted?

This Cross Reference
"Clues the Student In"
On Other Promising Headings ———————

**MARS (planet)**
➤ *See also*
**Space flight to Mars**

**Atmosphere**

Mariner 6: origin of Mars ionized carbon dioxide ultraviolet spectrum. A. Dalgarno and others. bibliog il Science 167:1490-1 Mr 13 '70

Red snowflakes on Mars? il Time 95:52 Mr 23 '70

**Mass**

Martian mass and earth-moon mass ratio from coherent S-band tracking of Mariners 6 and 7. J. D. Anderson and others. bibliog il Science 167:277-9 Ja 16 '70

**Photographs from space**

Mariner 6 television pictures: first report. R. B. Leighton and others; discussion. bibliog il Science 167:906-8 F 6 '70

**Radiation**

Bright flares on Mars. Sky & Tel 39:83 F '70

**Surface**

Hills and dales of Mars. Sci Am 222:60+ Mr '70

Mars surface processes studied. B. M. Elson. il Aviation W 92:61+ F 9 '70

Red plastic snow. Sci Am 222:46 F '70

Red snowflakes on Mars? il Time 95:52 Mr 23 '70

*FIGURE 5–8. Cross reference in* READER'S GUIDE. (*Reprinted by permission from* READER'S GUIDE TO PERIODICAL LITERATURE, *LXIX, No. 22. Bronx, New York: The H. W. Wilson Company, 1970, p. 187.*)

——— (7) For each promising article, does he make a 3 x 5 bibliography card—with the facts the same and in the same order as he will need them for his final bibliography?

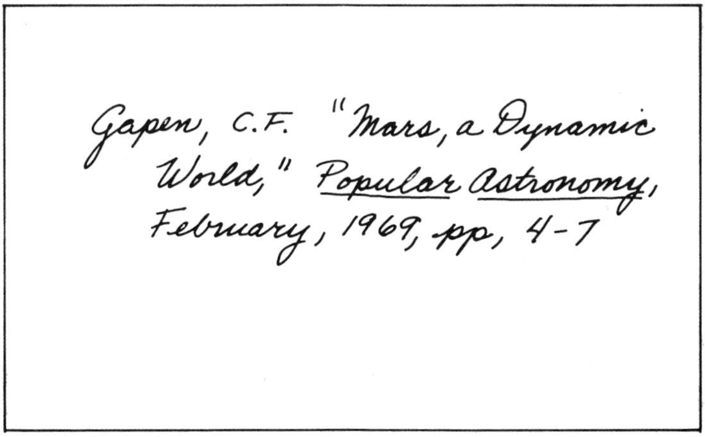

Gapen, C.F. "Mars, a Dynamic World," Popular Astronomy, February, 1969, pp. 4-7

*FIGURE 5–9. Sample bibliography card for periodical article.*

_____ (8) Does he understand that magazine and newspaper references are often of value when recency is *not* the consideration and that the *Reader's Guide* is the key which unlocks for him the vast storehouse of information in periodicals of the past?

_____ b. Is he aware that there are "reader's guides" in various specialized areas—guides in social studies, science, art, music, education, and other fields—and that these will unlock for him the contents of thousands of specialized articles? (Example: *Social Science and Humanities Index, New York Times Index*)

_____ c. Does he consult the Information (or Vertical) File as another promising source of current information? Has he ever explored its large drawers, often well stocked with pamphlets and clippings?

_____ d. Is he aware of other possible sources of current information such as

Encyclopedia yearbooks, recording major increments to knowledge within the past year

Almanacs and political handbooks

*Information Please Almanac*
*World Almanac*
*Statesman's Year-Book*

_____ e. As he moves from one library tool to another, does he compile his own "working bibliography," making a note of those references that look most promising?

_____ 8. Does the student select readings on an appropriate difficulty level?

We have mentioned the encyclopedia as the source of a quick overview of a topic and a promising starting point in an investigation. This strengthening of background information can be extremely valuable to less able readers. An inconspicuous word of guidance from the teacher can often insure "the right encyclopedia for the right student" and help to reduce discouragement and frustration.

The following annotations of encyclopedias commonly found in school libraries may be useful.

*The World Book Encyclopedia* (Chicago: Field Enterprises Educational Corporation, 1969)

Intended for students at grade level 4 and up, *The World Book* offers high interest reading matter that many poor secondary school readers can grasp. In many of the articles, the reading difficulty advances within the single article. Handicapped readers can often handle the opening section, which is approximately fourth grade level. Bibliographies are well chosen.

*Compton's Encyclopedia* (Chicago: F. E. Compton and Company, 1969)

Intended for upper elementary and secondary school use, *Compton's* offers readable material within the reach of many less able high school readers. The abundant full-color pictures with their easy captions appeal to under par readers. Many of the articles conclude with graded bibliographies.

*Britannica Junior* (Chicago: Encyclopedia Britannica, Inc., 1969)

This set, designed for pupils in grades 4–8, will also serve older students whose reading ability is not up to grade level.

*Collier's Encyclopedia* (New York: Crowell Collier and Macmillan, Inc., 1969)

This encyclopedia offers articles appropriate for many students in junior and senior high school as well as college. An "in-between" encyclopedia, *Collier's* is more advanced than the "juveniles" but less advanced than the *Americana*. Each article begins with a brief explanation. After that, the material gradually increases in sophistication. The style is popular, clear, and direct. Graded bibliographies are grouped together in the last volume.

*Encyclopedia International* (New York: Grolier Incorporated, 1969)

This, too, is an "in-between" encyclopedia, designed primarily for the high school or college student but appropriate also for many capable junior high school readers. The articles are usually short; the style popular, clear, and concise; the illustrations, abundant.

*Encyclopedia Americana* (New York: Americana Corporation, 1969)

The coverage is broader and the information more detailed than in the sets previously mentioned. Capable high school and college readers will use this encyclopedia to advantage.

*The Encyclopaedia Britannica* (Chicago: Encyclopaedia Britannica, Inc., 1969)

This, of course, is an advanced encyclopedia with contributions written by eminent scholars. Capable high school and college readers can use it to advantage.

_____ 9. Is the student aware that in reference reading it may be desirable to arrange his readings in an easy to difficult sequence?
      _____ a. When appropriate, does he first select a relatively easy source to get a general orientation to his subject? Does he realize that broadening one's background information is a *major factor* in increasing power of comprehension and that once he has strengthened

his background, he may be able to stretch and handle reading matter otherwise beyond his reach?

_____ (1) Does he recognize that the encyclopedia is sometimes the ideal place to get this easy introduction, this "instant background"—and that if he is planning to consult several encyclopedias, a desirable sequence is from easy to more difficult —perhaps *The World Book,* then *Collier's,* then *Americana?*

_____ (2) When appropriate, does he arrange the sequence of his magazine reading from popular to scholarly—first, for instance, a readable article for laymen in *Science Digest,* then a more learned and technical article in *The Scientific American* or *Science?*

## CAN THE STUDENT USE THE TABLE OF CONTENTS AND INDEX AS AIDS?

Let's suppose that the student has narrowed his problem and stated it precisely, has analyzed it into its component aspects and set up reading targets, and has found some reference materials that look promising. He now holds a book in his hands.

How can he find out whether the book really contains the information he is seeking? Does he thumb through it haphazardly, examining many unnecessary pages? Or does he take advantage of two ready aids—the table of contents and the index—to help him learn what the book has to offer?

_____ a. Does he turn to the table of contents for an outline, a concise, sequential listing of the major subject divisions covered in the book and the page on which he can find the beginning of a certain section?

_____ b. Does he utilize the index for instant finding of the precise page on which he will find a specific item from among the thousands of words in the book? Does he view it as the *sure way* to find all the help the book has to offer on his topic no matter how widely it is scattered? Is he aware that if he should overlook consulting the index, he may miss the very fact he is after?

_____ (1) Is he skillful at determining key words to help him find the sought-for information?

_____ (a) Is he aware that to dig out *all* the help the book has to offer, he may need to use more than one key word? (Examples: Mars, Mariner IV)

_____ (b) Does he realize that the index may not list the exact term he has in mind and that he may have to look under a synonym? Is he skillful at coming up with possible synonyms?

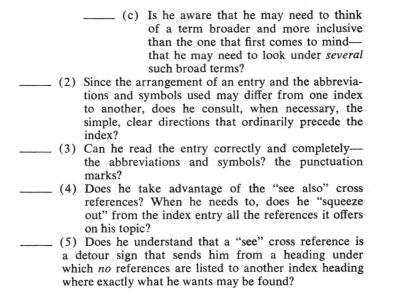

FIGURE 5-10. Index entry. (*Reprinted by permission from* AN INTRODUCTION TO ASTRONOMY *by Charles M. Huffer, Frederick E. Trinklein, and Mark Bunge. New York: Holt, Rinehart and Winston, Inc., 1967, p. 379.*)

_____ (c) Is he aware that he may need to think of a term broader and more inclusive than the one that first comes to mind— that he may need to look under *several* such broad terms?

_____ (2) Since the arrangement of an entry and the abbreviations and symbols used may differ from one index to another, does he consult, when necessary, the simple, clear directions that ordinarily precede the index?

_____ (3) Can he read the entry correctly and completely— the abbreviations and symbols? the punctuation marks?

_____ (4) Does he take advantage of the "see also" cross references? When he needs to, does he "squeeze out" from the index entry all the references it offers on his topic?

_____ (5) Does he understand that a "see" cross reference is a detour sign that sends him from a heading under which *no* references are listed to another index heading where exactly what he wants may be found?

_____ c. Does he discard from his working bibliography, cards for books which offer him no useful information on his subject?

## Papers, Oral Reports, and Class Discussions All Gain

A teacher who builds help with locational skills into the day to day work of his course in natural science, has this comment: "I guide my students in using the *Reader's Guide*—the index of a book—the card catalog—an encyclopedia yearbook—the specialized reference works of science—at the moment when they are caught up with the desire to solve an exciting problem and will get immediate results through using the new skill. Their papers, their oral reports, their class discussions all gain as they become increasingly at home among the reference tools of science."*

## CAN THE STUDENT SCAN A PASSAGE FOR INFORMATION?

Let us imagine that the student has located a book, has it on the desk before him, and has turned to a passage through which is interspersed information that will be useful. All he wants from these pages is the particular content that throws light upon his problem.

Many students have no approach other than starting at the first word of the passage and plodding through it line after line, page after page. They will add an extremely valuable reference skill to their collection when they learn the technique of scanning for specific information.

Here are some "trade secrets" of successful scanners:

*Have your reading targets clearly in mind before you begin your scanning.* Cement in mind all the elements of the question, both main topics and sub-topics.

*Watch for "highway signs."* Your author has put up conspicuous highway signs for much the same reason the road department builds these in unfamiliar country. Among these signposts are chapter division headings often in large capital letters, and side headings often in heavy (boldface) type. Such headings often announce the content of the section that follows. Some of these headings are saying, "This is promising hunting ground—you'll find what you're after here." Other headings are saying, "Speed right on past this section—there's nothing for you here."

If, for instance, you're searching for information on "What are the first Earthmen likely to find on Mars?" you can flash right on past a section headed Motion of the Planet. You'll slow down, though, and digest a section with the heading Is There Life on Mars?

*Zero in on paragraph openings.* The opening sentences of expository or explanatory paragraphs frequently flash signals as you are looking through a passage for specific information. You can often hop down the page, alighting on the first sentence or two of each paragraph, gathering up the gist of the paragraph quickly. Opening

---

* Hozinsky. Remarks to Thomas, May, 1970.

sentences may tell you, "Reader, slow down for this paragraph and search it carefully." Or they may say, "Bypass this paragraph—it isn't related to your problem."

Let's take an example. Suppose you're intent on finding just what temperatures the first Earthmen are likely to find near the equator on Mars. You'll speed right past the first paragraph below, but zero in on the second.

**TEMPERATURE**

The only practical means of determining the temperature of a body (such as a planet) millions of miles from earth is indirect: by measuring the heat or radiant energy it transmits to earth. The hotter a body is, the more heat it radiates, and the amount of heat received at any point depends upon the distance from the source of radiation. The heat of a candle, for example, can be felt a few feet away. On the other hand, the sun's radiation is perceptible even at a distance of 93,000,000 mi. If one can measure the amount of heat a body radiates per unit area of surface, one can calculate the temperature of the body from the laws of radiation. The absolute temperature is proportional to the fourth root of the energy radiated. The heat radiated from a planet is exceedingly weak but can be measured by sensitive detectors placed at the focus of a large telescope.

Radiation received from a planet is of two kinds: the sunlight reflected from its surface and the true planetary radiation resulting from the temperature of the emitting surface. The two kinds

This Opening Is a "Detour Sign."
The Paragraph Appears to Deal
Not With the Actual Temperatures on Mars
But With How Scientists Study
The Temperatures on a Faraway Planet.

Radiometric measures were made on Mars in 1954 with the 200-in. telescope at the Palomar observatory by John Strong and William M. Sinton. They found that the temperature at the equator reaches 25° C., while the sunrise temperature on the equator is at least as low as −50° C. They also found that the maximum temperature occurs about 12:30 P.M., instead of about 3:00 P.M., as on Earth. This slight lag, they concluded, results mainly from thermal conduction into the ground. This "greenhouse effect" is produced by the blanketing effect of water vapour and carbon dioxide in the Martian atmosphere, and is consistent with the theory that the surface of the planet is covered with dust. They estimated the average night-time temperature as −70° C.

These Opening Sentences Flag You.
They Say, "Here's What You're After —
The Actual Temperatures on Mars."

*FIGURE 5–11. Scanning signals. (Reprinted by permission from the* EN-CYCLOPAEDIA BRITANNICA, *Vol. 14, article "Mars." Chicago: Encyclopaedia Britannica, Inc., 1963, p. 959.)*

*Examine summary paragraphs at the close of chapters.* Here the author often wraps up the main points he has made in the chapter. If, judging from the summary, the chapter appears to offer what you're after, you may wish to turn back to the more detailed discussion.

Opportunities to help students scan for answers to live questions arise in day to day course work. A progression through increasingly difficult levels of scanning is desirable.

*Level 1.* Scanning for a bit of information that stands out easily—the date of some historic discovery about Mars, the university with which a certain scientist was affiliated.

*Level 2.* Scanning for an answer that is worded like the question.

*Level 3.* Scanning for an answer that is worded differently from the question.

### Using Scanning Techniques for the Unit on Mars

A teacher might share insights like the following, or elicit them from students, when a long unit like the one on Mars confronts the student with the necessity for frequent scanning. The students scan to find answers to questions from the current assignment.

"You will often need to use a book to search out a single fact, the answer to a single question, or one aspect of your topic. High speed scanning can *save you time* in study. You can learn to crack the printed page, moving your eyes down the page swiftly to the heart of what you want.

"First, fix in mind exactly what you're looking for. Hold this in the forefront of your mind. Flash your eyes down the page for this information only.

"Once you've found lines in the passage that *may* yield what you're seeking, stop scanning instantly. Shift gears into careful reading as you weigh whether you've *really* found what you're after."

What a teacher might do and say in helping students become skillful scanners on all three levels mentioned above is suggested in the section on scanning in Chapter 4.

### CAN HE DISCRIMINATE BETWEEN RELEVANT AND IRRELEVANT?

(*Note:* The suggestions given previously for practicing the technique of scanning are also applicable here.)

"Students often need to sharpen up their selectivity," teachers observe. "In reports and discussions, they waste their time and that of the class offering unrelated information. At the same time, they fail to include vital information."

The instructor's special guidance in selecting passages that are really relevant to the problem at hand should help students become discriminating reference readers. Suppose, for example, students are working at the moment with the question, "What *terrain* are the first Earthmen likely to find if they land near the Martian equator?"

They will need to hold in mind that precise question—to resist the lure of information that is "spectacular" but has no real bearing on their problem.

The pages before them may offer a confusing choice of diverse information.

the cratered surface

the origin of the craters

the intense wildness and loneliness

a desperate shortage of water

a hushed, deathly silence

the expanses of dusty "desert"

the color and type of soil

the curving surface and nearness of the horizon

bright white polar caps

the "blue-green" areas

components of the atmosphere

severity of the conditions for living things

and other information

They should learn to concentrate on their precise topic (the *terrain* of Mars at the equator), to reject unrelated information (the polar caps, which are not near the equator), and to resist vivid and dramatic but irrelevant information (the eeriness of the Martian landscape).

## DOES THE STUDENT SELECT OR REJECT AFTER CRITICAL EVALUATION?

The critical reading skills in the following check list are vital to the student in deciding which information contributes soundly to the solution of his problem.

### CHECK LIST ON CRITICAL EVALUATION

_____1. Does the student note the recency of the copyright date? Is he aware that since *Mariner IV*'s picture-taking probe made startling revelations about the atmosphere of Mars, he must search out sources with a publishing date recent enough to include these findings?

_____2. Does he thoughtfully appraise the qualifications of the writer and/or the investigator whose findings are reported?

_____3. Does he constantly ask, "What is the evidence that supports this statement? Is it soundly supported or is it just opinion—pure speculation passed off as fact?" What is the evidence, for example, for the statement that hot springs may provide water on Mars and warm the temperature?

_____4. Does he consider whether the statements made stem from emotion, bias, or a desire for sensationalism? As he probes the "great canal mystery," is he aware that the conclusion that intelligent Martians survived by building waterways carrying water from melting polar caps may have overintrigued a popular writer?

_____5. Does he weigh the writer's conclusions, inferences, and generalizations? What about the mysterious blue-green areas of Mars with their seasonal changes? Does the theory that they are advancing and retreating tracts of vegetation appear to be well supported?

_____6. Does he resist the impulse to accept the first plausible solution to the problem? Does he suspend judgment—asking, for example, "Are there alternative hypotheses about the changing appearance of these blue-green 'tracts of vegetation'?"

_____7. Does he accumulate sufficient information? What about those widely debated canals? Does he explore deeply enough to learn that the closeup photographs of *Mariner VI* and *VII* revealed no sign of them? Does he weigh the conclusion that optical illusion may have created "canals" as the human eye joins up disconnected spots and streaks into canal-like lines?

_____8. Does he read widely, looking for and welcoming different points of view? Does he understand how to proceed when the viewpoints of authorities are in conflict?

---

Teachers working with processes of logical thinking may wish to consult the following sources.

Altick, Richard D.   *Preface to Critical Reading* (New York: Holt, Rinehart and Winston, 1963)

Bilsky, Manuel.   *Logic and Effective Argument* (New York: Holt, Rinehart and Winston, Inc., 1956)

Hayakawa, Samuel I.   *Language in Thought and Action* (New York: Harcourt, Brace and World, Inc., 1949)

Ruby, Lionel.   *Logic: An Introduction* (New York: J. B. Lippincott Company, 1960)

Shepherd, David L.   *Effective Reading in Science* (Evanston, Illinois: Row, Peterson and Company, 1960)

Sund, Robert B. and Leslie W. Trowbridge.   *Teaching Science by Inquiry in the Secondary School* (Columbus, Ohio: Charles E. Merrill Books, Inc., 1967)

Washton, Nathan S.   *Teaching Science Creatively in the Secondary Schools* (Philadelphia: W. B. Saunders Company, 1967)

Werkmeister, William H. *An Introduction to Critical Thinking* (Lincoln, Nebraska: Johnsen Publishing Company, 1957)

Zahner, Louis, Arthur L. Mullin, and Arnold Lazarus. *The English Language* (New York: Harcourt, Brace and World, Inc., 1966)

## CAN THE STUDENT MAKE NOTES EFFICIENTLY FROM SCATTERED SOURCES?

Let us imagine the student at the stage where, with promising reference materials piled on the desk before him, he has located in one of these some highly important information. He wants to make notes on this and include it in his report or paper. Here, for many students, is a critical point in the research-study process.

All too often adequate preparation in the making of notes, if offered at all, is delayed until the final year of high school, when a major research paper is assigned in English. Yet on every secondary level, assignments in the content subjects confront students with the necessity for frequent notemaking. Left to devise their own notemaking systems, many students are handicapped for years by methods that are helter-skelter.

### Motivating and Teaching Notemaking

Let us picture a teacher holding a sendoff session when the problem requires notemaking from scattered sources, offering students some of the following insights and eliciting insights from students.

"As you do your reading on Mars, you'll want to take down important information. Of course you'll be making notes on all the different aspects of your problem. Have you considered the simple device of topical note cards? You'll complete your project better and *much faster* if you use these. [The teacher projects the card shown on page 196 on a screen.]

"Suppose you reach for a note card and begin jotting notes on several different aspects of your subject at random on that single card."

The teacher goes on, "This student's notes could hardly be more confused if they had been mixed up with a Mixmaster! Notes on seven different aspects of the Mars problem are jotted on that single card!

"Notes that you *scramble* as you take them, as this student has

| | WHAT FIRST EARTHMEN ARE LIKELY TO FIND ON MARS |
|---|---|
| Here's a jotting on "canals" ———→ | *Mariner IV revealed no canals,* |
| Here's one on pull of gravity ———→ | *Gravity – 2/5 ths that of earth.* |
| Here's one on length of day ———→ | *Day – 24 hours and 40 minutes* |
| Here's one of surface features ———→ | *Desert-like, dust-covered* |
| Here's one on Martian moons ———→ | *2 moons – Phobas and Deimos* |
| Here's one on atmosphere ———→ | *Only minute traces oxygen* |
| Here's one on possibility of life ———→ | *Low forms of animals –certain anaerobes– may be able to survive.* |

*FIGURE 5–12. Note card with badly scrambled jottings.*

done, must be painfully *un*scrambled later—at the cost of adding *greatly* to your research time. Later you must reread and reconsider your notes, one by one, and thoughtfully assign each note to its proper classification.

"Instead, why not sort out your notes *as you do your reading* —reaching for a separate note card whenever you make a note on a new sub-topic? You'll find this a most effective speed device in study."

The teacher projects on a screen the topical note cards that follow. Of course the "pattern" cards should be appropriate for the student's purpose, his level of advancement, and the time to be allotted to the project.

"Through your topical note cards, you've saved yourself time, trouble, and bother—simply by sorting out and classifying your notes as you go along!

"You'll find it greatly to your advantage to make notes only *on one aspect of your topic* and *from a single source* on each card. [Students may need to think about and discuss the *why* of this.] Later you can re-sort, regroup, and rearrange all the bits of information conveniently without the wasted effort of recopying. You can shuffle and reshuffle your cards with complete freedom as you contemplate different ways of organizing your material for your final presentation. You can easily add a new note on a topic or throw away notes you've taken which later prove to be worthless.

"As you're making the note, decide on an identifying topic label —one that closely fits the information on the card. [Students may

```
Make a note of
the subtopic here.



        Make a note(s) on a single aspect of your topic and
    from a single source here.



Make a condensed note of your
source here--author's last
name, a shortened title, and
the page(s) where you found
the information. (You already        You might want to record
have the complete data on your       here a cross reference to
bibliography card.) OR you           information noted else-
might number each bibliography       where. ("See also"
card and write just the cor-         another of your note
responding number here.              cards.)
```

*FIGURE 5–13. Note card for a single sub-topic.*

want to think about and discuss the value.] You can often pick up labels from the topics and sub-topics in your target outline—those reading goals you set up before you began reading. Print this heading in the upper lefthand corner of the card.

"It's handy to write on one side of the card only. Later you can spread out a number of cards on the desk before you while you're working and have in full view all the information you've gathered on a topic.

"Keep your cards arranged in alphabetical order according to their topic labels. Insert each new card at its appropriate place in your packet. Now you can quickly locate any card you want."

**Use Your Own Words—Unless**

"It's generally advisable to take down the author's thoughts in your own words. You may wish, though, to record the writer's *exact* words under certain circumstances:

1. If you think your paraphrasing will alter the original meaning.
2. If you wish to quote directly a writer who has expressed an idea more vividly, persuasively, or compactly than you could express it.

ONLY NOTES
ON
ONE TOPIC
AND FROM ONE SOURCE
WILL GO ON
EACH CARD

CLIMATE-TEMPERATURE

Colder than earth

At 7 A.M. on equator during Martian summer — —60°F.

At high noon — higher than 80°F.

Gallant, *Exploring Planets,* pp. 56-57.

POSSIBILITY OF LIFE – ANIMAL

In experiments, certain new forms – with little need for oxygen or water – grew and survived in an environment which simulated that of Mars.

Unlikely higher forms of animal life, as we know it, could exist in cold, and, oxygenless world.

Wright and Richardson, "Mars," *Encyclopedia Britannica, p. 954*

FIGURE 5–14. *Sample note cards.*

3. If you wish to quote an authority directly to reinforce an argument.

"Some students crowd and clutter their note cards by recording identical information two or three times. Be alert to recognize repetition when it's disguised in different phrasing."

### "Where Do Your Own Ideas Come In?"

"Where do *your* ideas come in during all this reading? What about your own observations, impressions, and conclusions? Of course you'll want to make notes on your own interpretations. If it's a case of interjecting your own ideas into notes you are making from another source, enclose your own ideas inside brackets. If you use separate cards to record your own ideas, flag these cards in some way so that you recognize *yourself* as the source. You might write the word ME with a circle around it—or your initials—in the lower corner where you usually make a note of the published source. Place the cards with your own reflections *with* related material from published sources.*

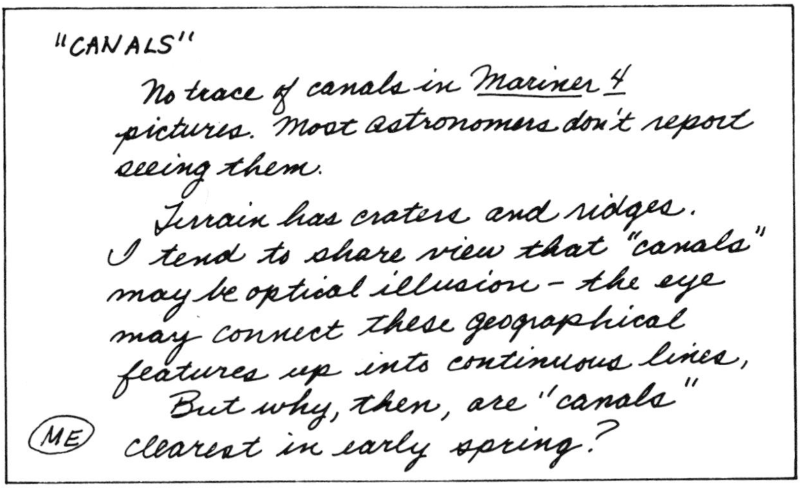

"CANALS"

No trace of canals in *Mariner 4* pictures. Most astronomers don't report seeing them.
    Terrain has craters and ridges. I tend to share view that "canals" may be optical illusion – the eye may connect these geographical features up into continuous lines. But why, then, are "canals" clearest in early spring?
(ME)

*FIGURE 5–15. Note card with student's reflections.*

In summing up, the students might review and discuss values of the topical note cards. Among the other plus factors, they are likely to mention the values below.

---

### WHY USE TOPICAL NOTE CARDS?

---

1. If your assignment is a written report, you'll now find much of the task of organizing already done. Your paragraphing will be much easier. You've already grouped together all the bits of information on each sub-topic. You can locate these sets of related facts quickly.
2. If your report is to be oral, you'll probably talk from notes, and you'll want to recast the notes on your cards into an outline. Here again, you'll find much of the assembly job already done.

---

* Louis A. Leslie, Roy W. Poe, Charles E. Zoubek, and James Deese, *Gregg Notehand*, Second Edition (New York: Gregg Division, McGraw-Hill Book Company, 1968), pp. 212–213.

## CAN THE STUDENT BRING HIS NOTES TOGETHER INTO AN ORDERLY PRESENTATION?

After collecting their notes, students may be at a loss in bringing them together into the final report or paper. Although assignments that call for presenting the results of reference reading are routine in many courses, the student's preparation is often "too little and too late."

The following guidelines for students direct attention to steps the student must take as he transforms his notes into the final presentation. For more thorough coverage, the reader may wish to refer to the following sources.

> Leslie, Louis A., Roy W. Poe, Charles E. Zoubek, and James Deese. *Gregg Notehand,* Second Edition (New York: Gregg Division, McGraw-Hill Book Company, 1968)
>
> Perrin, Porter G. *Writer's Guide and Index to English* (Chicago: Scott, Foresman and Company, 1965)

Instructors will wish to adapt these procedures to the level of advancement of their students, insuring early mastery of appropriate skills.

## TIPS FOR TRANSFORMING NOTES INTO YOUR FINAL PRESENTATION

You will often be called upon to present your library research findings in the form of a paper or report. To do so, you must bring many bits and pieces into a unified, orderly statement.

The notes you have made on cards are not yet in their final sequence, and you have probably made slight attempt to show levels of subordination. If you have used the one-note-on-a-single-card system so that there is not much overlapping, you can now sort, group, and arrange topics, sub-topics, and sub-sub-topics conveniently without the wasted effort of recopying. You can shuffle and reshuffle your cards until you are satisfied with the final arrangement.

The following suggestions are likely to be helpful.

1. You have already grouped your note cards by their topic labels. Now *look through your notes to identify the main topics under your general problem*. These will become the "highest value headings"

in your outline. You already know the identity of some of these main topics from your original reading targets and your topical note cards. Should other main topics now be added in the light of all your reading?

2. *In what order should these main topics be discussed in your final presentation?* Arrange them in the order you decide on, leaving plenty of space to insert sub-topics. Number these main topics with Roman numerals.

WHAT THE FIRST EARTHMEN ARE LIKELY TO FIND ON MARS
NEAR THE EQUATOR

   I. Surface features
  II. Features of sky
 III. Force of gravity
 IV. Atmosphere
  V. Weather
 VI. Life forms (if any)
VII. Perils to human survival

3. *Working with one main topic at a time, look through your note cards for points that develop, explain, or support that topic.* These of course will become sub-topics in your outline. Arrange these sub-topics in the order in which you plan to discuss them in your presentation. Label them with capital letters, as you would in any outline.

As you work with the main topic "Surface Features," for example, you may decide that you will discuss four sub-topics in the order that follows:

I. Surface features
   A. Terrain
   B. Soil
   C. "Hot spots" (?)
   D. Canals

Working on down to the main topic "Life Forms," you conclude that the logical sub-topics are definitely "Plant Life" and "Animal Life." You will now identify subordinate points that drop into slots under these sub-topics. Number these with Arabic numerals, as in the usual outline:

VI. Life forms
   A. Plant life
      1. Possible types
      2. "Hot spots" favorable to other types?
   B. Animal life
      1. Experiments simulating the Martian environment
      2. Higher forms possible?

    4. *Don't start writing too soon.* The organizing you are doing calls for strenuous logical thinking. Do not try to hurry this! Weigh the alternatives carefully—then make your decision. Do not hesitate to change your mind.*

    5. Your final outline may appear something like this:

WHAT THE FIRST EARTHMEN ARE LIKELY TO FIND ON MARS
NEAR THE EQUATOR

   I. Surface features
     A. Terrain
     B. Soil
       1. Type
       2. Color
     C. "Hot spots" (?)
     D. Canals
       1. Proof of advanced life?
       2. Natural features?
       3. Optical illusion?
  II. Features of sky
     A. Appearance of solar system and stars
     B. Sun
       1. Length of day
       2. Length of year
     C. Moons
       1. Deimos
       2. Phobos
 III. Force of gravity
     A. Comparison with Earth
     B. Effect on weight
     C. Effect on movement
 IV. Atmosphere
     A. Composition
     B. Pressure
     C. Humidity
     D. Color of sky
     E. Cloud formations
       1. Yellow clouds
       2. Bluish-white clouds

* John E. Brewton, R. Stanley Peterson, B. Jo Kinnick, and Lois McMullan, *Using Good English, 12* (River Forest, Illinois: Laidlaw Brothers Publishers, 1962), pp. 134–155.

   V. Weather
      A. Seasonal variation
      B. Daily variation
  VI. Life forms
      A. Plant life
         1. Possible types
         2. "Hot spots" favorable to other types?
      B. Animal life
         1. Experiments simulating Martian environment
         2. Higher forms possible?
 VII. Perils to human survival
      A. Insufficient oxygen
      B. Intense cold
      C. Ultraviolet radiation
      D. Life-support systems needed


   6. With your note cards now arranged in the order in which you plan to present your information, *write your rough draft* (or prepare the notes for your talk), using your outline and note cards as guides.

   7. At this stage you'll be extremely thankful for those bibliography cards on which you took down the essential facts about your reference sources in the exact order in which you'll need them for your bibliography. Now you can quickly *convert these cards into your final bibliography*.


## DOES THE STUDENT KEEP AN OPEN MIND FOR LATER EVIDENCE?

   The student should of course regard his final report as something less than "final." In the 1970's, solutions in the field of science, social studies, and other areas, may not long remain solutions. The fly-by of some future space craft near Mars—the probings from some lunar laboratory—an unmanned vehicle that touches down on the surface of the red planet, may disprove much that the student has searched out so carefully about the planet Mars.


## BIBLIOGRAPHY

Brewton, John E., R. Stanley Peterson, B. Jo Kinnick, and Lois McMullan, *Using Good English, 12.* River Forest, Illinois: Laidlaw Brothers Publishers, 1962. Pp. 134–155.

Goldsmith, Stephanie, *Library Tools, Reader's Guide to Periodical Literature.* Chicago: Independent Learning Project, the Laboratory Schools, University of Chicago, 1969.

Goldsmith, Stephanie, *Library Tools, the Card Catalog.* Chicago: Independent Learning Project, the Laboratory Schools, University of Chicago, 1969.

Goldsmith, Stephanie, *Library Tools, the Encyclopedia.* Chicago: Independent Learning Project, the Laboratory Schools, University of Chicago, 1969.

Moore, Patrick and Francis Jackson, *Life on Mars.* New York: W. W. Norton and Company, Inc., 1965.

Leslie, Louis A., Roy W. Poe, Charles E. Zoubek, and James Deese, *Gregg Notehand,* Second Edition. New York: Gregg Division, McGraw-Hill Book Company, 1968. Pp. 212–213.

McKee, Paul, *The Teaching of Reading in the Elementary School.* New York: Houghton Mifflin Company, 1948. Pp. 425–530.

*Reading, Grades 7, 8, 9, A Teacher's Guide to Curriculum Planning,* Curriculum Bulletin No. 11. New York City: Board of Education of the City of New York, 1957. Pp. 30–51.

Rossoff, Martin, *Using Your High School Library.* New York: The H. W. Wilson Company, 1964.

Spache, George D. and Paul C. Berg, *The Art of Efficient Reading.* New York: The Macmillan Company, 1966.

# MATHEMATICS

*This section was prepared with the help of two consultants: Richard Muelder, mathematics teacher at the University of Chicago Laboratory School and former Head of the Mathematics Department; and Max S. Bell, Associate Professor of Mathematics Education, University of Chicago.*

Many of today's textbooks in mathematics confront the student with page after page of specialized, often rigorous reading. With a frequently recurring pattern of a passage of analytical exposition followed by a set of problems, these textbooks make new demands on reading power.

What a sudden adjustment the student must face if he has acquired only a once-straight-through approach to reading! He must now draw out the meaning from extremely dense analytical passages. He may find telegraphic explanations that require his filling in the inner steps—passages that call for visualizing or sketching—reading that requires a back-and-forth shifting of his eyes and thoughts between a verbal explanation and a diagram. If he continues reading in the old familiar way, parts of his textbooks may lose him before he has read two or three sentences.

Clearly, the classroom instructor who provides this student with appropriate reading guidance is helping to insure his success in the immediate course and in all his advanced mathematics work. And, in an age of exploding mathematical knowledge, he is helping to prepare him for self-education in any occupation involving mathematics. Some of the specifics in a course in mathematics may become obsolete tomorrow. *The reading competencies that enable students to update those specifics are not likely to become obsolete.*

We have included in this chapter two items for your consideration. In the first item we offer you a miscellany of possible procedures for upgrading reading. Here a successful mathematics teacher discusses how, early in the course, he starts his students on the road to better reading. The second item deals with what many students consider their "disaster area" in mathematics—word problems. You will find suggested here an assortment of possible techniques for trouble shooting word problems.

## HELPS FOR IMPROVING MATHEMATICS READING

*Here are some tools for learning what students need as they read mathematics—then starting them along the road to better reading.*

How can a mathematics instructor get insights into the reading competencies of his students? How can he upgrade their mathematical vocabularies? Help them read their textbooks better? Encourage mathematical thinking in their lives outside the classroom? Help create lifetime readers in the field of mathematics? A few suggestions are offered here with the thought that the resourceful teacher will find them suggestive—improve them—and increase and multiply them.

### Standardized Reading Scores Talk to the Mathematics Teacher

Even before he meets his classes on the first day, the mathematics teacher can take steps to improve his students' reading. Through the standardized reading scores in their cumulative folders, he can have a preview of the diversity in reading levels he will face within his classes. Even in "homogeneous" classes a span of six full years is not unlikely. One teacher of high school sophomores, whose reading scores were spread out from sixth-grade level all the way to college freshman, commented: "I try to put myself in the position of the students at the different levels. I try to imagine how the sixth-grade-level reader will react to being faced each day with a high school sophomore's text and whether the college-level reader is likely to be challenged by that same high school sophomore's textbook."*

Students' folders often include sub-scores in vocabulary, com-

---

* Richard H. Muelder, "Helping Students Read Mathematics," in *Corrective Reading in the High School Classroom,* eds. H. Alan Robinson and Sidney J. Rauch, Perspectives in Reading Series, No. 6 (Newark, Delaware: International Reading Association, 1966), pp. 102–103.

prehension, and speed of reading. These scores talk to the teacher about possible trouble spots; by looking at these he can begin to get some rough insights into the problems of individuals. By noting low vocabulary scores he can identify students whose deficiency in general vocabulary may possibly block their comprehension in reading mathematics. Through noticing the combination of high speed scores with low comprehension scores he can discover those who may possibly need help in adjusting their speed downward for densely packed passages in mathematics. Low comprehension scores suggest that there may be a difficulty in important comprehension skills. Such insights can be followed by appropriate steps to help the student.*

Standardized reading scores can help teachers match the reading abilities of students with the materials they read. They are a factor to be considered as teachers select textbooks to be used by various homogeneous classes and as they search for the textbooks best suited for heterogeneous classes. They are a special aid to those who are selecting reading materials for enrichment. No matter how wide the diversity of reading levels within a group, the teacher can often get the right book into the hands of the student through supplementary materials. With guidance, the poorest reader can experience some measure of success, and the most highly gifted can read books that stimulate and challenge.† Word problems that are beyond a disadvantaged reader's reach can sometimes be rewritten on a level easier with respect to reading. Here, too, knowing his general reading level, even as roughly as represented by a standardized test score, is an advantage.

In schools that do homogeneous grouping, standardized reading scores are one factor to be considered in assigning students to the appropriate group. Traditionally, achievement and aptitude in mathematics, grades in mathematics, and intelligence scores have been considered. Modern textbooks confront the student with many pages of reading on the analytical aspects of mathematics; thus another factor predictive of success in mathematics is reading achievement.

### How Well Can a Student Handle a Textbook Passage?

While offering useful general insights, standardized tests are silent on important questions: What are the students' special reading competencies for mathematics? How strong are their mathematics vocabularies? Ordinarily the vocabulary section of reading survey

---

* Muelder, "Helping Students Read Mathematics," p. 103.

† Muelder, "Helping Students Read Mathematics," pp. 103–104.

tests covers only general vocabulary. And the comprehension section does not test the student on passages with mathematical content.

Is there a way a teacher can assess students' competencies in handling the actual textbook explanations they will be assigned all year? Having selected a passage the students might be expected to handle alone, you might direct them: "Study this passage right here in class as if you were preparing for a test on what it says. A little later, you will have some questions. Use a scratch sheet, if you wish, to make notes and jottings."

Students who fail to complete the passage within the time given should note on their papers the point to which they read. All should hand in their scratch sheets. The quality of each student's jottings on his scratch sheet, his answers to the quiz questions, plus your observations while he is working should provide important insights.

1. Can the student handle the textbook, or does it appear to be beyond him?
2. Can he master clearly explained technical terms independently? grasp key concepts? get the message of diagrams and figures?
3. Does he use a scratch sheet to study actively—to jot down important ideas, make his own sketches, fill in the inner steps of explanations?
4. Does he appear to be an extremely slow reader?

### Pre-Teaching To Remove Vocabulary Blocks

Teachers can remove blocks *before* their students read an assignment by searching through the assigned reading beforehand, pulling out words that will cause difficulty, and teaching them in advance —in the context in which they will be encountered.

*Example:*\*

In assigning pages on the properties of numbers, a possible block to understanding might be the word *commutative*. The word is placed on the chalk-board—its syllables marked off with vertical lines or short dashes:

com | mu′ | ta | tive

\* Paul Moulton, former Laboratory School mathematics teacher. Remarks to Thomas, May, 1969.

The students are guided in pronouncing the word part by part. At every opportunity the teacher points out to students that long, formidable mathematical terms often have familiar parts.

With *commutative*, he asks, "Can you see a word you know within this word?" Students quickly respond, "Oh, commute." Next he asks, "What does *commute* mean?" Then he guides the class in learning the technical meaning, the word's length no longer making it appear forbidding. As he encourages students to examine word parts he is helping to alter the habits of the many poor readers who are inclined to glance at the first few letters of a forbidding word, then dismiss it with "Too hard for me."

Numbers of words can be brought within the reach of readers through part by part analysis.

### Greek and Latin Word Parts

Greek and Latin word parts enter into the formation of many technical terms in mathematics. Mastering the easy-to-learn number prefixes *mono-, pent-, oct-, dec-, cent-, mill-,* and the others is, of course, a stride ahead. Students are often fascinated with the way Greek and Latin parts set off a chain reaction. Teach them the Greek prefix *poly-* in *polynomial,* and they already have a hold on *polygon, polyhedron,* and others. Teach them the Greek root *-hedron* in *dihedron,* and they have a handle for grasping *tetrahedron, pentahedron, octahedron,* and others. Teach the Latin prefix *inter-,* meaning *between,* and you help them unlock *interpolate, intersect,* and *intercept.* Teach the Latin prefix *co-* or *con-,* meaning *with* or *together with,* and you give them a hold on *coefficient, coordinate, collinear, coplanar, cosine, cotangent, conjugate,* and *conjunction.* You can help them grasp the formidable looking term *trichotomy* through the Greek parts *tri-* and *-tom,* meaning *cut.*

Terms like the following are likely to repay this sort of analysis, especially with students who have rich language backgrounds: *subscript, transpose, circumference, rectangle, equilateral, equivalent, bisect, perimeter, symmetry, diameter, concurrent, tangent, cotangent, finite, infinite, geometry,* and *permutation.*

### Students Should "Meet Their Textbook"

Today's publishers are providing students with textbooks with superior helps for reading and study. Many of these, however, will be

lost on students. There is good evidence that even superior students
do not make good use of such facilitative cues unless they are given
special instruction.* Time spent early in the course on a "meet your
textbook" session will reward students with an improved caliber of
independent study.

Students should come to know and *use* these study helps in their
new textbooks:

> The table of contents with its concise, sequential listing of major
> topics covered
>
> Lists of mathematical symbols for easy reference
>
> Large-size or boldface headings that announce the content of a
> section
>
> Italics, boldface or color used to signal "official" terms
>
> Italics, boldface, or color used to call attention to concepts, rules,
> or principles that should be learned and to flag these for easy
> reference
>
> Typographical danger signals of pitfalls to avoid
>
> Aids for pronouncing and accenting difficult new terms (if these
> aids are present)
>
> Chapter summaries that wrap up big ideas
>
> Self-check tests at the close of chapters
>
> Table of squares and square roots
>
> Reference list of axioms
>
> The glossary
>
> The index

Once these study aids have been pointed out to the student in
connection with a single chapter, the student should have them at his
command as he studies all the chapters that follow.

### Help Students Step Into a Unit

As students approach new work, it is well to help them step
into their reading by previewing the coming unit. Too often new
work is simply taken up detail by detail with little thought of relating
the details to the structure of the whole. Through this preview the
students should see the main concepts and principles in their relations to each other and to previous work. The preview can be a well
organized talk by the instructor—in most cases, it need not be a

* Francis P. Robinson, "Study Skills for Superior Students in Secondary School,"
*The Reading Teacher*, XV (September, 1961), p. 30.

long one.* In addition to helping the class view the total picture, the preview provides background understandings—and these, too, make for better reading.

## Make Dramatic Assignments

"Do the problems on page 37," the student is sometimes told. "And, by the way, read the two or three pages just before the problems." He may drudge through the two or three pages, his highest motivation to get the reading over with—if indeed he reads the pages at all.

Contrast his reading with that of the student whose teacher pulls out a dramatic "believe it or not" problem from the coming assignment:

*Example:*

> "What is the probability that among you twenty-five people in the class two have the same birthday?" To the surprise of the class, the teacher then proves that there is an even chance that two have the same birthday. Next he adds another class and works with fifty students. He proves that it is statistically certain that two have the same birthday. Now the minds of many students are alive with questions: "How can we calculate the probability that a certain event will occur?" "What are the reasons behind this type of calculation?" "Just what is meant by statistical certainty?" As they leave class the teacher reminds them, "You'll find all the answers in your reading for tomorrow."

Even students who are not mathematics oriented sometimes "dig into" this assignment.†

## Guiding Questions

Teachers can help students get through a difficult assignment by examining it ahead of time for points of probable difficulty, then supplying guiding questions that will help them work their way past these difficult spots. Niles suggests another reason for formulating

---

* Charles H. Butler and F. Lynwood Wren, *The Teaching of Secondary School Mathematics* (New York: McGraw-Hill Book Company, 1965), p. 134.

† Richard H. Muelder. Remarks to Thomas, June, 1970.

preliminary questions: "Asked *before* students read . . . , such a question should help *develop* comprehension. If the same question were not asked until *after* students had read a passage [unless the students return to the passage and analyze it], comprehension would be *tested* but not developed."* One would naturally expect students to comprehend better if they approach their reading with purpose questions—if, instead of reading in the dark, they know what they are to understand, and know, and be able to do at the completion of the reading.

## Hold "How to Read Your Textbook" Sessions

Today's textbooks *talk directly to the students*. Frequently there is a recurring pattern of explanation followed by a set of problems. Once students have been given adequate guidance, many can accept a share of the responsibility for their own learning through reading.

One teacher reports good results from sessions like this:

*Example:*

"Early in the course—the first time the class is faced with some pages that introduce new material—I make an assignment that is 100% reading. The students are given no problems to work for next day. I have two definite purposes in assigning 'pure' reading: (1) to emphasize for the class the importance of becoming successful readers of mathematics, and (2) to set the stage for giving some reading instruction. During part of the class hour we discuss why reading in mathematics differs from reading in other school subjects. Then I suggest some procedures to help the students become successful readers. (The procedures suggested are those reported in the example on the next page. They also include adaptations of the Read Step of the PQ4R approach in Chapter 3.)

"Early the next class meeting, before the reading is explained or discussed, there is a short quiz. This serves three purposes: (1) to help me evaluate my instruction in reading mathematics, (2) to jolt overconfident students who weren't quite convinced of the need to read and reread mathematical content, and (3) to reemphasize my conviction that reading in mathematics is something to work on.

* Olive S. Niles, "Help Students Set a Purpose for Reading," *English High Lights,* XX (April-May, 1963), p. 2 (Chicago: Scott Foresman and Company).

"The results, by the way, have convinced me that a one-shot effort is not enough—that I must reinforce, remind, and review in classroom and in conference."*

## "How You *Should* Have Read It" Sessions

The same teacher suggests that a classwide disaster brought on by careless reading of an assignment may be the right moment to walk the students through a model reading:

*Example:*

"Begin by having the class read the assignment through once, at a moderate speed, to get the general drift. Then briefly discuss the major ideas. Discourage too much detail—the purpose of the pre-reading was simply to get the broad picture. Then have students, in turn, read parts of the assignment aloud—slowly. Interrupt at crucial points—when the student should stop and draw a picture, when he should do some figuring, when he should find another example, when he should shift his focus to a diagram. Interrupt the reader—and let students do so—to ask questions. When the students have finished this slow rereading, have them all reread the assignment a second time at a moderate pace.

"Finally, have them close their books and take a quiz on the content covered in this 'model' reading, and reveal the answers immediately. Most of the students will be delighted at the results. Compare their success this time with past 'disasters,' and suggest that perhaps their improved scores are the result of their more careful, more thoughtful, more intelligent reading. All through the year, in emphasizing how students are expected to read an assignment, their experiences doing this model reading can serve as referents."†

## Guide Under-Par Readers to Easier Textbooks

Textbooks in introductory mathematics courses vary considerably in the reading demands they make on students. Some are expressly designed to meet the needs of below average readers and

---

* Muelder, "Helping Students Read Mathematics," pp. 104–110.
† Muelder, "Helping Students Read Mathematics," p. 111.

carefully control the level of reading difficulty throughout the book. When sections of a textbook are clearly beyond some readers, they may profit from reading the corresponding sections in a textbook easier with respect to reading. Possibly, with their background understandings thus strengthened, they may be able to extend their reach and handle their "too difficult" textbook.

Top readers, too, should not be overlooked. They can be sent to an advanced textbook—one which presents them with a challenge to "stretch their reading muscles."

### Mathematical Thinking Outside the Classroom

Clear, penetrating thinking in the world outside the classroom was never so vital as today. In an age of bewildering and complex problems, tremendous forces are at work to confuse thinking. Training in critical reading in mathematics could be a counterforce. Although all instructors hope for the transfer of habits of critical thinking and reading developed in mathematics class to the student's life outside the classroom, little is found in most mathematics textbooks to encourage this transfer. Perhaps it should be more than a byproduct to be hoped for—rather a definite outcome to be worked for.*

Classes should find it fascinating to practice applying techniques of deductive reasoning acquired in mathematics class to the affairs of daily life. *What's wrong with this thinking?* can become the watchword as they examine the reasoning that underlies excerpts from magazines and newspapers, from TV broadcasts, from conversations heard around school: Are there unstated premises here? Are they valid? Is this a case in point? Does the conclusion necessarily follow? The class might cull examples from their reading and listening and make notebooks or placard the classroom with displays of ads and clippings.

Certainly, few other teachers command the expertise of mathematics teachers in developing discerning readers of statistics. Students are inclined to revere statistics. They are likely to be unaware that in popular media and elsewhere, statistics, with their aura of objectivity and authority, can be highly misleading, that reports bulwarked with figures as "evidence" can be used to distort political, economic, and social trends, opinion polls, business conditions—even the census! Darrell Huff opens the bag of statistical tricks in an article in *Harper's,* "How to Lie with Statistics."† He alerts the reader to such mischief

* Butler and Wren, *The Teaching of Secondary School Mathematics,* p. 155.

† Darrell Huff, "How to Lie with Statistics," *Harper's Magazine,* CCI (August, 1950), p. 97.

makers as "the sample with built-in bias," "the truncated or gee-whiz graph," "the well-chosen average," "the unwarranted assumption or post hoc rides again," and others. Advanced high school readers and college level readers are likely to enjoy and profit from this article. A paperback book, *How to Lie with Statistics* by Darrell Huff and Irving Geis, is also available (W. W. Norton, Inc.).

An assignment like this can have appeal and value:

*Example:*

> As you come across statistics in your reading and listening this week, jot down some of the statistics or bring the clippings to class. Cull examples from your daily paper, your weekly news magazine, from speeches of legislators and political candidates, from TV newscasts, panel discussions and interviews, and from advertising. Do these statistics appear to be sound? Do any of the reports appear to misinform? How much attention should be paid to this evidence? Ask your classmates to weigh the possibility of distortion. Be prepared to comment yourself.

Such an assignment might be ongoing, with the clippings deposited in a growing critical reading file.

Current affairs materials offer a promising opportunity for team teaching between a mathematics teacher and a social studies teacher. In a joint assignment students might be asked to analyze the speech or public statement of some prominent figure—a speech or statement citing statistical evidence.

## Create Readers in Mathematics for Life

A library of attractive and inviting books on mathematics within the classroom—on instant call there—can be a daily stimulus to enjoy reading, practice it, and make it a lifetime habit. Books that convey the fascination of mathematics span an exceptionally broad range of reading levels. The colorful, profusely illustrated *Wonderful World of Mathematics* by Lancelot Hogben is within the reach of many below-standard readers. A book to stretch the reading power of top level readers is George Gamow's *One, Two, Three Infinity. Mathematics on Vacation,* edited by Joseph S. Madachy, opens a world of mathematical fun with its mathematical puzzles, pastimes, and curiosities, as does the advanced *Hungarian Problem Book,* translated by Elvira Rapaport. *Mathematics Teaching as a Career*

(National Council of Teachers of Mathematics) invites the reader who wants to evaluate his qualifications for a life work in the mathematics classroom. A teacher might speak to the class intriguingly about books like these, giving a thumbnail sketch of the content or reading aloud an inviting passage. Readers who would never voluntarily reach for a book in English class may reach for one here. They may find these books hard to put down and spend many hours in reading outside of class—with all the gains this added practice brings.

Through this "library," specialized reference materials in mathematics can be on instant call within the classroom. As students turn to these, the teacher has an opportunity to guide them in the techniques of searching out answers for themselves in the field of mathematics—thus strengthening their equipment for continuing their mathematics education long after school courses are over.

Books from the school library may sometimes be available, on long term or short term loan, for classroom collections. The lists below, available from the National Council of Teachers of Mathematics, offer "book bait" for students reading on a wide diversity of levels:

> *Mathematics Library—Elementary and Junior High School* by Clarence Ethel Hardgrove and Herbert F. Miller. This is an annotated bibliography of enrichment books from Grades K–9, classified by grade level.
>
> *The High School Mathematics Library* by William L. Schaaf. This annotated bibliography of enrichment books includes about 800 entries, classified by topics, which cover the principal areas of today's high school mathematics. A list of periodicals with a directory of publishers is included.
>
> *A Bibliography of Recreational Mathematics* by William L. Schaaf. Works are classified under 113 headings, including mathematics in nature, art, club programs, cryptography, string figures, and others.

## TROUBLE SHOOTING WORD PROBLEMS

*Word problems are one of the real trouble spots for students in mathematics. Reading guidance may be part of the solution.*

Ask students the most difficult part of courses in general mathematics and introductory algebra, and they are likely to answer, "Word problems." With many of these students their approach to the *reading* of the problem is a source of difficulty. Some have developed a deep-seated dread of these problems. After a reading that is inadequate, they are inclined to panic. Some are impatient. They dismiss a problem with "too hard for me" if they cannot see and organize the relationships almost instantly. Many are not aware of the close, concentrated reading that word problems demand. They do a helter-skelter reading, then strike out blindly.

Reaching all these problem readers of word problems taxes the resourcefulness of any teacher. Some possible ways of trouble shooting word problems through improving reading are offered here.

## One Step at a Time

Encouraging a step by step procedure may persuade superficial readers to give word problems a more deliberate reading and may help to "tranquilize" those who are fearful. Of course, students should not feel locked into a rigid progression of steps, nor should they conclude that there is only one acceptable way to solve a problem. What is of value is learning to analyze the problem situation systematically.

A step by step sequence like the one below should help students learn to attack word problems. (Modifications would have to be made before it could be applied in algebra.)

Let us suppose, for example, that problems about major league baseball players and batting averages are timely and that students are going to work with the following problem:*

> Willie Mays has 31 hits for 48 official times at bat. If he goes
> 5 for 5 in today's game, by how many points will his batting
> average increase?

*Step 1: Read the problem thoroughly, asking, "What is this all about?"* Size up the problem situation. Is there a word you don't know? Now is the time to check up on its meaning. A single word left unknown—a slip-up because of one *un*clear meaning—may make the rest of your efforts ineffective.

The student's thinking should run something like this, "This problem is all about batting averages and comparing two of them." If he does not know what "he goes 5 for 5" means, he must find this out before he can proceed further. Of course, students should have the background information that batting averages are decimal fractions between zero and one, rounded to three places.

* Richard Muelder, University of Chicago Laboratory School mathematics teacher and former chairman of the mathematics department, devised the baseball problem and helped apply the sequence of steps to it.

*Step 2: Reread the problem, asking, "What am I to find here?"* Make sure you understand precisely what the problem asks for.

The student should say to himself, "I need to figure two batting averages—one for Mays' present record and a second after today's game. Then I'm to figure the increase."

*Step 3: Ask yourself, "What facts are given?"* What information is already supplied you in the problem? Make jottings.

The student might think, "I know the number of Mays' hits and times at bat right now, and I know that he adds 5 to each of them in today's game."

*Step 4: Next, plan your attack.* Read the problem through once more, asking, "What processes will I use?" and/or "What formulas will I need?" Plan the steps you'll take in finding what's required. Continue to make jottings.

The student's thinking should run something like this, "I must divide the total times at bat into the number of hits to find the batting average. First, I'll divide 48 into 31 so that I can get Mays' first average. Then I must add five to each of these in order to learn his new record. Then I must divide 53 into 36 to determine Mays' new average. And last, I must find the difference between his first and his second average."

*Step 5: Estimate the answer.* Ask yourself, "What would a reasonable answer be?"

The student might possibly estimate something like this: "Both 31/48 and 36/53 are batting averages over .500. So their difference will be a decimal fraction less than 1/2."

*Step 6: Carry out the operations.* Now the student carries out the operations he has planned. Hopefully, he will obtain, as his answer, an increase of .033 in Mays' average.

*Step 7: Check your work.* Compare the answer you arrived at with your estimated answer. Go back to the original problem and check your results against the conditions of the problem. See if your answer fulfills those conditions.

No one can bat over 1000. Thus, if the student gets the spectacular increase of over 3300, he will know that something is wrong! He will need to check by asking, (1) Was my error caused by a simple error in arithmetic? or (2) Did I misunderstand the problem?

It should be noted that with the mature problem solver there is no dichotomy between reading time and figuring time. He reads and figures—getting notions, discarding one, trying another—not one and then the other but "all mixed in."*

* Max S. Bell, former chairman of the Laboratory School mathematics department. Remarks to Thomas, August, 1970.

In summing up, students may reach the answer on a ladder of these steps:*

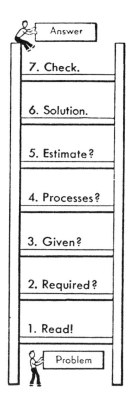

*FIGURE 6–1. Ladder of steps.*

Word problems in algebra can be attacked by using a modified version of the strategy described above. The flow chart on the following page illustrates how to set up a problem with one variable.† In time, the student will find himself going through these steps automatically. He is likely to improve his speed and accuracy tremendously. Such a flow chart will be most effective if its use is illustrated with specific problems, if practice is provided, and if students *see the results* in arriving at solutions efficiently.

* William Betz, A. Brown Miller, F. Brooks Miller, Elizabeth Mitchell, and H. Carlisle Taylor, *Everyday General Mathematics,* Book One, Revised (Boston: Ginn and Company, 1965), p. 71. Reprinted with special permission.

† Richard Muelder contributed the flow chart for solving a word problem in algebra.

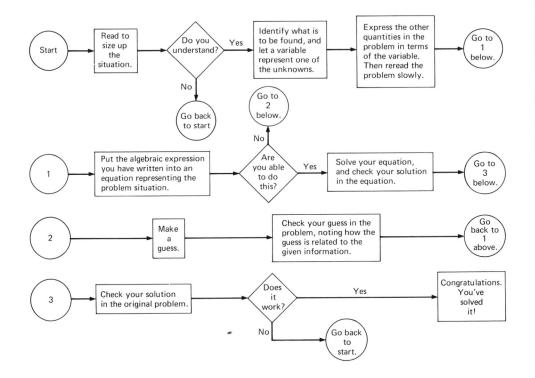

*FIGURE 6–2. Flow chart for solving a word problem in algebra.*

**Try Data Diagrams**

It may be helpful to draw a picture or a simple sketch of just what is going on in the problem. On a data diagram, like the one that follows, the student sets down, as briefly as possible, all the facts that he is given:

> Mr. Greene is to land at the airport at 9 p.m.
> Mrs. Greene, who lives 20 miles from the airport,
> is to meet him.   If she leaves at 8:15 and averages
> 30 mph, will she be on time?

| SHE | | HE |
|---|---|---|
| LEAVES | ←—— 20 MILES ——→ | → ARRIVES |
| 8:15 | 30 MPH ——→ | 9:00 |

*FIGURE 6–3. Data diagram. (From Dunstan Hayden and E. J. Finan,* ALGEBRA ONE. *Boston: Allyn and Bacon, Inc., 1961, pp. 275–276.)*

Through the diagram, the student sees the problem situation *visually,* and as he does so, he can often detect relationships and formulate mathematical expressions of them.

### Good Guesses Help Toward Solutions

The step by step procedures previously suggested include an extremely helpful guessing step. Unless the problem situation is too involved, students often move closer to the solution when they ask themselves, "What is a reasonable answer in the light of the facts given?" Formulating an informed guess leads students to *really think through* the problem situation and to detect elements and see relationships they can use in moving to a solution. The instructor should point out the difference between a *good guess* based on systematic consideration of the data and a *haphazard guess* based on little thought. He should make clear that he is not teaching students that they can get quick answers by guessing.

"It's not important," one teacher observes, "that the student's guess be accurate. What is important is that he test his guess with the data given, and in so doing see how the data are related to the answer wanted. After having done this, he can often set up a problem using a variable, replacing his previous guess with the variable. He can then proceed to solve the problem."*

Students can be given extra "guessing practice" through problems with multiple-choice answers. Problems can be dittoed with several estimated answers printed below each problem. Students are asked to think through the problem data carefully—cross out answers that would be ridiculous—and arrive at their choice of "guesses."

### Verbal Check—Superior Reading Practice

Showing students how to make the verbal check—how to rethink the problem situation—can be excellent reading practice—in many cases, teachers find, fully as valuable as the original problem solving itself.† Students should appreciate the *why* of the verbal check.

"Don't be satisfied with substituting the answer you arrived at in an equation you made yourself. This, of course, is *not* a

* Muelder, "Helping Students Read Mathematics," p. 112.

† Margaret Matchett, Laboratory School mathematics teacher. Remarks to Thomas, November, 1971.

check for verbal problems since you may have made an error in writing the equation in the first place. If you are satisfied merely to substitute in the equation, any errors in *thinking through the information* will, of course, escape you.

"A complete check, therefore, should include (1) a *mathematical check* to catch any errors in your computations, and (2) a *verbal check* to verify your thinking through the information.

"Now is the time to substitute your answer in the equation in order to catch any errors in the mechanics of your computations.

"For your verbal check, return to the original problem. Check your results against the conditions of the problem. Substitute according to the original conditions and see if your answer fits into the picture. If it does fit, you are likely to have solved the problem correctly."

## How-to-Read-It Sessions

Try holding sessions in which you concentrate on guiding students through the reading of verbal problems—through the stage of formulating the open sentence but no further. Guide them through a sequence: reading for the drift of the problem—asking, "What am I to find?"—noting what is given—making a "data diagram"—planning their strategy, and so on. In these practice sessions, have them concentrate only on *reading and thinking through the information.* They need not spend time performing the computations.

It may help to encourage students to imagine themselves as participants in word problems. *You* are in the speeding car which must come to a stop when traveling a certain number of miles per hour. *You* are in racing boat A which may or may not overtake boat B.

## Try Pre-Reading Sessions

One instructor sets aside class time for students to pre-read word problems that have just been assigned for tomorrow. While the students are in her presence, she has them read the problems silently. This is *reading* practice—they stop short of carrying out the computations. They are encouraged to ask questions at points where they foresee difficulty and to work out their trouble spots while they are still in class. She also holds post-reading sessions in which the students discuss freely the difficulties they had reading last night's problems. She reminds her students, "If you slight the reading, you'll make hard work for yourself as you strike out blindly, make errors, and have much to do over."*

### Is a Once-Through Reading Enough?

To prove dramatically the necessity for rereading, students might be given an interesting problem and asked to read it through once *at their normal reading speed*. Only this single reading is permitted. Then, without looking at the problem again, they are to answer questions on the conditions described in the problem. When the students have tried *all* the questions, they are to check their answers with the original problem.† The message comes through loud and clear, that close reading and several readings are essential to "pull out" all the information in a problem.

### "Translate" the Words into Symbols

Write out the statement in the problem across the chalkboard in one long line. Then show, just below, how the verbal statement can be written in a mathematical statement by substituting the right mathematical symbols for the words. This "translation device" is often effective.‡

### Try Reading Problems Orally

Another teacher finds oral reading to have special values: "When a student comes to me for help with a word problem, I often have him read the problem to me orally, assisting him when it seems appropriate. As he reads aloud, I learn something about the nature of his reading blocks. The student whose difficulty with a problem results from a reading disability is often able to solve the problem if he *hears* it. The emphasis in schools on silent reading leads students to think it's somehow wrong to read aloud to oneself. This not the case with word problems. I suggest to students that they bring all possible learning channels to bear, including hearing."§

---

* Gladys Junker, formerly of the Laboratory School mathematics department. Remarks to Thomas, June, 1970.

† Hayden and Finan, *Algebra One*, pp. 275–276.

‡ A. M. Welchons, W. R. Krickenberger, and Helen R. Pearson, *Algebra, Book One,* Annotated Edition (New York: Ginn and Company, 1970), p. 42.

§ Muelder, "Helping Students Read Mathematics," p. 112.

### Try the "Easy Numbers" Technique

The extremely helpful "easy numbers" technique can be suggested to students: "Have you ever read a problem, thought it too complicated, and just guessed what to do? We have already suggested rewriting a problem in your own words. Another way to rewrite a problem is to substitute 'easy' numbers for those in the problem. 'Easy' numbers give a quick solution and show how to solve the original problem."*

*Example:*

> An airplane averaging 238 miles per hour flies from New York to Detroit in 2¾ hours. How far is it from New York to Detroit?

*Solution:*

> REWRITE An airplane averaging 200 miles per hour flies from New York to Detroit in 3 hours. How far is it from New York to Detroit?
>
> Do you see that the answer to this easy problem is 600 miles? It must have been found by 3 × 200. Therefore, we solve the original problem by 2¾ × 238.

### Simplify Problems for Under-Par Readers

When word problems are beyond handicapped readers, they can sometimes be rewritten on a level easier with respect to reading, then dittoed for the students. The general vocabulary can be made easier, the sentence structure simplified, and the sentences shortened. Reading consultants can suggest methods of bringing verbal material within the grasp of below average readers. A teacher's growing folders of simplified problems will enrich his resources year after year.

### Tap Student Interests

Through original problems, it is sometimes possible to tap the interests of students, to bring problems within the range of their everyday experience, and to make these problems seem real. Students whose world is cars might be asked: "How much can Al save on his new

---

* Allen L. Bernstein and David W. Wells, *Trouble-Shooting Mathematics Skills* (New York: Holt, Rinehart and Winston, Inc., 1969), pp. 301–302.

accessories—6-volt spotlight, turn signals, new rear view mirror, and so on—when these are on sale at a 20% reduction?" "What is the percent of increase in the cost of liability insurance for a male driver under 25?" "What was Bill's average annual depreciation per mile?" "What was the average asking price of the cars Tom considered while shopping for his car?"*

Students may think of sports events as worlds away from mathematics. If students are sports minded, problems about sports can tie the two together while capturing a bit of the excitement of the sports event itself: "Which yacht, *Seawind, Spray,* or *Green Wave,* won the race when the elapsed times were corrected?"

Problems about sports can take on interest through timeliness—they can ride the crest of seasonal enthusiasms: "Which of the two old rivals—Grantley High or Williams—had the better final standing in the North Central Football Conference?" "How many hits must ace shortstop Bill Rawls get his next 25 times at bat to average .300?"

Problems which are real and practical, which are within the comprehension and experience of students, and which are solvable by elementary algebra, appear to be very scarce. Teachers will wish to detect, select, and create such problems.†

## Relate Problems to Job Ability

In communities where graduates are likely to be looking for work within the community, students or the teacher might ask prospective employers, "What problems would you like your employees to be able to solve?"‡ A student hopeful of becoming an auto mechanic might feel genuine interest in solving a live problem supplied him by a professional mechanic. File folders containing problems related to a variety of types of jobs can be built up over the years.

## Have Students Bring in Live Problems

Students can be encouraged to bring in live problems—those that confront them in their personal lives. The problems they come up with are likely to be practical, to have teen appeal, and to testify to the fact that mathematics does meet personal needs.

* The ideas related to problems of interest to students are from Nila Banton Smith's *Be a Better Reader,* Book IV (Englewood Cliffs, New Jersey: Prentice-Hall, Inc., 1963).

† Butler and Wren, *The Teaching of Secondary School Mathematics,* p. 383.

‡ Stephen S. Willoughby, "Issues in the Teaching of Mathematics," in *Mathematics Education,* ed. Herman Richey, Sixty-ninth Yearbook of the National Society for the Study of Education (LXIX, Part 1, 1970), p. 276.

## BIBLIOGRAPHY

Butler, Charles H. and F. Lynwood Wren, *The Teaching of Secondary School Mathematics*. New York: McGraw-Hill Book Company, 1965.

Herber, Harold L., *Teaching Reading in Content Areas*. Englewood Cliffs, New Jersey: Prentice-Hall, Inc., 1970.

Herber, Harold L. and P. L. Sanders, eds., *Research in Reading in the Content Areas: First Year Report*. Syracuse, New York: Reading and Language Arts Center, 1969.

# 7

# SCIENCE

If science teachers were to list the characteristics of today's "ideal graduate" in science, they would probably name *maturity in reading* as a major attribute. Some of the specifics in science courses are likely to go out of date several times within a student's lifetime—for in this field, change is a constant. On the other hand, the skills he has developed in the reading of scientific materials will probably remain quite firm.

In this chapter we share with you an approach to the reading of laboratory procedures developed through the team efforts of a reading consultant and Mr. Jerry Ferguson, biology teacher in the University of Chicago Laboratory School. Mr. Ferguson found that many students were coming to lab sessions unprepared. Though the procedures for the experiment had been assigned for reading the night before, many students were reading them carelessly—if indeed they read them at all. He wondered if some reading pointers would be helpful. The approach that was developed, and the results in the laboratory, are shared with you.

Of course, directions for laboratory procedures are only one of the specialized patterns of writing that confront students as they learn from the printed page in science. They will profit from their teacher's help in handling other demanding patterns. In fact, the section on upgrading students' textbook reading in Chapter 3 was originally developed for use in Mr. Ferguson's classes because of his concern for helping students approach their new textbooks early in the course. "Giving students study reading techniques," he comments, "is a necessary and rewarding introduction to the course—it pays dividends all year in increased efficiency for students."

The section on reading skills for problem solving (Chapter 5) was also prepared with the needs of science students in mind. Because of the close similarity between reading in science and in mathematics, most of the approaches and devices suggested in "Helps for Improving Mathematics Reading" in Chapter 6 will be equally helpful in science.

## UPGRADE STUDENTS' READING OF LABORATORY PROCEDURES

*"My students used to read their laboratory procedures carelessly—then muddle through their investigations," Jerry Ferguson, Laboratory School science teacher, reports. "Then I upgraded their reading and changed lab day into a smooth operation."*

Picture a laboratory into which students walk on lab day having read the assigned procedures only superficially—indifferently informed about the activity ahead—uncertain about their objectives. Their experimenting time slips away as they try, at the last minute, to find out what they are to do, leaning on their teacher or on each other, and asking unnecessary questions. They lose time correcting errors and perhaps doing the investigation over. As the bell rings, some have failed to finish the experiment.

Picture another lab where students arrive oriented to the investigation ahead and informed about how to proceed. They quickly secure the materials they need, operate without pressure, correct fewer mistakes, work with appropriate independence, and finish the investigation on schedule. What makes the difference? Several factors. Probably among the foremost is the degree of expertise the students have developed in reading the procedures.

Because the activities that occur in the laboratory are the heart of many science courses, and the laboratory is the place where students *practice* the scientific method rather than merely read about it, proficiency in reading investigative procedures is likely to be an important plus for the student.

### Reading May Require a New Look

Why is reading likely to call for a new look as the student in a new science course tries to read the procedures he must carry out in the laboratory? A pattern of writing never before encountered may confront him. He must grapple with the directions for carrying out a process—often a long and complicated process involving many steps. The sequence of steps may be crucial. A single word left unknown may throw off the entire experiment. Drawings, diagrams, and photos take on special importance—convey a vital message.

Perhaps for the first time in his experience, the student must translate reading into action within a rigid time limit. His reading time must not encroach upon his doing-the-job time. The student must read the direction pattern with in-depth comprehension. Perhaps nowhere in all his years at school has he had a chance to *learn* to cope with this type of reading. If he reads his lab instructions as he has done his reading in the past, he may lose out before he has read two or three steps.

### Teacher and Consultant Develop Guidelines

Intent on improving efficiency in the laboratory, Jerry Ferguson, University High School science teacher, enlisted the help of the reading consultant. In the laboratory instructions that confront his students all through the year, an identical pattern of writing occurs scores of times. Perhaps proficiency in handling this pattern might be developed relatively quickly during the opening weeks of the course in the fall. Perhaps together teacher and consultant might work out some this-is-how-to-read-it suggestions.

The guidelines that evolved were entitled "A Scientist's Approach to Reading Laboratory Procedures" and were printed as a four-panel foldout, which students would keep for reference in their looseleaf notebooks and to which they could refer while doing their advance reading of the procedures at home. A complete set of instructions for a laboratory investigation—one which the teacher had selected as representative—was reproduced, with permission of the publisher, in the two center panels of the foldout. The pointers for efficient reading appeared on either side. Highway signs, SLOW, STOP, and WARNING—in attention-catching red or yellow—were positioned appropriately, adding page trim and color.

To bombard the class with the guidelines, a striking "billboard" was hung on the rear wall, where it dominated the laboratory. So that the guidelines might be enlarged to this billboard size, they were abridged, typed on an IBM Executive typewriter, and reproduced by a photo blowup process.

The content of the students' foldouts is offered here under "A Scientist's Approach to Reading Laboratory Procedures."

# A SCIENTIST'S APPROACH TO READING LABORATORY PROCEDURES

**Study** the **title.** ▶―――――▶―――――▶―――――▶―――――▶

It quickly "clues you in" to the type of activity ahead.

**Read** the **introduction.** ▶----▶----▶----▶----▶----▶----▶

This orients you—may supply critical information—charts your direction.

It helps you to set your over-all purpose, lets you know the why of the who e procedure.

Ask yourself: "How does this relate to what I've studied?" "Where am I going in this investigation?"

**Note** mentally **materials** you'll need. ▶━━━━━▶━━━━━▶━━━━▶

*Try This Approach for a Detailed Procedure:*

1. **"Pre-read"** the **entire procedure** and also the **discussion questions.**

   Read these through "once over lightly."

   Ask yourself, "What, in general, am I to do?" Now each step in the process takes on meaning. It falls into place in relation to the whole.

2. **Read** the **procedure** a **second time**—step by step—with great care!

   **Make** a complete **stop** after reading each sentence or each step, whenever necessary, to make sure you understand just what you are to do.

   "Thought time" is needed in addition to reading time.

   Are you having difficulty concentrating on a complicated step? It may help to **form** a **mental picture** of yourself performing the step.

   Seeing yourself perform the step may help you to rivet your attention on the meaning—forces you to take in what's being said.

   If you read without this visual image, your reading may be passive—with your thoughts worlds away.

   **"Read"** the **diagrams** as well as the text.

   As you read, you'll find frequent references to diagrams. These are often quick, vivid, easy-to-grasp—give you instant "how-to-do-it" insights—save you working time.

   When you are first referred to the diagram, shift your attention

to the diagram. Read the caption, then examine the diagram
carefully, noting each label and its corresponding part. Whenever a subsequent sentence mentions something that is pictured in the diagram, look back at the diagram, if you need to,
after you've read the sentence.

Diagrams often clarify methods and processes for you every step
of the way—show you what to do and what not to do.

### 5-4   Investigating the composition of water. *

In this investigation you will see a compound broken down
into the separate elements that form it. You will split water into
two gases by passing an electric current through it. This process
is known as electrolysis (e-lek-TROL-uh-sis). The gases will be
collected and tests will be made to identify them. Your observations should help you to understand the relationship between
atoms and molecules and between elements and compounds.
These observations will also help you to understand the nature of
chemical changes.

### Materials

Electrolysis apparatus (See Figure 5-5.)
  Water-acid solution (100 parts water mixed with two parts
  concentrated sulfuric acid)
DC power supply (or two 6-volt dry cells connected in series)

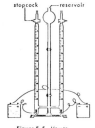

Figure 5-5   How to
set up the electrolysis
apparatus.

### Procedure

1. With the stopcocks open, pour the water-acid mixture into
the reservoir until the liquid level reaches the bottom of the stopcocks. (See Figure 5-5.) Pour the acid mixture carefully. Close
the stopcocks.

2. Connect the wires from the electrodes to the terminals of the
DC source. If you use a DC power supply, start with a low voltage and increase to a higher voltage. If you use dry cells, connect each pole to one of the electrodes. Do you observe any
reaction? Next, connect another battery in series with the first.
Use only one wire to connect the two batteries, the positive pole

* Reproduced with permission from *Biological Science, Molecules to Man*, Blue
Version, by Biological Sciences Curriculum Study. Boston: Houghton Mifflin Company, 1968.

of one to the negative pole of the other. Connect the remaining poles directly to the electrodes as in Figure 5–5.

3. Observe the process closely for 15 minutes. List at least ten observations. Be sure that they are really observations and not assumptions.

4. Your teacher will perform tests for two common gases to help you identify some of the substances that were produced in the process.

### Discussion

1. Did you notice bubbles rising from the electrodes? How do they differ in each tube? Do they rise to the surface at the same rate?
2. What happened to the water in each tube? Form a hypothesis to explain your observations.
3. What is the ratio of the volumes of gas in the two tubes? Did this ratio remain constant during the observation time?
4. What is the probable ratio of hydrogen particles to oxygen particles in a molecule of water?
5. What is the relationship between the volume of gas produced at a terminal and the electrical charge on that terminal?
6. What is the effect of the increase of voltage? What would you expect with further increase in voltage?
7. What is the function of the electric current in the electrolysis of water?
8. As the teacher opened the stopcock to collect the gases, which test tube was held upside down? What can you tell about the gases from this technique?
9. Write a short paragraph summarizing the results of the tests.
10. Complete the equation to show how many atoms of each gas would be produced by splitting two molecules of water.

$$2H_2O \longrightarrow ? + ?$$

**Terms in *boldface italics* say, "Stop! Look! Learn!"**

These are highly important "official" scientific terms. The authors "signal" other important terms with italic type without the boldface.

Reach for your dictionary, when necessary, for unfamiliar general terms.

Make sure you <u>know</u> the meaning of <u>abbreviations</u> and <u>symbols</u>.

A single word left unknown—an imprecise meaning—may <u>ruin</u> your entire <u>experiment.</u>

You can have "instant access" to forgotten technical terms through the index of your textbook.

> LEARN TO HANDLE EXPERIMENTAL PROCEDURES LARGELY ON YOUR OWN. COME TO LAB PERIOD ALREADY INFORMED ON WHAT TO DO. YOU'LL NEED THE ENTIRE PERIOD FOR EXPERIMENTAL WORK.

### ◄ Note warnings!

*Italic type*—with or without the word CAUTION—is sometimes a "danger flag" alerting you to possible "traps." (See Step 1 under "Procedure" for the experiment.)

Overlooking a warning may

> Cause injury to yourself or a classmate.
> Ruin your experiment.
> Damage expensive equipment.

Anything **quantitative** is a possible **danger-spot.** "Zero in" on amounts, distances, timings, and temperatures—and later make your measurements with precision.

**Reread** as often as necessary.

> Note that each step is built on full understanding of preceding steps.
>
> A single error in any step may throw off the rest of the process.

3. **Add** a last quick **"run-through"** to **fix** in mind the **procedure** as a **whole.**

4. During laboratory period, **carry out** the **steps** to the **letter** in the **order given.**

> Timing for "15 minutes" means precisely 15 minutes by the second hand. (See Step 3 under "Procedure" for the experiment.)
>
> The sequence of steps is critical.

If **something** goes **wrong:**

> Rethink the purpose, reread the procedure, and recheck your actions.

**STOP**

### No question should remain unanswered.

> Jot down questions to ask in class.

> Precision reading of the directions for an experiment is an essential tool of learning in science. It should enable you to work through experiments far more accurately and quickly. Clumsy reading does not pay as you strike out blindly—blunder—then lose time correcting errors and perhaps redoing the experiment.

**Classes Profit From How-to-Read-It Sessions**

In September, before his students had an opportunity to fall into inefficient habits, the teacher acted to develop *efficient* habits.

On the day before the first laboratory session, he stressed expertise in reading laboratory procedures as a must for the course ahead: "You'll need to come in tomorrow with what you are to do *already fixed in mind*. Your experimental work will fill the entire period. Time used in class for *reading* the procedures is time lost in the *doing* of them. As the course progresses, the investigative procedures will become more complicated. Reading in class will be out of the question— you'll hardly have time to say 'Good morning'! If you try to crowd your reading into the lab period as your fifty minutes are ticking away, you may have chaos. If you read the procedures *before* you come, you'll be more confident and efficient."

Having distributed the foldouts, the instructor then guided the class through the suggested reading approach, using the investigation assigned for the next day. He concluded, "Does anyone have the procedure perfectly in mind—just what you are to do tomorrow? No? That's understandable—this is rigorous reading. So you'll want to reread it tonight.

"Of course, your memory for the details will not be perfect. You should *expect* to look at the printed procedure during the experiment tomorrow. But you'll look and say, 'Oh, I remember—I cut the corks now.' This will take *minimal* time compared with the time it would take you to do an initial reading. Perhaps you'll want to give the procedure a quick run-through just before class tomorrow."

As the instructor observed the students' performance during the next day's lab session and later examined their written lab reports, he noted continuing reading needs. These he discussed with the class a day or two later. There was guidance as needed during the first two or three months of school.

**Classes Help Develop Guidelines**

There is no intention of straightjacketing students into a rigid procedure. The guidelines are offered as tips that are likely to prove helpful. A teacher may prefer to involve his students in developing the guidelines. He might project on a screen before the class a set of laboratory instructions, then pose the question, "Suppose you wished to read these directions, then carry out the investigation without a word of help or explanation from your teacher. How would you read the directions *ideally?"* When students focus their attention on how to read procedures *ideally,* they often come up with highly practical suggestions. These the teacher can combine with his own expertise to evolve the final guidelines.

### Have Students Improved Their Reading of Procedures?

How has "Operation Reading" worked out? The instructor comments: "In the years before we had the 'directions drive,' many students had no approach other than a hit or miss reading. Now most of them come to the lab prepared. The many students who follow the guidelines on the foldout are confident, efficient, and pleased with the results. They find that they can work steadily, yet not hurriedly, and do not get lost in the process of working. They do not have to correct as many mistakes but can proceed smoothly and without much pressure. The few who start out by ignoring the outlined reading procedure become confused and pressured enough to have to start over, or find themselves wasting too much time, or frequently find that they cannot complete the work at all. The truth becomes evident to them, and the vast majority of these doubters reform their reading procedures before many sessions have passed.

"Periodic reminders to follow the successful procedure must be given—though with decreasing frequency—as the first semester progresses. Once a student has panicked under the stress of not being prepared, he serves as his *own* moving spirit. The long range result of our project has been more efficient laboratory sessions and a saving of countless hours of working time."*

### When Students Design Their Own Procedures

Students who have learned to read experimental procedures precisely have an advantage later in the course *when they design their own procedures.* They are likely to make sounder decisions because they have observed with what precision, with what rigorous preparation, with what logic a scientific investigation must be devised.

### Isn't a Compelling Interest in Laboratory Work Enough?

Isn't a compelling interest in the activities of science class enough to bring about efficient reading? Surely, genuine drives for reading are

* Jerry Ferguson, "Teaching the Reading of Biology," *Fusing Reading Skills and Content,* eds. H. Alan Robinson and Ellen Lamar Thomas (Newark, Delaware: International Reading Association, 1969), pp. 118–119.

of immense importance in the reading development of students. But do these automatically insure that the students will develop the most rapid, labor saving, and effective techniques? When students caught up with interest in an exciting problem have the added advantage of their teacher's guidance in the most effective techniques, an ideal situation is created. The immediate need motivates the student to learn the facilitating skills. He is likely to react, "That really works!" His satisfaction leads to his continued use of the skill and to its reinforcement.

Neither powerful incentives for reading nor the teacher's guidance in reading approaches is fully effective without the other. Together, they can be a potent force for giving the student a complete collection of reading skills for science.

# INDUSTRIAL ARTS AND
# VOCATIONAL EDUCATION

*Herbert Pearson, Laboratory School industrial arts teacher,*
*served as a consultant for this chapter.*

Students with reading difficulties often gravitate to technical courses, hoping for a haven at school where reading is not demanded. Instructors express concern over the gap between the reading competencies these students bring to their courses and the demands that will confront them from day to day. Teachers without formal training or experience in teaching reading can take action to narrow this gap—in the daily work of the course with no undue investment of additional class time. There should be these dividends for students: (1) better mastery of the immediate course, and (2) better reading for advanced technical courses and apprenticeships and for self-education after school courses are over.

The problem of upgrading reading in technical courses is a special one—but *so is the opportunity*. Where, if a boy is interested in technical subjects, is reading closer to "doing his own thing"? In woodshop, the printed words on the page before him may be related to making a pair of water skis—in electronics, to checking out what's wrong with his transistor radio or portable phonograph—in metal shop, to improving his scuba diving equipment—in auto mechanics, to getting more "go" out of his motor bike or car. Here reading ability can be turned into *job* ability. The student realizes that he *must* be able to handle technical reading or be shut out of the job market for all but the simplest manual labor.

In this chapter we offer for the consideration of the teacher first a section suggesting approaches and devices which should help readers (particularly those less capable) handle the heavy vocabulary load in technical courses. The second item presents a strong case for a technical library right in the shop or classroom. Here students can acquire find-it-yourself procedures to keep their technical knowledge up to date and growing—for life. And here, in fascinating how-to-do-it books and colorful popular magazines, there will be a silent reading teacher daily inviting them to *practice* reading.

## HELPING STUDENTS LEARN TECHNICAL VOCABULARY

*The vocabulary load in technical courses is crushing for many students. There's an urgent need for effective vocabulary learning.*

In technical courses, difficult vocabulary terms—sometimes hundreds of them—come crowding upon the student. A precise working understanding is often crucial. Not knowing the difference between *drilling* and *counterdrilling* can mean disaster for that study desk the student is making. The new technical terms pile up and must be mastered from day to day. To the last day of the course, they will be precision tools for grasping essential new knowledge.

In some respects there is a unique opportunity in the technical classroom for effective vocabulary learning. Here, daily, there are live experiences with words. The student *sees* the referent for many printed symbols right there before him in wood, metal, plastic. As he learns the new term *engine lathe,* he sees, hears, touches, and manipulates the actual machine. As he learns the term *knurling,* he observes, then performs the process. When he meets *micrometer caliper,* he picks up the instrument and holds it in his hand *to do a job.* Here a "print-shy" reader may change his attitude toward words. As he turns the pages of a popular magazine on mechanics, printed symbols on the page may stand for fascinating parts of his mini-bike—and printed words tell him how to repair it.

It might be argued that the school shop or the technical classroom should provide a reading-free environment—a place at school where the discouraged reader can succeed *without* the printed word. But this is not realism. Let us rather examine the possibility of exposing him to powerful reading stimuli—indeed, of bombarding him with printed words. A miscellany of possibilities for increasing his technical word power through many such exposures is now offered.

## Take Down the Obstacle Course

You can remove roadblocks *before* your students read by searching through textbook or job sheet beforehand, pulling out significant words that will cause difficulty, and teaching them in advance—in the context in which they will be encountered. As you do so, you will be taking the chill off the reading, and discouraged readers may take hold.

Numbers of technical terms can be brought within the reach of student readers through part by part analysis. A word like *superconductivity* may appear overlong to some readers. They are likely to be frightened by its seven syllables and give up. It is immensely helpful simply to show students that long, difficult-appearing words often have familiar parts—here, the obvious *super* and *conduct*. This takes just minutes. Students are likely to "see into" words as you analyze them if, on the chalkboard, you mark off longer words into easy to manage parts:

super / conduct / ivity

With *carbonaceous,* students might be asked, "Can you see a word within the word?" as you print the word on the board. Some will discover *carbon* quickly. You might highlight the base word on the board in some way, perhaps by underlining:

carbonaceous

Then the class can move on to learning the technical meaning—the word's length no longer making it appear forbidding.

With *dynamometer* printed on the chalkboard, you might ask, "Is there a part you know?" Students are likely to respond, "Oh, dynamo!" They now perceive that the long word *dynamometer* is a not too difficult word with *meter* (which may already be familiar) tail-ending it.

If *commutator* should be a hurdle, you might suggest, "Can you strip this one down?" When the students discover *commute,* you might ask, "What does *commute* mean?"—then guide them in mastering the specialized meaning.

Printing the term on the board accents its appearance and spelling and helps the student to "take a mental picture." If in future reading he is to recognize the new term instantaneously, he must have this "mental picture."

The terms that follow, found in various technical textbooks, lend themselves to the question, "Can you take this word apart—break it into its building blocks?"

| | |
|---|---|
| set-over | demagnetize |
| spotfacing | electromagnet |
| setscrew | variometer |
| casehardening | variocoupler |
| monotype | magnetometer |
| ultrasonic | equipotential |
| photosensitive | interelectrode |
| photoconductive | transconductance |
| micrometer | electrodynamometer |
| autotransformer | microminiaturization |
| accelerometer | radiometallography |

Familiar parts discovered in these words are handles to take hold of in remembering their meanings. Terms that lend themselves to part by part analysis are numerous in technical courses.

### Teach Jackpot Word Parts*

Students who master the easy-to-learn Greek and Latin word parts for numbers take a stride ahead in technical vocabulary. In a few moments of turning through the index of two or three technical textbooks, one can find all these derivatives: unipolar, unishear, monoblock, monotype, monochrome, bimetal, bilateral, binary, trimetric, quadrant, quadrilateral, tetrahedron, pentagon, pentagrid, hexagon, hexahedron, hexode, heptagon, octagon, octahedron, octode, nonagon, decagon, dodecagon, dodecahedron, centimeter, millimeter, and others. Here, again, the familiar part gives the student a peg on which to hang his retention of the meaning.

### Multimeaning Terms Call for Special Handling

Many words take off their easy, familiar meanings and put on difficult technical meanings the minute the student walks through the door into the shop. Words like *lap, polish, rack, tolerance, quench,*

---

* Ward S. Miller uses the term "jackpot" vocabulary lessons in *Word Wealth* (New York: Holt, Rinehart and Winston, Inc., 1967).

*cast, dog,* and *boss* suddenly take on technical meanings that must be learned with precision. *Hard* and *tough* look like everyday words to students and are likely to be thought similar in meaning. Now they become important in describing certain properties of metal and must be carefully differentiated. Since students must relinquish their preconceived ideas of such terms as easy, some of these terms may call for special handling through emphasizing their technical meanings during explanations and demonstrations.

**Meet Your New Shop**

The more numerous his exposures to a printed word, the more likely the student is to form the visual image necessary for him to incorporate it into his vocabulary. On the first day in a new shop class, when interest is high, a floor plan of the shop can be given to each student.* On it various pieces of equipment—engine lathe, shaper, milling machine, table saw, jointer, planer, and others—are located and numbered. The machines themselves have identification signs conspicuously attached. Eager to learn about the equipment they will be using, the students move around the shop with their floor plans. As they circulate, they complete a numbered sheet, writing the name of each machine after the number corresponding to that on the floor plan.

**Safety Signs Send Out Verbal Stimuli**

Shop safety signs, which students will live with from day to day, further expose students to the stimuli of printed words. As the teacher directs attention to a prominent sign and forcefully drives home its message, students may come to retain an image of the printed symbols. For still another exposure to words, bulletins on shop safety might be read aloud to under-par readers as they follow the printed words silently.

**Label Everything in Sight!**

Almost everything in the shop or classroom can be conspicuously labeled. The tools on the tool racks can be labeled. The materials in

* Gordon Funk, "Reading and Industrial Arts; Interview," *Industrial Arts and Vocational Education,* L (October, 1961), p. 25.

drawers or in storage cabinets can be prominently labeled.* Each time a student removes a tool from a rack—or replaces one—or opens the door of a cabinet, he is pelted with words. He may come to associate the symbol with the object, retain a mental picture, and make the word his own for future reading.

One teacher demonstrated the use of a machine—a squaring shear, for example—with eye catching name cards attached to important parts.† Small magnets designed to hold cards were used to attach the labels. Interest was caught by this novel and effective way of presenting vocabulary. Later the name cards were removed, and the students were asked to reattach them to the right parts. As they manipulated each label, they strengthened their visual image of each term—*extension arm, cutting blade, bed, foot treadle,* and others.

Bulletin boards, too, can teach vocabulary. One teacher displayed a wood selection chart with 48 kinds of hardwoods and softwoods, each of these conspicuously labeled. His boys could be seen lingering before and after the class hour, studying this chart. Colorful charts supplied by industry expose the student to additional verbal stimuli.

Dittoed job sheets are often accompanied by diagrams and drawings. These provide still another opportunity for prominent labels.

### Demonstrations Are an Opportunity Plus

The instructor's frequent demonstrations of equipment and processes in technical courses offer a superlative opportunity. Is there a better setting for synchronizing *hearing* the word and *seeing* it, a coordination conducive to acquiring vocabulary? Auditory memory is involved as the student hears his teacher use the word during the demonstration. Most important if his reading is to benefit, his visual memory is involved, if, at the same time, he sees the word displayed during the demonstration. Here again he has a chance to photograph the word in his mind's eye—and add it to his sight vocabulary. If demonstrations are conducted without printed words, this special opportunity is lost.

How can a teacher spotlight printed words while he has his hands full giving a demonstration? Classroom-size flip charts with pages that flip over easily can present the terms to view. A portable stand, which can be moved anywhere in the shop, makes displaying the charts quite

* "The Reading Program and Industrial Arts," *Workshop for Reading in the Content Areas* (El Monte Union High School District, California, 1966), p. 9.

† Howard R. Schramm, "Helpful Teaching Aids for Industrial Education," *Industrial Arts and Vocational Education,* XLIII (October, 1954), p. 278.

easy. As the teacher demonstrates knurling on an engine lathe, he can direct attention to the term *knurling* in large print on a chart nearby. As he demonstrates the uses of the circle saw, the important new terms *ripping, crosscutting, mitering, dadoing, beveling,* and others—each one in turn—take the spotlight. Students can sometimes profit from helping prepare the charts.

In reviewing terms just taught, a teacher working with younger children pointed to the printed terms on the chart. The students enjoyed getting the actual objects—nail, screw, dowel, and others—and holding them up beside the printed symbol.*

The same instructor found it helpful to have tools as well as words in full view during a demonstration. He constructed a simple portable chalkboard with a handy magnetic toolholder held by a strip of plywood to the top of the chalkboard. The magnet held up small hand tools. The background of the chalkboard permitted him to label the tool and its parts with prominent printed labels. A "Magnagrip" toolholder can be secured from the Phelon Magnagrip Company, East Longmeadow, Massachusetts 01028.†

Another teacher had an ingenious way of spotlighting a term at just the right moment.‡ Have you ever wished, he asked, that you could reveal the name of each part of a tool or machine just when you need to during a demonstration? To solve the problem he prepared large size drawings of various tools and machines, omitting the names of the parts. Then he covered the drawings with clear cellulose acetate. As he proceeded with his demonstration of the actual equipment before the class, he printed the name of the part he was explaining, using a china marker. For emphasis, he sometimes printed the labels in color, using different colored china markers. The pencil markings could be easily removed from the acetate. The drawings were on hand for follow-up reinforcement and testing and for use year after year.

Contrast reading oriented demonstrations like the ones just described, with those in which the student simply hears the word and there *is* no printed symbol. Printed words thus spotlighted should add up to better reading.

## Turn Job Sheets into Better-Reading Devices

As their teachers can substantiate, many students lack the reading power to handle the job sheets which are intended to guide their

* Anthony J. Ferrerio, "Try Industrial Arts for Retarded Readers," *Industrial Arts and Vocational Education*, IXL, No. 2 (February, 1960), p. 19.

† *Industrial Arts and Vocational Education*, XLIII, p. 278.

‡ *Industrial Arts and Vocational Education*, XLIII, p. 279.

work in the shop from day to day. It may be possible to transform these guide sheets into better-reading devices.

Handicapped readers often shy away from the printed word. They prefer to depend on the spoken word, to get by without reading by turning to their teacher for information. But since drawing out meaning from printed material is vital to their success as technical workers, they should be led back to the printed page as a source of information whenever possible.

One teacher developed a type of lesson intended to help students handle their immediate job sheets and improve in reading, too.* Picture his groups confronted with a job sheet that started like this:

**Unit—How to Turn Tapers by the Offset Tailstock Method**
**Topic—Checking Offset with Dividers**
1. Set the legs of the dividers to the required offset. Adjust set-over screws until the distance between the index line on the base and the index line on the tailstock body corresponds to the setting of the dividers.

And this was just the first step!

First, the teacher demonstrated the required processes orally, introducing the class to the equipment with which they would be working. Attention was directed to the chalkboard where the teacher had printed the key words of the job. Among these were the following:

1. required offset

2. set-over screws

3. corresponds to the setting

4. tailstock body

5. index line

and a number of others.

As a check on understanding, the teacher pointed to the phrase on the board and asked a student to indicate the equipment (set-over screws, for example) and to give the function, or to demonstrate or explain the process. Again, headlining the phrases on the board concentrated attention on their appearance and spelling. Sometimes the teacher erased the words and called on certain students to write them in again, asking the others to watch the board and be ready to help their classmates. After this thorough pre-teaching of key vocabulary,

---

* Isidore N. Levine, "Solving Reading Problems in Vocational Subjects," *High Points,* XLII (April, 1960), pp. 22–24.

the teacher or a student read the job sheet aloud while the students followed along silently. As they did this, their understanding of words they could not recognize on the page was made possible by the *heard* word. Many proceeded with their work, now capable of reading their job sheets for themselves. Of course, all this support for students— this oral-silent reading procedure—is appropriate only for those who have problems reading the job sheets.

### Elicit the Use of New Terms

Students can be led to *use* the new terms immediately. A shop teacher who has just demonstrated mitering a board asks his class, "What did I just do to this board?" The students reinforce their new learning as they answer individually or in chorus. Holding up the miter-gage or the push-stick, or pointing to the rip-fence, he asks, "What did I just call this?" Again, there is the opportunity to say and to hear the new words.

### Bring Job Sheets into Closer Reach

When job sheets, textbook directions, and the like are beyond the reach of certain readers, they can be rewritten on an easier level. The general vocabulary can be made easier and the sentences can be shortened to include only a single direction in each. A reading consultant can suggest ways of bringing directions more nearly within the grasp of under-par readers. Resources of simplified materials can be enlarged year after year.

### Non-Print Materials Can Reinforce Reading

For individuals who need further reinforcement in recognizing important terms and following directions, the teacher might record a series of directions on a tape. Using earphones, the students read the words on the page silently while reinforcing their reading through listening. They play and replay the tape as often as necessary. Through this reading-hearing procedure, they come to associate the word they see printed on the page with the word they hear. After this reinforced reading some students can proceed with their work away from the tape recorder using only the printed directions. Thus they are grasping the directions for their current project and learning to read better besides.

Films and filmstrips can be used to introduce new terms. During the film the students both hear and see the key terms and see the tools and materials pictured.

### Can You Answer the Boss's Note?

The teacher clips an advertisement for a carpenter's assistant from a newspaper.* He asks, "If you were to get this job, what do you think you would have to do?" The students talk this over.

The teacher goes on, "Here is a copy of a note you might get on the first day of your new job," and he projects on a screen a blow-up copy. The note is read aloud, and here is the boss's message:

> I am up on the tenth floor. Bring me the following tools:
>
> | | | |
> |---|---|---|
> | mallet | gouge | pliers |
> | chisel | hammer | coping saw |
> | brace | hand drill | hacksaw |
> | bit | plane | clamp |
>
> *Hurry!*

The teacher then asks, "What will you need to know to be able to answer the note?" The students respond, "The tools the carpenter mentioned."

The tools the carpenter needs are laid out on a work bench. Their names have been printed on large size word cards. The students are asked to match each name card with the corresponding tool.

After the tools and cards have been matched, the teacher removes the tools but leaves the word cards. The students now work only with the printed symbols. Asking the class to keep in mind the *use* of each tool, he suggests that certain words can be grouped together because their use is similar. He continues questioning until the name cards have been arranged into five groups:

> mallet—hammer
>
> chisel—gouge
>
> pliers—clamp
>
> coping saw—hacksaw
>
> brace—bit—drill

In summing up, the class discusses the question, "How can this help you to be a good carpenter's assistant?"

---

* "The Reading Program and Industrial Arts," *Workshop for Reading in the Content Areas* (El Monte Union High School District, 1966), pp. 10–11.

## Name That Tool!

The teacher introduces the class to tools, parts of tools, types of lumber, varnishes, stains—whatever is needed to complete a project. As he does so, the printed names are displayed and stressed. Later he hangs a number on each item and gives each student a numbered sheet. The student is asked to write down the name of each piece of equipment or material. The teacher is enlisting kinesthetic (muscular) learning, which in many individuals is one of the strongest of all learning channels. The motor act of writing the new term, in and of itself, is likely to strengthen the learning.

## Record New Terms

Supply houses are often generous with large-size advertising calendars. As one more way of enlisting motor memory the student might write on today's date the new technical words he learned that day. If spelling is a problem he might print the word's trouble spots in extra-large letters or in color.* Students might also prepare their own individual calendars to help develop a key word list.

Some teachers suggest that students record words for special study in a vocabulary notebook. They might group them under various classifications: cutting tools, hammering tools, electric tools, and so on.

Flash cards offer another possibility for enlisting "muscular memory." The student prints the term by itself on one side of a 3 x 5 flash card and writes the meaning on the reverse side. In checking, he looks at the new term and asks himself, "Do I know its meaning?" Or he operates the other way, reading the meaning and asking, "Can I supply the new term?"

## Play Up "Words of the Week"

A sign with movable letters, which can be shifted to spell out words, is displayed before the class.† Each week crucially important words are highlighted. The teacher plays up these words in demonstrations and discussions, and they turn up on quizzes. The sign is just one more way to underline for students the importance of building their technical vocabularies.

* *Industrial Arts and Vocational Education,* IXL, No. 2, p. 20.

† Arnold P. Ruskin, "Teaching Vocabulary in Industrial Arts," *Industrial Arts and Vocational Education,* LV (February, 1966), p. 45.

### Point Out the Index for Easy Finding

As already mentioned, some students are "allergic" to print. They want *spoken* answers and like to get these by leaning on their teacher, turning to him often with "What does this word mean?" Such questions are an opportunity to ask, "Have you tried to find out?" If the student starts leafing absently through the pages of a book, guide him to the index. Demonstrate its value as an aid to instant finding. If necessary, assist him appropriately as he reads the explanation of the term. If the book has a glossary, alert him to its value.

### The Dictionary Is a Vital Tool

Classroom dictionaries to which students can turn for unknown general terms should be part of a vocabulary "tool kit." Helping the student *use* this tool is strengthening his power to read and learn independently *for life*.

Simplified dictionaries should be standard equipment in classrooms where there are deficient readers. What is to be gained if a student deficient in vocabulary looks up *automatic* and finds the meaning *done without volition?* Too often a shabby college-level dictionary which has been knocking around the classroom for years is the only one to which poor readers can turn. For younger and less able readers, elementary and junior high school dictionaries should be within reach. The reader will find easy-to-use student dictionaries listed in Chapter 2.

## A SHOP LIBRARY CAN TURN ON READERS

*Herbert Pearson's technical "library" is often the busiest part of the shop.*

You can get a good thing going in a shop or technical classroom "library." Boys who would not be caught reaching for a book in the school library may reach for one here. Here, each time they come to shop, attractive how-to-do-it books and colorful popular magazines can invite boys to *practice* reading.

Picture a turned off reader—yet a boy geared up with mechanical interests—walking into this library. Reading in English class was never like this! On a bookshelf he sees the brightly colored new *Honda Repair and Tune Up Guide*. On display, as in the corner magazine store, are *Popular Mechanics, Mechanix Illustrated, Science* *and Mechanics, Popular Science,* and others. The shiny cover of one offers him a preview of the cars and drivers slated to appear at the Indianapolis speedway. The equally bright cover of another invites him to build a sailplane from a kit. He turns the pages and finds plans for building himself a combination desk and workbench, or tips for choosing the right caulking for a boat. He leafs through another and finds suggestions for sprucing up his car to make it pay more at trade-in time. He sees a pamphlet, "Careers in Technical Occupations," and looks it over. It invites him to check out his abilities and limitations, size himself up, and perhaps make some plans for *the* job someday.*

With his teacher's guidance, he soon comes to regard the library as a technical know-how center. The doors of the tall cabinet of how-to-do-it books are always open. Books with hundreds of easy-to-grasp diagrams and pictures ease the way to solve his in-class (and sometimes out-of-class) problems. There is no period of waiting, no cooling of enthusiasm or drop in interest while he runs to find a book in the regular school library. His need is right there and right now, and so is the book. He can reach for *Experiences with Electrons, General Shop for Everyone, Modern Metalworking,* the bright-colored *Chilton's Automobile Repair Manual.* The pamphlets supplied by industry are inviting. One of these, the *ABC's of Hand Tools* (General Motors), clarifies the use and care of small hand tools through Walt Disney drawings. He may gain a new view of what is between the covers of a book. Answers he is seeking are right there for him—in *printed words.*

Through this "library," reference skills for reading technical material can be taught *right in shop,* at the time the student is caught up with a problem. In minutes his instructor can teach him to value and use a book's index as an aid to instant finding of what he is looking for from among the many thousands of words in the book. With guidance he can learn to scan pages rapidly to find his target information. These find-it-yourself procedures will be a built-in part of his learning equipment when confronted with "exploding" technological advances after his schooling is over.

Simple check-out procedures encourage him to practice out-of-class reading. He writes his name on the card, then leaves the card with his teacher or a student librarian. The loan period is flexible—in keeping with his current project and the demand for the book by others. Books that everyone needs at once do not circulate—they must be read in the "library."

The books span a broad range of reading difficulty levels. They

* Lists of free or low-cost pamphlets on vocational opportunities in technical fields are available from the United States Printing Office, Washington, D.C. A list will be mailed on request.

are processed in the school library, yet considered a permanent part of the classroom collection. Paperbacks on a variety of technical and practical subjects are available at low cost through the Popular Science Book Club, 44 Hillside Avenue, Manhasset, New York 11030.

### Benefits of a Shop Library

Staggering sums are required to reclaim students who leave the doors of their schools without reading power and without earning power. The sum expended to finance a shop library is an investment in *prevention*. Here are some of the benefits it may bring to turned off readers:

1. A boy's strong interest in shop-related subjects can help remove psychological blocks to his reading progress.

2. The world of words has never been his world. Now, for the first time, he may spend many hours in the world of printed words. He meets new words repeatedly in similar and different settings, often with a little increment of meaning with each encounter, and gradually incorporates them into his vocabulary. His reading practice tends to strengthen his comprehension.

3. An impelling interest in a subject may enable him to handle "far too difficult" books and to stretch his reading power.

4. As he learns to search out answers for himself in books, he is better able—through reading—to continue his technical education.

5. The inviting do-it-yourself projects in popular magazines and in books often lead to home hobbies.

6. A young person's self-concept can be altered when he experiences success. Success through and with reading in shop class sometimes helps him succeed better in the broader school situation.

## BIBLIOGRAPHY

Bamman, Henry A., Ursula Hogan, and Charles E. Greene. *Reading Instruction in the Secondary Schools,* pp. 200–210. New York: Longmans, Green, 1961.

Coston, Frederick E., "Reading and Vocational Education," in *Fusing Reading Skills and Content,* eds. H. Alan Robinson and Ellen Lamar Thomas, pp. 145–150. Newark, Delaware: International Reading Association, 1969.

# TYPEWRITING AND BUSINESS EDUCATION

*The reading helps in this section were prepared with Faynelle Haehn, Laboratory School typewriting teacher.*

One day a reading consultant asked a typewriting teacher, "What bothers you most about the reading of your students?"

The teacher answered, "They read directions superficially—even my class of particularly bright seniors. It's the major block to their progress in typewriting."

Together the typing teacher and the reading consultant examined the frequently missed directions in the textbook—then decided to involve the classes in an intensive directions-reading drive. The methods and materials they developed—including detailed guidelines for students—appear in this chapter.

Did the "directions drive" prove effective? Was there an observable change in the reading behavior of students? On the following pages the teacher makes some encouraging observations.

Here is the teacher's unsolicited comment: "I like teaching reading. So will you! You will find it one of the most rewarding areas of teaching typewriting."

## BUSINESS EDUCATION TEACHER UPGRADES READING DIRECTIONS

*There's a "directions explosion" in business education. The future secretary, typist, file clerk, office manager, operator of office machines, and data processor must*

> *grasp countless directions for carrying out a process—*
> *often a complicated process involving many steps. Fre-*
> *quently they have only hit or miss procedures for this*
> *critically important type of reading.*

There's a "directions explosion" in the typewriting textbook. In one widely-used text more than 1200 directions confront the students. Teachers observe that careless reading of directions is a frequent roadblock to progress in typewriting. Upgrading direction-reading techniques should mean time saved to the last day of the course as students eliminate nonessential questions, require less supervision, and work through practice after practice more accurately and quickly.

### The "Right Moment" to Teach the Reading of Directions

At University High School the typewriting teacher capitalizes on the right moment to give instructional guidance.

1. Students return to school those opening days in September with high resolves, "This year I'll do my very best." In a how-to-do-it session shortly after textbooks are distributed, the instructor accents competency in reading directions as a must for success in the course ahead.

2. A classwide catastrophe in practice work brought on by misreading directions may offer the opportune moment.

3. Instruction or reinforcement may be appropriate at a point in the textbook where the difficulty of directions increases sharply.

4. Reinforcement may be desirable at the stage where the work becomes individualized and students are expected to complete their practice work independently. Now, do-it-yourself techniques become critically important.

### Classes Help Develop Guidelines

Concerned that many students used no approach to directions other than haphazard reading, the typewriting teacher and the reading consultant went into action. Together they decided to involve the classes in developing their own guidelines. They planned a lesson in which the students were confronted with rigorous directions for aligning and typing over words, a complicated procedure involving a series of numbered steps. These directions were projected onto a screen before the class with the opaque projector.

The instructor asked each class, "Suppose you wished to follow these directions without a single error and without a word of help or explanation from your teacher. How would you go about reading them?" With their attention focused on how they would read the directions ideally, the students came up with some highly practical pointers. These the teacher recorded in shorthand. The suggestions of the students were then combined with the expertise of the teacher and the insights of the reading consultant to evolve the final guidelines.

### Students Observe "Road Signs"

The guidelines which follow were printed as a colorful three-panel foldout. Sample directions from the textbook (those for aligning and typing over words) were reproduced in the center panel of the foldout. The guidelines were printed on either side. Highway signs SLOW, STOP, and WARNING, in red and yellow, were positioned appropriately, adding page trim and color. As an added, constant, and powerful stimulus, the guidelines were abridged, typed on an IBM Executive typewriter, enlarged by a photo blow-up process, then placarded on the classroom wall on a striking 4' × 8' "billboard." The foldout was kept for reference in the students' individual typewriting folders.

## CAN YOU DO PRECISION READING OF DIRECTIONS IN YOUR TYPEWRITING TEXTBOOK?

1. **Study** the **title.**

   It quickly orients you. In just a word or two, it "clues you in" to the type of activity ahead.

2. **"Preread"** the **entire procedure.**

   Read it through "once over lightly." Ask yourself, "What, in general, am I to do?"

   Now you've set your direction. Now each step in the process takes on meaning. It falls into place in relation to the whole.

3. **Read,** then **carry out each step**—with great care!

   Adjust your speed of reading to the difficulty of the step.

   Make a complete stop, if necessary, after reading each difficult step, to be sure you understand just what you are to do in carrying out that step.

   "Thought time" is needed in addition to reading time.

   Are you having difficulty concentrating on a difficult step? It may help to try to form a mental picture of yourself performing the step.

   Seeing yourself perform the step rivets your attention on its meaning—forces you to take in what's being said.

   If you read without trying to form this visual image, your reading may be passive—with your thoughts worlds away.

   Reread as often as necessary. Each step is built on full understanding of preceding steps.

   A single error in any step may throw off the rest of the process.

---

Precision reading of difficult directions is an essential tool of learning in typing. It should enable you to work through practices *far more accurately and quickly.* Clumsy reading does not pay as you strike out blindly—blunder—then lose time correcting errors and perhaps doing entire practices over.

---

**Unknown terms** say "Stop! Look! Learn!"

A single word left unknown—an imprecise meaning—may necessitate redoing the entire practice.

You can have "instant access" to forgotten meanings through the index of your textbook or the diagram of typewriter parts.

Consult your dictionary, when necessary, for unfamiliar general terms.

# 45E: Aligning and Typing Over Words*

**LOCATE:** Aligning Scale **33**; Variable Line Spacer **3**.

1. **Type** the following sentence but do not make the return:

   I think I can align this copy.

2. **Move** the carriage so the word *think, align,* or *this* is above the scale. Note that a white line points to the center of the letter *i* in the word.

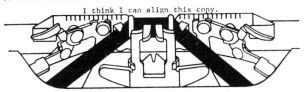

3. **Study** the relation of the top of the scale to the bottom of the letters with down stems.

   *It is important for you to get an eye picture of the exact relation of the typed line to the top of the scale so you will be able to adjust the paper correctly to type over a word with exactness.*

4. **Remove** the paper; reinsert it. Gauge the line so the bottoms of the letters are in correct relation to the top of the aligning scale. Operate the variable line spacer **3** if necessary to move the paper forward or backward. Operate the paper release **16** to move the paper to the left or right if necessary when centering the letter *i* over one of the white lines on the scale.

5. **Check** the accuracy of your alignment by setting the ribbon control **22** for stencil position and typing over one of the letters. If necessary, make further alignment adjustments. *Return the ribbon control to typing position.*

6. **Type** over the words *think, align,* and *this* in the sentence, moving the paper forward or backward, to the left or right, as necessary for correct alignment.

7. **Repeat** Steps 1, 3, 4, 5, and 6.

* Reprinted with special permission from *20th Century Typewriting* by D. D. Lessenberry, T. James Crawford, and Lawrence W. Erickson, South-Western Publishing Co., Cincinnati, 1967.

◄ ‧‧‧‧‧◄ ‧‧‧‧◄**Note warnings.**

In your textbook, <u>italic type</u> is often a "danger flag," alerting you to possible "traps."

**Focus** full attention on **drawings** and **diagrams.**

These are quick, vivid, easy-to-grasp—give you <u>instant "how to do it" insights</u>—save you working time.

They may <u>clarify procedures</u> every step of the way—show you what to do and what not to do.

Far from repeating what the words have already said, they sometimes convey a message words could not possibly express.

**Carry out** each **step** to the letter—in the order given.

The <u>sequence</u> of steps is <u>critical.</u>

If **something** goes **wrong:**

<u>Reread</u> the procedure and <u>recheck</u> your actions.

---

LEARN TO HANDLE DIRECTIONS LARGELY ON YOUR OWN. EMPLOYERS LIST "FOLLOW-THROUGH" WITH THEIR DIRECTIONS AS ONE OF THE TOP ASSETS OF EMPLOYEES.

---

## How-to-Read-Directions Sessions

Aware that the printed foldout was not likely to mean much to students unless accompanied by instruction, the teacher planned how-to-read-directions sessions. There was follow-up then and later as she guided the class through the suggested procedures under supervision.

There was no intention to lock students into a rigid procedure. The guidelines were intended to convey the idea that difficult directions should be approached with system, to discourage the impression that a once over lightly reading is enough, to inform students that rereadings are not only expected but desired. Students were encouraged to view the guidelines as tips that were likely to prove helpful, and to use these flexibly, adapting them to the demands of the task before them at the moment.

Has the reading effort proved effective? From the first how-to-read-it session, the instructor observed a tendency to approach directions more carefully, to eliminate careless errors, and to work more independently.

## Students Assess Their Own Skill

The Self-Evaluation Check List for Reading Directions, reproduced below, centered each student's attention on need areas and pointed the way to improvement. The classes had a part in developing this check list. One day they were asked to think about their own areas of need and to write these down on an index card. From these cards and the discussion that followed, the teacher and the consultant evolved the check list.

# SELF-EVALUATION CHECKLIST FOR READING DIRECTIONS

| NAME | PERIOD | DATE |
|------|--------|------|

This check list is intended to focus your attention on any need areas and point the way to improvement. Your teacher, too, will evaluate you.

Consider how you stand on each of the points below, then rate yourself from 1 to 10 in the space before the numeral.

### Points to Consider

_____ 1. Do you focus full attention on directions in whatever format you find them—itemized lists with numerals, brief directions out in the margin, directions inserted right into the copy, etc.?

_____ 2. At the end of an especially difficult step, do you stop, reflect, and reread, if necessary, to make sure you understand just what you are to do?

_____ 3. Do you make sure you understand the meaning of unfamiliar key terms?

_____ 4. Do you examine the photographs and drawings?

_____ 5. Are you moving in the direction of independence in handling directions largely on your own?

_____ 6. Are you gradually eliminating errors due to superficial reading of directions?

_____ 7. Are you gradually eliminating redoing practices because of superficial reading?

Now that you have considered your specific strengths and weaknesses, give yourself a general rating on the scale below. Place a single check mark at the appropriate point on the scale.

### Your Own General Evaluation

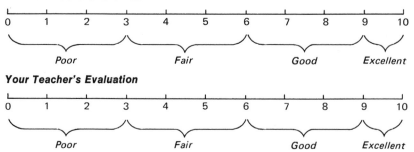

### Your Teacher's Evaluation

### Set Your Own Goals

What general rating do you hope to attain before the next evaluation? Place numeral here: _____.

The students evaluated themselves at intervals and filed their check lists in their individual folders. The instructor evaluated the student's competency on an accompanying scale and discussed with individuals any marked disparity between their own evaluations and those of their teacher. Each student set as his personal goal the rating he hoped to attain on his next evaluation. The teacher was alert for the first signs of progress and accorded these recognition and praise. Improvement was reflected in grading.

### Students Zero In on Directions

The directions in the textbook, the teacher noted, appear in a variety of types, sizes, and colors. Some of these directions are simple and present no reading problems. Nonetheless, they are frequently missed, often through carelessness and oversight.

Students were asked to search selected pages of their textbook with these questions in mind: "How does the author focus your attention on exactly what you are to do? Does he catch your eye through the type and the size of the print? through the use of color? by other means?" Students were quick to spot in their particular textbook the following types of attention catchers: marginal directions in eye-catching red, red italics inserted right into the copy, headings in bold-face type, black italics specifying line length and spacing, boldface terms that signal warnings, instructions boxed off in black lines.

The different formats for directions were then illustrated on a wall poster with the heading "Zero In on Directions—Wherever You Find Them." Full textbook pages that illustrated the various ways the author calls attention to directions were displayed on the poster. Each type of attention catcher was conspicuously labelled out in the margin of the poster. A vivid red cord caught the student's eye and led it from the label to the sample direction. Daily this placard sounded an alert.

### Teacher Projects an "Aid-less" Page

To dramatize the value of aids for grasping directions provided them in their textbooks, the teacher projected on a screen before the class a page with all these aids "Snopaked" (whited) out. Conspicuously *missing* from the page were the marginal directions in color, boldface "warning" type, numerals indicating a series of steps, boldface headings that give directions, directions inserted into the copy to be typed, and drawings clarifying exactly what to do.

The class was encouraged to react to this "aid-less" page. One student commented: "It isn't friendly. It doesn't talk to you. It doesn't come to help you. You have to fight with it to pull out what it wants you to do. You have to tussle with it."

When, in contrast, a page complete with all these aids was later flashed upon the screen, the students had a new appreciation for the help these aids had to offer. They realized that typographical and other helps they had sometimes overlooked were clearly important and would reward their close attention.

### How-to-Do-It Insights from Drawings

The teacher also projected on the screen directions from the textbook *with* a drawing showing how to reach for the letter *t,* followed by the same directions from which the drawing had been removed with Snopake. She commented, "It may cost the publisher several times as much to reproduce a drawing as it does to use regular type. If you don't notice the drawing, this money's lost. Why does he go to all this expense?"

**REACH TECHNIQUE FOR T**

Reach the *left first finger* to **t** without arching the wrist or moving the hand forward.

tt tf tf tt ftf tf tt ftf

tf the flat the left that

*FIGURE 9–1. An important drawing. (Reproduced with special permission from* 20TH CENTURY TYPEWRITING *by D. D. Lessenberry, T. James Crawford, and Lawrence W. Erickson. Cincinnati: South-Western Publishing Company, 1967, p. 8.)*

One student reacted: "You quickly see *exactly* how to reach for the *t*. It would take a good many words to tell you just how to hold your wrist and fingers, and even then the words couldn't possibly tell you as well as the picture."

## Students Build "Bank Accounts"

Progress was dramatized through "bank accounts" of points. Students started with a "deposit" of one hundred "direction points." They might increase this deposit by following accurately an exceptionally challenging set of directions. If they succeeded in following these without an error, they "deposited" ten points to their account. For each error in following directions, one point was deducted from the "deposit." An impressive "bank balance" at the end of a marking period was reflected in the student's grade.

It should be added that the points penalty is not invoked until the student is oriented to difficult new practice work. With business letters, for example, there are no deductions before the students' third experience.

## Dividends from the Directions Drive

Students were quick to note certain plus values as they sharpened their directions-reading skills:

1. More of their practice exercises were going right the first time— not the second or third or fourth.
2. They were saving many hours of working time as they eliminated errors and typed fewer practices over.
3. On occasions when the work was individualized, they were more productive.
4. Their stepped-up proficiency was bringing an improvement in their grades in typewriting.
5. They were acquiring an asset vital in many careers—the ability to read and grasp directions and to follow through.

The dividends are high. As the year progresses, there is less page trim in red pencil. There is a decreasing tendency for students to lean on the teacher and ask nonessential questions. The time spent in the directions drive has been saved many times over through more efficient, more productive class sessions.

# 10

# HOME ECONOMICS

*The reading helps in this section were prepared with Dorothy Szymkowicz, home economics teacher in the Laboratory School.*

One day a reading consultant was invited to visit a foods class. She found the teacher carefully pre-teaching vocabulary. The class was preparing to make spaghetti, and the teacher was painstakingly teaching *colander,* surrounded by chopped onions, tomato sauce, and Parmesan cheese! When, after the closing bell, the consultant expressed her delight at finding a part-time "reading teacher" in a home economics classroom, a cooperative venture to try to upgrade reading—a sharing of insights of classroom teacher and consultant over the years—was born.

The teacher posed their first problem: "Students tend to be over-confident with directions. How can we equip them to handle the directions on packaged products? Almost everything will be pre-packaged for the homemaker of tomorrow!" The procedures they worked out together are discussed in the first section of this chapter.

Next, they turned to the reading of recipes. "Here," the teacher commented, "deficiency in reading is disastrous to a successful food product." Could they work out ways to develop expertise in reading these? The procedures they developed, including a set of guidelines for students, are detailed in the second section of this chapter.

Next, the teacher suggested, "Can we help students handle the complicated—often bewildering—directions on a sewing pattern?" The reading guidance that resulted is explained in the concluding section of the chapter.

How has the reading venture worked out? Has there been a

change in the students' reading behavior? On the pages that follow, the teacher makes some interesting observations.

In these projects, the teacher had the enthusiastic help of intern reading consultants: Phyllis Brannan, Terri Heimann, and Joan Gilpatrick.*

## HOW TO READ DIRECTIONS ON PACKAGE MIXES

*A home economics teacher talks about her students' reading before and after her guidance.*

Ours is an "age of directions." In the future, nearly every food product for the home will be prepackaged with directions. Even today there are few commodities—either food or nonfood—offered to the homemaker without some kind of directions attached. She must read the directions on a package mix for party cupcakes, follow the directions for washing a delicate sweater, carry out the instructions for attaching a new accessory to her vacuum cleaner.

Directions on packages are often short and concise—*and highly deceptive.* These "simple" directions are densely packed with detail and require slow, precise, and thoughtful reading. Advertisers who give the impression that the result will work out perfectly often fail to stress that the directions must be followed precisely—*step by step* —if the perfect result is to follow. Students—and even experienced homemakers—tend to be overconfident when they see "simple" directions. They have simply never been briefed on the appropriate reading techniques.

To equip students to deal successfully with the directions on package mixes (and, more broadly, the directions on products for the home of any type), a home economics teacher and a reading consultant prepared a set of guidelines, "Direct Success with the Directions on Package Mixes." The teacher reports the results of a "before and after" experiment.†

---

* Miss Brannan is now Reading Consultant, Washtenaw Intermediate School District, Ann Arbor, Michigan. Miss Heimann is Language Arts Consultant for the Interrelated Language Skills Center, Milwaukee Public Schools, Milwaukee, Wisconsin. Mrs. Gilpatric was formerly Reading Specialist, Cabrini Learning Center, Chicago, Illinois.

† Mrs. Szymkowicz reported her reading activities with home economics classes at the 1969 International Reading Association Convention in Kansas City. Her complete paper is available in *Fusing Reading Skills and Content,* eds. H. Alan Robinson and Ellen Lamar Thomas (Newark, Delaware: International Reading Association, 1969), pp. 62–66.

"In the students' first experience with package mix, no special guidance in reading was given. The students were told only to follow the directions on the package. Their remarks were 'That's easy!' and 'No challenge in that!' As they worked, they paid slight attention to the directions. They merely glanced at a word or two now and then and guessed the rest, or asked one another what to do next. Some students never once looked at the printed directions. As the work progressed, students were beginning to look completely lost. With many, the final step was guessed, and the concoction was thrown into the baking pan in utter despair. Some ovens were not checked for the correct temperature. One oven was quite cold! Most students, having expected the mix to work perfectly, were very disappointed in the results. The conclusion of the group, to their own surprise, was that they had misjudged package mixes and that it was easier to make a product from scratch.

"A day or two later, the guidelines were used with the same group of students. This time I guided the class through a thoughtful reading of the guidelines, applying them to another set of directions on another, different package mix. After this 'reading lesson,' the students, on the whole, carried out the step-by-step procedures with much better results. Although there were still some difficulties, this time they involved practical skills, not reading skills."

The guidelines were kept for future reference in the students' looseleaf notebooks. There they were available to consult and review as needed. The teacher constantly broadened the application of the direction-reading techniques, encouraging the same precision with the directions on home appliances, on the labels of all household containers, and on the tags attached to ready-made garments.

How did the "directions drive" work out? As the weeks passed, many students read directions with never-before precision, asked fewer nonessential questions, and required less supervision. They became aware that the fine print on an inconspicuous label can mean the difference between delight in their purchase, or disappointment. When the course ended, these homemakers of tomorrow were better equipped to cope with the "directions explosion" that will confront them when they buy packaged products.

"Self-Evaluation Check Lists" can be used to focus students' attention on their need areas in reading directions and point the way to improvement. The reader will find an example, adaptable to home economics, in Chapter 9.

## HOW TO READ A RECIPE

*Students can improve their competencies in reading recipes relatively quickly. Better use of class time is one result.*

How many times will students follow a recipe in the course of a class in foods preparation! Here, day after day, they must read an almost identical pattern of direction writing. Without reading guidance, students tend to be "direction dropouts." They often glance at two or three words, then turn to their teacher with questions. *With* guidance, many can acquire recipe reading techniques relatively quickly. The results? Better food products, better use of both student and teacher time, and better foods preparation in the home after school days are over.

Using the guidelines, "How to Read a Recipe Successfully," a home economics teacher guides her students through a model reading of a recipe. The students discuss the how-to's and the why-do's of the suggested procedures; they talk over the critical importance of understanding each term; they become aware that a single punctuation mark can mean the difference between failure and success. The guidelines, printed on a colorful foldout, are kept for future reference in their notebooks. A striking wall-size billboard on which the guidelines have been enlarged by a photo blow-up process dominates the kitchen area of the classroom. Throughout the course the teacher refers to the billboard frequently. A single reading lesson with no follow-through, the teacher observes, has little permanent effect on student behavior.

After their directed reading of the recipe, most of the students read recipes more precisely and are more successful with their products. Some who have viewed themselves as scholastic misfits experience their first sense of accomplishment and confidence in foods class. The lift to their self-concepts through these experiences of success and approval could well lead to better achievement in the broader school situation.

### Tape Recorded Directions to the Rescue

Below-average readers often congregate in homemaking classes. For individuals who need reinforcement in recognizing the words of the directions, the teacher might record a series of directions on tape. Using earphones, the students read the words of the directions silently while reinforcing their reading through listening. They play and replay the tape as often as necessary. Through this reading-hearing procedure they come to associate the word they see printed on the page with the word they hear. After this reinforced reading, some students can proceed with their work away from the tape recorder, using only the printed directions. Thus they are grasping the directions for their current project, and learning to read better, besides.

# HOW TO READ A RECIPE SUCCESSFULLY

If the oven is to be used, **locate temperature** required.

    Think ahead! And at the appropriate time preheat your oven. Light your oven <u>before</u> assembling your ingredients. It will take about 10 minutes for it to reach the temperature desired.

### PART I—MATERIALS

**Read** through the **entire recipe** with special care.

    <u>Descriptive words sound an alert.</u> These are "key terms" to ►► cooking success.

    <u>Focus</u> sharply on <u>abbreviations.</u> ►- - - - - - ►- - - - - ►- - - - ►- - - ►

        Remember: <u>tsp.</u> mean teaspoon
                <u>Tbsp.</u> means tablespoon.

<u>Note</u> carefully <u>quantities</u> you'll need. ► ══ ══► ══ ══► ══ ══►

Unknown terms say **Stop! Look! Learn!**

    A single word left unknown may ruin your batch of cookies.

    The index of your cookbook or its "List of Terms Used in Recipes" should give you "instant access" to the meanings.

**Assemble** your **ingredients** and **utensils.**

    Then double-check. Reread Part I of the recipe to be certain you have everything you'll need.

**RECIPE FOR EASY SUGAR COOKIES**

*Part I*

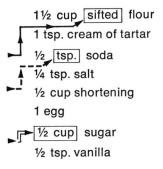

1½ cup sifted flour

1 tsp. cream of tartar

½ tsp. soda

¼ tsp. salt

½ cup shortening

1 egg

½ cup sugar

½ tsp. vanilla

OVEN TEMPERATURE 375°

**PART II—METHOD**

**Carry out** all the **steps** one by one in the **order given.**

Notice that the ingredients are conveniently listed in the order in which you'll use them.

Watch for special action words, for example: ▶━━━━━━━━▶

       Sift       Beat

       Cut in    Mix

and perform the technique called for. Remember that specific words are used for a purpose. Though some words may seem to differ only slightly, there's a decided difference in the action called for and a world of difference in the way your cookies may turn out!

Focus on descriptive words. ▶- - - - -▶- - - - -▶- - - - -▶- - -▶

"Zero in" on amounts, timings, temperatures.▶•••••▶•••••▶•••••▶

       Quantitative directions are "danger spots."

Carry out each step—with great care!

       For example, add the egg mixture to the flour, not the flour to the egg mixture.

Reread as often as necessary.

       A single error in any step may make your cookies not a delight but a disaster.

Then time precisely.

       Note the description of the finished product. 〉ooooo▶ oooooo▶ooo

> TAKE TIME for Precision Reading!
> SAVE TIME When Things Go Right!

*Part II*

1. Sift together flour, cream of tartar, soda, and salt.
2. ‾Cut in‾ shortening until like fine crumbs.
3. Beat egg with sugar and vanilla.
4. Add egg mixture to flour mixture and mix well. Dampen the hands with water, and roll into balls the size of a walnut.
5. Place balls one and a half inches apart on an ‾ungreased‾ cookie sheet.
6. Flatten first cookie with bottom of dampened glass tumbler.
7. Dip tumbler into the sugar and then press all the cookies.
8. Bake in a moderate oven 375° ‾until pale brown—about 6–10‾ ‾minutes.‾

## HOW TO READ A SEWING PATTERN

*Through guiding students in reading, a home economics teacher frees her own time for better service to her students.*

Anyone who opens a sewing pattern for the first time is likely to be bewildered by the many pieces, the different "views," the marking symbols, the cutting layout, the special language of the sewing guide, the detailed steps. How confusing all these must be to the beginning student!

Aware of the special need for instruction in reading such complicated directions, a home economics teacher and a reading consultant developed "Guidelines on How to Read a Sewing Pattern." Intended as an insert for students' looseleaf notebooks, they supplement and reinforce in-class instruction.

There's excitement in the air on the day the students bring to class their newly purchased fabric, their zippers, their buttons, and their intriguing new patterns—all to go into the making of THE dress. As the period starts, the teacher passes out the guidelines and sets the stage for the reading instruction.

> "You've bought your materials and your pattern, and you're eager to go ahead. That sixty-five cent pattern is a gold mine of information—but it's no use to you if you can't understand it. Knowing how to read it will help you become a make-it-yourself expert. You'll go home and sew just as well *there,* where you no longer have me to help you. How easy it will be for you to make a becoming dress for yourself—*when* you've learned how to read your pattern! You'll work ahead faster here in class, too. You won't have to ask unnecessary questions or lose time waiting in line for me to answer. How much time can I give each one of you if all of you, instead of consulting your patterns, come to me at once with questions!"

The teacher now leads the class through their study of the reading guidelines, applying them to the parts of the pattern: the envelope, the general directions, the marking symbols, the diagram of pieces, the cutting layout, the sewing directions, the symbols on the pieces themselves. As a step along the road to independence, she introduces the students to a colorful sewing resource book, *The Simplicity Sewing Book,** in which they can find the answers to many of their ques-

* Simplicity Sewing Book (New York: Simplicity Pattern Co., Inc.), 1970.

tions. This, she explains, will always be close at hand—theirs to reach for at the moment of need. She points out the clear "this-is-how-to-do-it" illustrations and the simple, easy-to-grasp explanations of sewing terms they may not know. Reinforcement of the newly acquired techniques is ongoing during the weeks and months that follow.

Does behavior change as a result of special instruction in pattern-reading techniques? The teacher comments:

> "*Without* instruction, many students are question-prone. They look for the easiest and quickest way to learn a new technique, and that is to try to get all the answers they can by asking their teacher. Searching out information for themselves on their pattern or in a sewing resource book may not have occurred to them. *With* guidance in reading a pattern, they are likely to require much less supervision and to work with an appropriate degree of independence. My time is freed to give essential instruction in construction techniques. The students usually find their first encounter with a pattern rewarding rather than frustrating, avoid mishaps with their garments, and experience the satisfaction of successful on-their-own accomplishment. Many, in future years, will be able to make quality garments without professional help. Their pattern reading expertise will enable them to continue their sewing education after school days are over."

# MUSIC

*This section was prepared in consultation with Frank Tirro, former music teacher and Chairman of the Music Department of the Laboratory School.*

Music courses often demand an extraordinarily high level of reading competence, and it is frequently the student's ability to read—not his musicality or intelligence—that determines his success or failure in music. This is the observation of Frank Tirro, teacher of music theory and music history.

He emphasizes the rigorous reading that confronts students in certain textbooks: "A music theory textbook is almost in a class unto itself. Each word of explanation, each note or other symbol on the musical staff, must be carefully considered, tasted, swallowed, and rechewed like a cow's cud. One does not really *read* a theory book. One grapples with it in a life-and-death struggle. Perhaps in all reading situations the teacher is well advised to introduce students to the particular reading techniques of the discipline in question. In music it would be sadistic not to do so."*

He urges other music teachers to become part-time reading teachers and reports his own activities in helping students digest their music textbooks: "It becomes obvious that early in the year, time must be taken to study and prepare an assignment in these courses. Instead of dictating the assignment traditionally, then sending

* Mr. Tirro reported his reading activities with music students at the International Reading Association Convention in Kansas City. His complete paper appears in *Fusing Reading Skills and Content*, edited by H. Alan Robinson and Ellen Lamar Thomas (Newark, Delaware: International Reading Association, 1969), pp. 103–107.

the student home or to the library with no further instruction, it becomes clearly preferable to make the assignment and then dedicate the next few class periods to the actual preparation, the teacher demonstrating how he would attack the chapter—previewing, questioning, reading, self-reciting, and so on—and then supervising the students in the same processes. This approach is preferable to leaving the preparation of the assignment to chance. The teaching of method and technique is infinitely more important at this stage of the course than attempting to move directly to content. When method is faulty, the acquisition of knowledge in any form is likely to be faulty."

Two of the areas Mr. Tirro focuses on are discussed specifically in this chapter, essentially through pragmatic tips for the student. In preparing these tips, Mr. Tirro and the Laboratory School's reading consultant combined their insights. First, we consider the reading of musical examples and then study-techniques for the vocabulary of music. The reading-study approach to which Mr. Tirro introduces his students early in the school year is explained in Chapter 3, in the section on PQ4R. Instructors of music appreciation courses, too, can take advantage of this approach to make their students more efficient readers of their textbooks.

## READING TECHNIQUES IN THE TEACHING OF MUSIC COURSES

*In certain areas of music education, it is the student's reading competence that determines his success or failure.*

The opening weeks of a course in music theory, music history, or music appreciation are the right time to help students learn to handle the heavy load of musical terminology in their textbooks. A special need—indeed, a crucial need—is a strategy for reading a *musical example*. A musical example is an explanation of a term or concept, not in words, but in notes and symbols on the musical staff (see Fig. 11–1, Inversion of intervals). Students often barely glance at these examples or bypass them completely. A reading technique that is highly specialized—in fact, unique to music—is called for. Only the music teacher has the expertise to develop highly skilled readers of musical examples.

And, of course, students need guidance in music, as well as in other disciplines, in learning to cope with the multitude of new terms and concepts explained in words, and sometimes not explained at all. The remainder of this chapter, therefore, consists essentially of tips: tips for reading a musical example and tips for learning key technical terms. These tips, when made meaningful for students in a teaching-and-practice situation, help students pull out the meanings and make the new examples and terms permanently theirs.

# TEN TIPS FOR READING A MUSICAL EXAMPLE

As you read your textbooks in music courses you will meet explanations of new terms or concepts followed by clarifying examples. These examples—unlike those in your textbooks in other subjects—are not written in words. Instead, they are *printed in notes and symbols on the musical staff.* Bypassing these examples can be disastrous to your understanding of the term or concept.

You're likely to need a special strategy for attacking musical examples. The tips that follow should prove extremely effective for the student who is seriously bent on mastering the vocabulary of music.

Of course, you will not need to use every technique suggested with *every* new term. Use as many of the techniques as necessary—or all of them—to grapple with the new term and grasp its meaning.

1. Most musical examples flash a warning signal—REDUCE SPEED *in reading.*

2. Read the author's words of explanation with special care.

3. When the author refers you to the musical example, *shift* your eyes and thoughts *to the musical staff.* Note whether the passage is a musical excerpt or a devised textbook example.

4. When key signatures, notes, intervals, and the like are mentioned in the verbal explanation, locate these on the musical staff. *Continue* this *back-and-forth reading* as needed.

5. *Hum* or *whistle* the *passage* (or part of it) or *play it* on a musical instrument.

   (a) Note the clef, the key, the meter, and the tempo.

   (b) If the passage consists of a sequence of single notes instead of chords, hum or whistle the melody to yourself.

   (c) If the rhythm is important to your understanding of a term or concept, you will find it helpful to tap the rhythm. Use your finger, not your foot. Finger tapping is more likely to to be a conscious gesture. Foot tapping usually degenerates into unconscious motion.

   (d) Chordal passages should be played on the piano.

6. *Read and reread* as often as necessary. Complete stops are called for. Thought time is needed in addition to reading time.

7. Read with pencil in hand and staff paper before you. Try to *make up* on staff paper an example of your own that fits the author's specifications. Now compare your own example with the author's and with the verbal explanation. Have you indeed "translated" the words into a musical example?

   Creating your own example is a powerful technique. It helps bring hazy understandings into sharp focus. If you study the

# TEN TIPS FOR READING A MUSICAL EXAMPLE

### The Inversion of Intervals

We have already mentioned the fact that notes which have the same letter name are regarded as equivalent. This is evident in the following theme.

**Example 26.** MOZART: *Symphony in D major, K.385 ("Haffner")*

Do back-and-forth reading between printed words and musical staff.

The half note D in the second measure is not different from the first note of the theme, but merely another occurrence of the same note in a different octave. Both notes are called D. Similarly, all the notes in the third measure are C#'s and all the notes in the final measure are A's. This reflects the operation of the principle of 8ve equivalence previously described (page 8). *Inversion*, a primary technique of chord generation, is dependent upon the principle of 8ve equivalence. We shall consider chord inversion in subsequent chapters; here we limit discussion to interval inversion. This is shown below.

**Example 27.**

Unison = 8ve

*FIGURE 11–1. Inversion of intervals. (From Allen Forte,* TONAL HARMONY IN CONCEPT AND PRACTICE. *New York: Holt, Rinehart and Winston, Inc., 1962, p. 15. Reprinted by special permission.)*

verbal explanation, then "illustrate" it—watch it develop—see it build up—the new term or concept should take on full, clear meaning.

You might also make up an example that does *not* fit the author's specifications and think through the reasons why it does not fit. Bring your example to class and discuss it with your teacher and classmates.

8. Turn on "the most powerful study technique known to psychologists"—*self-recite* on the new term.* Cover the words of explanation. Look at the musical example and see if you can supply the explanation in actual words—your own words. If you can't, recheck the explanation.

Now operate the other way. Expose the words, cover the musical example, and see if you can "see" the musical example.

* Walter Pauk, *How to Study in College* (Boston: Houghton Mifflin Company, 1962), p. 25.

9. All through this process, *turn on triple-strength learning*—visual, auditory, kinesthetic. If you try to learn a musical term with your eyes alone, you'll be using just one-third of your sensory channels for mastering the printed page. Use your eyes—then add your ears and muscles.

   Learn with your *eyes* as you *read* the words of explanation and the musical example. Strengthen learning with your *ears* as you hear yourself *hum* or *play* the example. Now you've brought to bear your auditory memory. Add *muscular learning* as you *write* out your own example on staff paper. Now you've involved motor memory—one of the strongest learning channels for many students.

10. Make an effort to *use* the musical term or concept. Whenever you hear a musical selection on TV or radio, on a record, or at a concert, apply and reinforce your new learnings. Now the term is likely to be *yours to stay.*

---

**In Summing Up—**

1. Reduce speed.
2. Read the words of explanation.
3. Focus on the musical example.
4. Do back-and-forth reading.
5. Hum, whistle, or play the passage.
6. Reread.
7. Make up your own example.
8. Self-recite.
9. Turn on triple-strength learning.
10. USE your new term or concept.

---

# SOME STUDY TECHNIQUES FOR THE VOCABULARY OF MUSIC

As you begin to study music seriously, it may seem as if you're learning a foreign language. Difficult and unfamiliar technical terms come crowding. Once an unfamiliar term is defined, the author will use it again and again—assuming ever after that you understand it.

Rote memory is not enough. You must acquire a "working understanding"—learn to use the new word tools rigorously and intelligently. Pass over these new terms lightly, and word blocks will obstruct your learning—your reading will become an obstacle course. Learn the new terms thoroughly at the time they're introduced, and you'll have precision tools for grasping essential new knowledge to the last day of the course—and beyond it.

Clearly, your vocabulary competencies now become a tremendous asset. Fortunately, learning experts at a number of universities, in actual experiments with students, have researched learning and retention techniques. Some of the procedures suggested here are based on years of experimentation in the psychology of learning.

FIGURE 11-2. Hurdles!

**How Will the Author Alert You to Important Terms?**

When key terms and concepts are first introduced to you in your textbook, the author flags you with a conspicuous signal. The signal used is likely to be *italic* or **boldface** type. Words so designated are highly important "official" terms or concepts.

In the passage below, the author makes important terms stand out on the page by using italic type.

### *TIPS FOR LEARNING KEY TECHNICAL TERMS IN MUSIC*

1. *Attend to each new term* when first it appears. Read reflectively to grasp what the explanation is saying—not to memorize by rote but to gain a real appreciation of the meaning.

2. *Read and reread* as often as necessary. Reading-once-straight-through patterns are no longer appropriate. Complete stops are called for frequently. Thought time is essential in addition to reading time. Even your instructor, with his broad background and long experience, finds that he must read difficult new material extremely slowly.

3. Suppose, as you're reading the explanation of a new term, you encounter a musical term you've already met whose meaning now escapes you. We all forget! You have the meaning of many such terms at your fingertips—through the *index* of your textbook. It offers you instant access to the original, the full textbook explanation of many terms.

4. You may wish to *consult a dictionary of musical terms* for those not included in your index. A reference that offers you clear, readable explanations is Willi Apel's *Harvard Dictionary of Music*. Music textbooks of high quality are often difficult. General vocabulary *terms* which you do not know may be frequent. To remove these roadblocks to your understanding, consult your general dictionary.

5. The author's definitions of new terms are almost always followed by musical examples. *Examine* these *examples* critically and figure out how they follow the definition. You'll find a special strategy for reading musical examples earlier in this chapter.

6. *Challenge the author.* Try to think of exceptions. Stop often and ask, "How does he have a right to say that?" "How does he justify saying that?" If you read on thinking, "I'll accept that without question," you may soon forget what the author has said. But if you've *questioned* it and convinced yourself it's right, you're far more likely to remember. Does your own musical experience support the author's contention? Bring your exceptions to class and challenge your teacher.

7. *Read* the explanation of the new term *with pencil in hand.* Make up your own examples on staff paper.

### The Auxiliary Note and the Passing Note

The Beethoven themes above also illustrate two melodic events of funda
mental significance to the study of harmony. First, in Example 15 attention is
drawn to the note marked *aux.*

STOP!
LOOK!
LEARN!

TOOLS
FOR
FUTURE
LEARNING

This abbreviation stands for auxiliary note, a note that stands at the
interval of a 2nd above or below two occurrences of a more important harmonic
note. In this instance the auxiliary note D stands between two C's, C being
the more important note since it belongs to the C major triad, which is the
keynote or tonic triad. The second melodic event of fundamental significance is
marked *pn* in Example 16. This abbreviation stands for passing note, a note
that passes between or connects two more important harmonic notes. Here D,
the passing note, stands between Eb and C, which belong to the C minor triad,
the tonic triad in the key of C minor. The passing note differs radically from
the auxiliary note. The auxiliary note departs from and returns to the same
note. The passing note connects two different notes.

Auxiliary notes and passing notes are often chromatic. In such cases
spelling depends upon the function of the note. For instance, in the Haydn
theme below we find a chromatic passing note which connects scale degrees 1
and 2. Since the passing note ascends, it is spelled G♯, not A♭. The latter
would be the correct spelling for a descending passing note.

**Example 17.**  HAYDN: *Symphony in G major, No. 94*

In the passage quoted below the chromatic auxiliary note is spelled F♯, not
G♭, since it ascends to the main note.

**Example 18.**  HAYDN: *Symphony in C minor, No. 95*

*FIGURE 11–3. Auxiliary note and passing note. (From Allen Forte,*
TONAL HARMONY IN CONCEPT AND PRACTICE. *New York: Holt, Rinehart
and Winston, Inc., 1962, p. 10. Reprinted by special permission.)*

Students often say, "I learn new terms, but I can't retain them." You may find it helpful to record the meaning, and perhaps an example, of difficult new terms on a flash card or in a notebook —not by rote but with full appreciation of the content. Take two or three minutes—that's all you'll need—to make each entry. If you were to do nothing more than *record* the new terms and definitions and then lost your flash cards, you would still have an advantage. The muscular act of writing, in and of itself, would have strengthened your learning.

8. *Self-recite.* Cover the words of explanation, and see if you can supply the explanation in actual words—your own words.
You may find a "List of Some Important Terms to Define and Memorize" toward the end of each chapter. You'll wish to check your understanding of these terms. The terms your author has selected for this list are crucial.

9. Some of your new technical terms will involve difficult musical concepts. Even with the systematic, effective procedures suggested here, the meaning of some of these terms will probably elude you. Your teacher will preview some of the most difficult terms in class *before* you read your assignment. Mastery of some will come about later as you work through the exercises or as your teacher explains the material or discusses it with you.
No question should remain unanswered. *Jot down questions* to bring to class.

10. Make an effort to *use* your *new* musical *terms.* Whenever you hear a musical selection on TV or the radio, on a record, or at a concert, apply and reinforce your new learnings.

---

**In Summing Up—**

1. Attend to each term.
2. Reread.
3. Use your index.
4. Consult your dictionary.
5. Scrutinize the examples.
6. Challenge the author.
7. Be active with a pencil.
8. Self-recite.
9. Bring questions to class.
10. APPLY YOUR NEW LEARNINGS.

---

# 12

# LIBRARY SERVICES

The library should be a vital communication center in every junior high school, senior high school, and college. Here students should be able to find materials, both print and nonprint, to help them complete their assignments as well as to suit their host of leisure time purposes. Here they should be conscious of a partnership between their classroom instructors and the library staff.

Librarians at the University of Chicago Laboratory School, and certainly in numerous other places, attempt to come to know their patrons, their reading levels, and their interests. The closer the liaison between the instructors and the librarians, the more the students will benefit. Librarians who are aware of assignments in advance can prepare the library environment so that students will make maximum use of its offerings.

Librarians everywhere face the persistent problem of coping with the individual needs of students in large school populations. Hour after hour, all through the school day, they attempt to get the right books into the hands of students. They will have an invaluable tool to assist them if they can have—on instant call—information about the general reading achievement of each student.

At the University of Chicago Laboratory School the reading consultant provides librarians with a simple, handy device—an "instant reading level file," with a card of useful information about the reading of each student. On the pages that follow we share with the reader how to make and use such a file.

## LIBRARIANS CAN LEAD THE SCHOOL IN "OPERATION MATCH-UP"

*With a handy "instant reading level file"\* librarians can translate impersonal standardized test scores into the personal needs of students. How often these scores gather dust in some remote file case! With quick access to these, librarians can often match the reading reach of students and the materials they read. And they can be a force for a far-reaching "Operation Match-Up"—all through the school.†*

Librarians are confronted hourly with a broad span in reading achievement. Among students crowding around the charging desk for books to do the same assignment—on, say, Shakespeare's theater— there may be one who should be guided to a book of sixth-grade difficulty and another who can handle college reading. Without guidance the poor reader may select books years beyond his reach and, deprived of practice, fall even farther behind. The gifted reader may mark time all year instead of moving closer to his full potential.

Through their daily contacts, librarians can influence the choice of reading materials throughout the school. They can sometimes make successful reading experiences possible for the school's prospective dropouts. And they can share with instructors in every classroom the conception of the school's reading range as an exciting challenge.

### Put Scores on Instant Call

Librarians can have insights at their fingertips through an "instant reading level file." It is a file of cards arranged alphabetically for every student in the school. On each card is test information that throws light on reading. At the Laboratory School, librarians consult

---

\* The "instant reading level file" was the subject of an article, "Instant Access to Students' Reading Levels" by Ellen Lamar Thomas in *School Library Journal,* XII, copyright © R. R. Bowker, 1966, pp. 49–52. Parts are reprinted here with special permission.

† Librarians guide students to successful reading experiences daily at the University of Chicago Laboratory School. They include Head Librarian Blanche Janecek, librarians Mary Biblo, Frances Fadell, Melissa Kern, Fylla Kildegaard, Winfred Poole, and also Floyd Fryden, Judy Geneson, Stephanie Goldsmith, Sylvia Marantz, and Susan Peters, formerly librarians in the Laboratory School.

such cards from day to day. Of course they recognize the file as only one tool in reading guidance—one which must be supplemented with all the resources of a trained librarian: a thorough knowledge of materials and their difficulty, and, most important, a knowledge of individual students. The limitations of standardized test scores are recognized, and the scores are regarded as just a suggestion of the student's reading level. It is also fully recognized that reading strength is not identical in all subject areas.

Since publishers' appraisals of the difficulty of books are often expressed in grade levels, it is convenient if the scores are stated in grade levels rather than, or in addition to, percentiles, and/or stanines. Many tests yield scores in grade levels. Of course, percentiles and stanines are equally suggestive of a student's relative standing. The breakdown into vocabulary, comprehension, and speed is useful in suggesting to the librarian the student's strengths and needs in these particular areas. "STEP" scores* in social studies and science are recorded because they have something to suggest about the student's

---

| | | *Confidential* |
|---|---|---|
| Student *Davis, Tom* | Class | *9* |

Gates-MacGinitie Reading Test, Form 1$^3$

| | Grade Level | I.Q. *106* |
|---|---|---|
| Comprehension | *7.2* | |
| Vocabulary | *6.9* | |
| Speed and Accuracy | | |
| Number Attempted | *9.2* | Interests: |
| Number Correct | *6.8* | *space* |
| | | *stock cars* |
| | Percentile Band | *wants to be* |
| STEP Social Studies | *17–37* | *auto mechanic* |
| STEP Science | *42–71* | |

FIGURE 12–1. *Instant reading level card. A card like this places at the librarian's fingertips insights into each student's reading power and his possible interests.*†

---

* *Sequential Tests of Educational Progress* (Princeton, New Jersey: Cooperative Test Division, Educational Testing Service, 1956–59).

† *Gates-MacGinitie Reading Test* (New York: Teachers College Press, Teachers College, Columbia University, 1965).

"reach" when reading books in these particular fields. Favorite pastimes, interests, and possible vocational choices are a useful addition.

### Other Resources Must Supplement the File

Gleanings from a student's card are adjusted in the light of all the librarian knows about the student, his motivation, his drive, his interests, his background on the subject, and other factors. No student is locked into books on a certain level. A student possessed with interest in a subject (stock cars, for example) may, by virtue of his background information and technical vocabulary, command far more reading power on this topic than his reading scores suggest.

### Help Rescue Retarded Readers

A stand-up tab on the card of each student enrolled with the remedial reading teacher can be a signal to librarians for "special handling." If a freshman is unable to read much beyond the level of a fifth grader, for example, his special reading teacher will give him materials and assignments with which he can succeed and progress, but can work with him only two or three hours a week. During the rest of the week—in English, science, social studies, and mathematics—his readings may be years beyond him unless the total curriculum is adjusted to his needs. Most often the curriculum is not altered, so he simply cannot cope with the rest of the school program. He loses hope and purpose. Librarians can help get the right books into the hands of this student, making a measure of success possible. They can help him overcome a failure mind set and help alter the damaging self-concept that has determined much of his reading behavior.

Of course poor readers are sensitive about their handicap and reluctant to accept materials that make them appear different. A book should not offend through its format, and there should be no notation of its difficulty. Librarians can guide these students inconspicuously, with casual comments:

"All these books are excellent. This one has some material that may be useful. Why not look it over and see if you like it?"

"You may want to read this as background before you read this."

"You can take this now, if you wish, but you'll probably enjoy it much more in a year or two."

Of course, multilevel print materials alone will not solve the problems of retarded readers. Multimedia materials should also be utilized. The scores on the cards can alert librarians to the less verbally oriented students. Having identified the students, they will sometimes find it appropriate to provide filmstrips, slides, or other nonprint materials. Suitable print materials should be complemented with instruction on essential reading skills in subject classrooms and through the school's special remedial services. Little is gained by supplying poor readers with easy materials and leaving them there, so that they never stretch their reading power. *The goal is a sequence of increasingly difficult readings with the student held to all he can do.*

A librarian often finds it possible to advance a student to a more difficult book when he is caught up with interest in a topic. One librarian comments: "I find the days just before a vacation a good time to suggest something more difficult. During the vacation the student will not have to hurry his reading. Other times I suggest a more difficult book on a try-it-out basis: 'Here's a book like the one you liked—only slightly harder. You might try a few pages and see how it goes.' "

### The File Can Spotlight Top Readers

The abilities of gifted readers often go unobserved. The reading levels in the file can help librarians identify these students. Top readers who habitually reach for an easy book can then be guided to works that broaden, stimulate, and challenge.

### Reading Scores Have Top Security

Of course the file should have a top security rating—out of the reach of student assistants. It would be shattering for a sophomore to come across his card and find a score on sixth grade level—or to learn this from a student assistant who had tampered with the file.

### Distribution Charts Can Alert a School to Its Broad Reading Range

Reading level distribution charts (see Fig. 12–2) for each grade in the school can show at a glance the spread in reading comprehension within each grade together with the number of students who scored on each grade level. When circulated far and wide throughout a school, these ditted sheets can have an impact on teachers who are selecting books for reading lists or considering new textbooks. The charts can be prepared in just an hour or two simply by turning through the cards in the file box and recording on the appropriate grade level a tally for each student.

```
                            FRESHMEN

Reading Comprehension Levels            Number of Students

      11th-grade or above       (14)   / / / / / / / / / / / / / /
      10th-grade                (11)   / / / / / / / / / / /
      9th-grade                 (20)   / / / / / / / / / / / / / / / / / / / /
      8th-grade                 (13)   / / / / / / / / / / / / /
      7th-grade                 (13)   / / / / / / / / / / / / /
      6th-grade                 (13)   / / / / / / / / / / / / /
      5th-grade                 (9)    / / / / / / / / /
      4th-grade                 (7)    / / / / / / /
```

*FIGURE 12–2. Reading level distribution chart. Reading level distribution charts reveal at a glance the spread of reading scores within a class and the number of students who scored on each level.\**

The message of the chart above comes through loud and clear. Instructors see their freshmen spread out over at least eight grade levels. The chart "nudges" them to provide enough sources—and enough copies—at the often neglected lower and upper extremes.

Librarians find the distribution sheets immensely helpful. After examining them, they can enter classes to "advertise" books armed with some knowledge of what the students in those classes can read. If librarians are searching out sources to list on a bibliography for groups working on a special assignment, they can gain from the charts insights into what those students can profitably use.

The reading level file becomes well worn during the school year through frequent use. In free moments some librarians even sit down with the box and study the cards. One reports: "Now when students come crowding and it is difficult to leave even for a moment, their reading levels click into mind."

* The reading levels illustrated are not those of the University of Chicago Laboratory School, but are representative of the distribution for a number of high school populations in public schools.

# 13

# FINE ARTS

A dedicated "reading teacher" is where you find one. In the University of Chicago Laboratory School there's one—of all places—in art class. There "Operation Reading" is a full-scale, year-long project, built right into the art curriculum. There, in the art history, design, and photography courses—courses where reading often plays a minor role—Robert Erickson, department chairman, sells his students reading, improves their reading, helps them find themselves through reading.*

What will you find if you look in on one of his reading oriented art classes? Books with colorful covers and intriguing content—shelves and shelves of them—are standard equipment—as much so as paints, paint brushes, and palettes. Students reach for a book to find a stimulating new idea for a project, to study a technique, to search out information related to an assignment, to explore a philosophy, or just to browse a while. The demand for books is so great that the instructor is often asked to unlock the book cabinet before unlocking the supply cabinet.

* Mr. Erickson reported the reading activities in his art class at the 1969 I. R. A. Convention in Kansas City. His paper is published in *Fusing Reading Skills and Content,* edited by H. Alan Robinson and Ellen Lamar Thomas (Newark, Delaware: International Reading Association, 1969), pp. 89–96. He discussed the contribution of the art teacher to the whole-school reading program in an article, "Art Class Book Collection Promotes Better Reading," *Journal of Reading,* XI, No. 5 (February, 1968), pp. 333–336.

"An art teacher has a special opportunity," Mr. Erickson points out, "to reach the unreached. Readers who have lost hope, including those most likely to become dropouts, often sign up for art, driven there by the fear of failing in reading subjects. They hope to find an activity centered class where reading is not demanded. I try to stimulate their enthusiasm for art, then use this interest to lead them to reading. Some students, for the first time in their lives, find something to value and enjoy between book covers." Mr. Erickson would like to see "libraries" like his in every classroom in the school—in music, science, industrial arts, physical education, and elsewhere.

In this chapter we present Mr. Erickson's approaches both to reading improvement and the development of the reading habit, as he uses them in his art classes.

## REACHING THE UNREACHED—THROUGH ART CLASS

*What can an art teacher contribute to the whole-school reading program? Robert Erickson, University of Chicago Laboratory School art teacher, spells out a practical answer.*

All through the class hour, powerful reading stimuli impinge upon the students in art class. Often, when a student needs the answer to an immediate and pressing problem, the teacher suggests a book.

"I'm having trouble drawing the legs of my lion in motion," a student comments.

"Do you think this book might help?" the teacher suggests, indicating the profusely illustrated *Animal Drawing* by Knight. "Here are pictures of the external features and of the muscle structure, and on this page the author gives you pointers."

"I don't know how to develop my roll of film."

"Where can I find information on that artist—what's his name—oh, Kandusky?"

"What is a *cliché verre?*"

"How can I take a photo of Jim shaking hands with himself?"

"Where can I find info on geodesic domes?"

There is no period of waiting—no cooling of enthusiasm—while the student runs to find a book in the regular school library. Instead, he finds in his hands an "instant book." As the students discover solutions to many of their problems in books, their instructor's time and energies can be directed elsewhere.

During the class hour a student may hold in his hands a dozen attractive books. While the class is discussing, say, twentieth century architecture, the instructor passes around ten or twelve books, with tabs inserted to mark some special reference ("p. 72, see 3"). Students often check out those books and take them home to read that night. Often a bright new book just added to the class library is put in the spotlight through the instructor's enthusiastic thumbnail sketch of its content, then left on the table for anyone to pick up and examine. An intriguing passage read aloud may make some student "captive." One day when the class was deeply involved discussing the basic question "What is art?" the instructor read aloud from Andreas Feininger's *The Creative Photographer*. A student checked out the book that night.

The *now* problems of young people searching for values in a society in ferment are grist for excited discussions. A thought provoking editorial may touch one off.

> Can a blindly angry young generation with its so-called documentary, protest pictures do much to better things? It is true that such pictures can motivate others to change things, that they are valuable as stark evidence of the neglect, poverty, and cruelty in the world. But will it not take people with a positive view of change, not simply a blindly angry view, to make the improvements that will really alter deplorable conditions?*

The question "How does this relate to your lives?" recurs from day to day as the teacher taps the strong interest of teenagers in ideals, values, and a life philosophy. One day he reads aloud from *The Wisdom of Confucius* or from Albert Schweitzer's *Out of My Life and Thought*. On another day he shares with students the vivid, intimate account of an artist's hopes, despairs, and thoughts about life in *The Daybooks of Edward Weston*.

### Start with a Handful of Books

The art library started with a handful of books, which barely filled one side of a small bookshelf over the teacher's desk—total cost, $10 or $15. Shopping with great discrimination, he had "scrounged" a dozen choice volumes in used-book stores, at sidewalk sales, at neighborhood rummage sales, and at Salvation Army and Goodwill stores. This small collection he supplemented by bringing in his own personal books from home. Later, funds from the Art Department's budget for supplies (about $30 to $50 each year)

* This quotation is slightly adapted from Norman Rothchild's "Offbeat," *Popular Photography*, LXVI, No. 6 (June, 1970), p. 20.

financed books for the ever growing library. Parents and teachers heard about the project and sent books. Windfalls came when school departments changed textbooks and donated what became resource books in science, drafting, or mathematics. In five years, a mere half a bookshelf had grown to quite an extensive collection—so many, in fact, that the books are now processed in the school library but kept on extended loan in the art classroom.

Simple checkout procedures encourage the student to do out of class reading. The student lists in a notebook his name, homeroom, the title of the book, the author, and the date borrowed. When the book comes back next day, the instructor crosses off the notation. So that all the books will be on hand each day for ready use, checkout privileges are offered only for overnight or for the weekend. The outflow to students is constant.

The subjects of the books are as far-ranging as the interests of the students, and these range over much of the field of art. It has been necessary to stock books on many subjects—collage, sculpture, painting techniques, architecture and city planning, drawing, cartooning, art history, product design, creative process, automation, handicrafts, toys and games, printing, typography, lettering, design, invention, structure, modern art trends, photojournalism, photo tricks, procedures in developing, printing and enlarging, movie making, night photography—and more. The latest issues of *Craft Horizons* and *Popular Photography* are also on the shelves.

As an aid for the art teacher in matching book and student, the reading consultant once coded the level of reading difficulty in each book. Each year she arms him with a handy score kit containing a card for each student with standardized reading scores and a suggestion of the student's reading grade level. "These cards," Mr. Erickson comments, "alert me to those readers who may need special assistance. The scores give me some idea, especially during the first few weeks, whether to hand a student a book of sixth grade difficulty or one on college level. More often, though, I work intuitively by finding material of vital interest and suggesting small segments to be digested."

## Can an Art Teacher Teach Reading?

How can an art teacher, with no special expertise in teaching reading, help less verbally oriented students learn from the answers in books? "Students let me know freely," answers Mr. Erickson, "when they don't understand a passage. Then I have a number of choices, or combinations of choices.

1. The class is often an activity period during which each student is working in a different direction. This gives me a chance to sit down with the student and read the passage with him. We work our way by small steps through difficult material. Often we read it sentence by sentence, stopping at the end of each and seeing what the student did or did not comprehend. I help him clarify terms he does not understand.

2. The reading consultant suggested that we strip a long, involved sentence down to its framework. When there are long, complicating subordinate phrases and clauses, we let these go for the moment and look for the main clause, or kernel of meaning. When this framework shows clearly through and we have a firm hold on the main idea or fact, then we can return and read the material again with all its trimmings to get the full sense.*

3. I can ask the student to read aloud to me. As he reads I discover something about his reading blocks: Does he give up completely before a word that seems difficult? Guess wildly at words? Should he try harder to figure words out? Can he handle the material at all, or is it hopelessly beyond him?

4. If the reading matter clearly exceeds his reach, I can direct him to simpler material.

5. Sometimes I supply a book I hope the student can understand and guide him to a small segment—a paragraph or a page related to what he is doing. I make it a point to observe him as he goes on with his work. When he seems to be having difficulty, I step in and help, discussing with him the troublesome part. Sometimes it's enough just to encourage him to persist—to read and reread the segment.

6. When a technical term is sure to overwhelm the student, I teach the term before he begins reading. Ted S., who was exploring the work of Jackson Pollock, would have been blocked by *abstract expressionist*. So I explained the term *before* he began reading. Students often search out answers for themselves in our well worn classroom copy of *Dictionary of Art and Artists*. A handy general dictionary is also within reach, and the students turn to it often.

7. Sometimes other students are a great help in explaining meaning in readings. I often ask students with greater experience and background to help those of lesser competence with the reading material and with the project itself.

* Walter Pauk, *How to Study in College* (Boston: Houghton Mifflin Company, 1962), p. 44.

"The subject teacher is not a reading specialist," Mr. Erickson goes on. "He is limited in what he can do. As time goes on, though, I notice that some poor readers can now read more difficult books. And I constantly observe how the driving interest of a student helps him to overleap barriers. When the desire to know is strong enough, the student can often dig the meaning out of difficult bits of material in highly technical books."

Especially in photography class students must often read directions, then carry out with the utmost precision the not-to-be-played-with procedures. Mr. Erickson resists spelling out for students exactly what they are to do. Instead, he equips them to read these directions and, in the process, moves them toward independence. He encourages the student about to mix a gallon of photodeveloper with: "Study the directions on the can with extreme care. They must be followed 100% in order for you to have a usable product. Overlooking a single direction in fine print may ruin your developer. Make brief jottings in your own words of the steps you're going to take, then check your steps with me before mixing your developer." The reader interested in detailed direction-reading techniques will find easily adaptable suggestions in Chapter 9.

### "Problems" Can Help

In problem centered art courses, the students are often caught up with exciting problems. Mr. Erickson frequently personalizes the problems, brings them close to the lives of his students; then these problems trigger the drive to read.

> Learn about the artist whose work most closely resembles your own.
> Investigate your own nationalistic, racial, and/or religious roots through art forms.
> Try to discover the work of some artist whose point of view most closely parallels your own. Point out the similarities.

Now reading skills for problem solving are germane to the art class. Acquiring these does not drain away time—many such skills can be taught in minutes. Student and instructor now narrow problems to manageable proportions and plan how to better organize material. Doors are opened to rich reading resources in art of which the student has been unaware. As he holds a promising book in his hand, he may learn to use the index as an aid to quick finding of what he is after from among the many thousands of words in the book. He may learn to scan pages and columns for information related to his problem, speeding right on past unpromising paragraph headings, then slowing down to examine a promising paragraph. He is likely to leave art class with more expertise for exploring problems in the field of art and for continuing his art education after the course is over. Readers interested in the skills essential for students in solving problems through reading can consult Chapter 5.

### Students Become Lifetime Readers

Students possessed with interest in problems in art are often led to rewarding experiences with reading.

One day Ricky, a not-so-eager reader, expressed an interest in architecture. I asked, "Do you know the work of Frank Lloyd Wright? of Eero Saarinen? of Antonio Gaudi?" We went to the bookcase together, looked through some choice books on architecture, and Ricky was attracted to Saarinen. We sat down together at a table with the book, talked over some of the plans, and read some of the descriptive material. During the course I saw Ricky turn to that book often— and then to others. He probably digested every book on architecture on the shelf. Later he talked about his life choice—and architecture seems to be the direction he has chosen.

Larry, a below-average reader caught up with science, wanted to photograph under the microscope tiny living things in a drop of water. Knowing nothing about taking photomicrographs, he now had a driving reason for reading. I suppose I might have *shown* him how to take these pictures. Instead I suggested, "Here's an explanation in *The Focal Encyclopedia of Photography*. Ask questions about any part you don't understand." Slowly digesting each paragraph and asking frequent questions, he read for four consecutive class sessions. At the end of the fourth day, Larry borrowed a microscope from the science lab and a 35 mm reflex camera from me and began his experimentation. The results were some good color photographs of tiny-celled creatures—and a greater potential for Larry in finding things out for himself.

Carl, a black student who had a reading problem, expressed interest in his own heritage in art. I directed him to books on tribes and forms of African art. He spent a good deal of time studying the illustrations and reading about his own people. We discussed the characteristics of the various tribal examples and together formulated some creative examples that challenged him and enabled him to depart from—yet use—the material he had studied. A year later, Carl still drops by the art room, browses through the books for hours, selects some to read, and takes time to talk over what he is reading.

Often students begin their own private library collections as a result of reading successes in the art classroom. Judy, a sophomore, in response to the assignment to find the work of some artist whose work most closely resembled her own, wrote a paper on her reactions to Picasso's work and brought in a new book on Picasso for me to see and to use as I marked her report. She commented, "The best thing about the assignment was that I added this book to my own collection!"

Charles, both retarded and reluctant as a reader, had great successes in art class but failures everywhere else in school. I encouraged him to look at work by other artists in our books. He started to look at slides and at color reproductions in the books, but he didn't read—at first. I read aloud, though, to his class, and he became curious about the ideas expressed by artists. He began to read small bits of information related to the artists whose work he admired. Later he joined an art book club and began to build up his own home art library. As each new book arrived, he would bring the precious volume to me so that I could share his newly found joys. He even selected books for me to read. I felt some real success with Charles.

### It Doesn't Take with Every Student

"Reading doesn't take with every student," Mr. Erickson has found. "Some are not reached at all. They are not anxious to read but only to *do*. They avoid reading suggestions and reading assignments. They take a grade of *F* on an assignment that involves reading rather than meet the requirement. And there is another problem—the problem of thefts. My classroom library used to be in the next room where students could quietly go and do research, browse, read, or just relax with a book. Many fine volumes were stolen, particularly those dealing with nudes, anatomy, photo techniques and with Dada and surrealist art. Such volumes are now kept out of reach in locked cabinets. These may be signed out for period use only. I have moved the art library into both the art and photo classrooms where I can constantly check the volumes. Thefts are less frequent, but they still occur. I hate to think of keeping the books locked up. I would rather take the attitude that the gains for students through having books easily accessible outweigh the losses. However, the books I bring from my own home are used only by the period. I do not loan them for overnight use."

**Dividends from "Operation Reading"**

Staggering sums are required to reclaim students who leave the doors of their schools without reading power and without earning power. The sum expended to finance an art class library is an investment in *prevention*.

1. A student's strong interest in art related subjects can help remove psychological blocks to his reading progress.

2. The world of words has never been the world of the poor reader. When a teacher guides him to a book right for him in difficulty and interest, he may, for the first time, spend many hours in the world of printed words. He meets words repeatedly in similar and different settings, often with a little increment of meaning at each encounter, and gradually incorporates them into his vocabulary. His reading practice tends to strengthen his comprehension.

3. An impelling interest in some aspect of art may enable him to handle "far too difficult" books and to extend his reading power.

4. He may do an about-face in his attitude toward books. Though the printed page has held little appeal for him, he may now view it as a possible source of solutions to his in-class and out-of-class problems.

5. The presence of the classroom collection daily builds toward voluntary and habitual reading.

6. Inviting do-it-yourself projects often lead to home hobbies, especially when there is the ability to read and follow simple directions. Some simple photo and art materials at home—a simple camera, a few pieces of charcoal, some stencils for lettering, a brush or two and some paints—can involve teenagers in constructive hobbies and, in urban situations, help to keep them off the streets.

7. A student's self-concept determines much of his behavior, including his reading behavior. A young person who views himself as an individual who cannot read tends to fulfill his own expectations. A damaging self-concept may be altered by successful reading experiences in art class and elsewhere. Success through and with reading sometimes helps a discouraged reader take hold, renew his efforts, and succeed better in the broader school situation.

# 14

# PHYSICAL EDUCATION

The development of lifetime readers is an obligation as well as an enjoyable responsibility of all teachers. The teaching of reading skills without the concomitant utilization of those skills for a multitude of purposes selected by the reader is of questionable virtue.

In many classes, such as physical education, the actual teaching of reading skills has little or no place. But the physical education instructor, the coach, has as much of a responsibility as any other teacher (perhaps more) for helping students make use of the reading materials related to his field. In fact, he has a remarkable *opportunity* for helping students turn to reading they will enjoy without bothering them about whether or not their reading skills are adequate.

Too much of the time the words in the opening paragraph above become educational lingo, often stated and infrequently followed. Throughout this volume, however, you are meeting teachers who *really believe* in the development of lifetime reading habits and have created procedures for doing something about them.

In this chapter you meet a physical education instructor and coach, Sanford Patlak, who is dedicated to the development of lifetime readers. We try to show here (a difficult job without the enthusiasm and spontaneity of Coach Patlak confronting you) the specific techniques he uses for getting all students, and particularly reluctant readers, to turn to books about sports—fiction, nonfiction, biography, autobiography, reference materials. Some specific book titles are referred to, but the reader should realize that they do not remain static; Coach Patlak adds new titles as he finds materials he feels will be exciting, valid, and pertinent. His most recent bibliography of books for easy reading was printed in *Fusing Reading Skills and Content.**

## COACHES CAN GET BOYS "HOOKED ON BOOKS"

*Sanford Patlak, whose part in his school's reading program is reported here, is basketball coach and physical education instructor at the University of Chicago Laboratory School. Coach Patlak sees opportunities in schools, particularly inner-city schools, for coaches to help rescue lagging readers and hold prospective dropouts. He catches his readers young.†*

Reading projects in physical education can contribute to the school's reading program. The status a coach's recommendation to read books has with his boys can change their attitudes toward reading. When a coach shares his enthusiasm, reading becomes manly instead of "for squares."‡

"There are opportunities," Coach Patlak points out, "with boys in depressed neighborhoods. Sports rate high in these areas. Suppose a boy thinks the coach is great. The coach might say, 'Jim, come into my office—I have this book. Can you look it over and see how you like it?' You just might give him a reading interest—a habit, maybe. You might help keep him off the streets. It just might work."

Boys can improve their athletic techniques through books. Publishers are offering outstanding how-to-do-its on every sport. By pushing these, a coach can have more playing power in his boys. Television is bringing sports events to millions, many of whom are ill-informed. Through books, boys can broaden their backgrounds and add to their enjoyment as spectators.

* Sanford Patlak, "Sandy's 99 Sports Books for Reluctant Readers," *Fusing Reading Skills and Content,* eds. H. Alan Robinson and Ellen Lamar Thomas (Newark, Delaware: Intenational Reading Association, 1969), pp. 201–204.

† Coach Patlak's work with students was reported in an article, "Books Are the Greatest," by Ellen Lamar Thomas in the *Journal of Reading,* XII (November, 1968), pp. 119–124. Parts are reprinted here with permission.

‡ Mrs. Lois Osberg helped Coach Patlak start his project when she was interning as a reading consultant in the University of Chicago Laboratory School. The reports of some of the coach's reading sessions are drawn from her notes. Mrs. Osberg is now Director of Reading, Duneland School Corporation, Chesterton, Indiana.

### The Sports Library—the Busiest Spot

At times Coach Patlak's library of sports books is the busiest spot in the gym. Comments the coach, "It's sports books where they belong." A traffic-stopping red and white highway sign invites a boy to STOP at the coach's bookshelves. A poster headed *"Have you read this?"* displays colorful dust jackets high in sports appeal—*Football Fury, Go Team Go,* and *Baseball Sparkplug.*

### A Coach Can Start a Library with Pennies and an Orange Crate

Coach Patlak started his library with little time and less money:

> Someone was getting rid of some bookshelves. I set them on an old training table. My first books were second-hand —had a lot of mileage on them. I asked my varsity boys and the boys in my classes to bring in old books. Mothers and dads heard about it and sent me books. The response was tremendous. And I bought books for pennies at rummage sales.
>
> You can start with a handful of books and an orange crate for a shelf. You can have a plush library—rows of clean, expensive books—but without someone's interest, boys may not reach for one. My library wasn't big, but it did the job.

Later the school's reading consultant paid for the coach's book orders by selling packets of locally made instructional materials to visitors. Hearing about the project, the school's director made a sum available. In other schools, a coach might interest a school service club or a leader of the PTA. School libraries often lend books for classroom collections. The possibility of federal or state funds can be investigated through the school librarian.

### Sports Books Invite the Hand of a Reluctant Reader

Coach Patlak's collection ranges over the entire field of sports. To help him select books, the reading consultant supplied book lists, which offered capsule summaries, interest levels, and reading difficulty levels. On the coach's shelves are action-packed fiction as well as how-to-do-it books on the major sports as well as on judo, camping out, life saving, scuba diving, fishing, and drag racing. There are colorful, attractive paperbacks, slim and trim enough to invite the hand of a reluctant reader. The books span a broad range of difficulty levels from grade four through college. The coach knows his books. He reads the how-to-do-its, skims the fiction, and makes it a point to remember student comments.

### "You Can Do Your Selling Job in Minutes"

Coach Patlak talks up books on the playing field, on the edge of the swimming pool, in the gym with the boys sitting around him on tumbling mats. "It takes hardly any time," he comments. "You can do your selling job in a few minutes at the beginning of the period." He pushes books hard with younger readers: "Catch a boy young—before he lags behind."

He "sells" books to seventh-graders lined up on benches alongside the swimming pool. He pulls books out of a carton, holds up each one, and keeps up a running sales talk. He paces back and forth around the circle, showing a bright paperback, *The Kid Comes Back.* "This is about a fellow who was captured after his plane crashed in wartime. He kept longing to play ball again. It tells how he escaped and became a big league player. It's a tremendous book!"

He reaches into the carton for *How to Star in Track and Field* and waves it before the class. "We'll be starting track soon. This one's topnotch. It shows you how to pace yourself, work up to distance running, improve your starts. A tip you pick up here may make you a better track man. Sports and books on how to improve your skills go hand in hand. You can learn in your own room at home. Is it easy? Right! You don't have to worry about hard words. Books are the greatest!"

Out of the carton comes *Strike,* a how-to-do-it book on bowling. "This is for a guy like you, Andy. Bowling is your thing. You'll learn how to have the right stance, how to pick up the ball the right way from the rack. *See* how to bowl. Are there good pictures! One picture may give you a pointer."

Last, he waves *Basketball Rules.* "You might want this one, Don. You're a good ballplayer, but there's a lot to learn about the rules. You can't play—you can't even *watch* intelligently—if you don't know the rules. Read just as much as you want to—maybe just ten or fifteen minutes. You don't have to read all of it, just the parts you're interested in. We've got a good deal going in these books. They're in the locker room with the balls. If you want one, just check it out after class."

## Checking Out Books Is Simple

The boys, showered and dressed, wait in line by the door for the passing bell, close to the locker room library—its door wide open. "Just take the card out of the book and write your name," suggests the coach, "then put it in the box on my desk." (Books can be processed with cards and pockets by student assistants.)

Star athletes sometimes start runs on books: "Sometimes a school hero carries a book out under his arm, and the lowerclassmen see him. They say, 'I want that book next time! Man, I've got to have that book!' After that, I just can't keep that book—it goes out with one boy after another."

## "Operation Match-Up" Guides Boys to Books

"Give a boy a book beyond his reach,"Coach Patlak comments, "and you'll lose him." The level of difficulty has been color coded in each book by the reading consultant. "Property of Coach Patlak" is entered in red for a difficulty level around grade 4, green for grade 6, blue for grade 8, and so on. In schools with no consultant, librarians can appraise difficulty.

"I know where the kids stand in reading," the coach explains. "The reading consultant gives me the scores. All the time it's going through my mind. 'You're a poor reader.' 'You're a good reader.' I cover up my intent. If I hand out books during class, the first one goes to a top reader. But later I maneuver so that the right book goes to the one who can't read well."

The coach has in mind sequences of books of increasing difficulty and likes to advance a boy through a series on some compelling interest like football or scuba diving. A boy possessed with such an interest can sometimes handle "far too difficult" books. It's great when he sees a reader "graduate" from extremely easy books to books that stretch his reading power. Top readers, too, crowd the library, often taking home a book from the coach's own professional collection.

## Book Reporting Starts Runs on Books

The boys respect a book tip from someone their own age. They sometimes trade tips out on the soccer field, sitting in a circle on the grass.

COACH    I'd like to talk with you a minute about the books you've been reading. Mark, you took one out the other day. Are you through with it? What was it about?

MARK    It was about football. The name of it was *The Keeper Play.*

COACH    Were there some exciting spots?

MARK    Yes. It was cool when they were doing this special play called "the keeper play."

COACH    Hold it! That's the whole thing—that special play! Don't tell about it. Let them read it and find out!

COACH    Do you think someone else here would like your book, Bob?

BOB    I think so. It's *How to Play Baseball.* It showed things you really need to know.

COACH    Did you like anything especially?

BOB    It showed me how to throw a curve ball.

COACH    Who in the class would like it?

BOB    I'd give it to Ron. He wants to be a pitcher.

COACH    Was it hard to read—hard words?

BOB    No, sir. It was OK.

### Books Can Help Mixed-Up Boys

In the library is an article, "What Man Can Be," by Bob Richards, clipped from *Guideposts* (October, 1968) and supplied with a bright construction paper cover. "When a kid gets hurt and is feeling low because he can't play again," observes the coach, "this one might be just right to talk about. Here you learn about stars who had setbacks. Take Bob Mathias. That guy really had heart. His foot was badly torn. Later it became his take-off foot in jumping. You learn about how great champs started up the ladder again. When a kid has a problem, I try to find a book about the same problem. I can talk up the book walking with him down the hall."

### The Sports Page Can Grab Boys

Coach Patlak rides the crests of sports enthusiasms, the surge of interest as a season approaches, the wave of excitement when a school team is having a winning streak, when the local pros are front-runners. "I catch the boys when they're geared up with a certain interest. Before class starts, I ask a question, 'What's the big sports headline today?' That starts a chain reaction: 'Did you see that article about so-and-so who was traded to so-and-so?' 'How did the Cubs make out?' 'Is their streak still alive?' 'Try to look over the sports page Sunday and remember the highlights. We'll have a little run-down Monday.'

"These questions take about a minute. It doesn't take much time to sell reading. I get my regular job done."

## The Bulletin Board Can Too

The bulletin board "grabs" boys as they enter the gym. A large placard spotlights the local "Players of the Week" and announces the reason these boys were selected. A series of pictures, with captions, on how to make a free throw invites reading. Displayed on large laminated cards are the Athlete's Creed, the Code of Sportsmanship of a nearby college, and the coach's Thought for the Week—"When the going gets tough, the tough get going."

## A Coach Can "Sell" Library Cards

The coach gives vacation reading a sendoff: "We don't want the kids to stop reading when they leave in June. I take five minutes near the end of school and say, 'Soon you're going home for vacation, and I know you're all interested in reading some more books. How many of you have library cards?' Those who have no cards are given applications. They fill these in at home and then bring them back to gym class. The last day of class in June I give out the cards to the boys personally. A student can do the leg work—get the application forms from the library, return these to the library, and bring me the cards."

## Coach and Reading Teacher Work Together

Sometimes the coach and the remedial reading teacher talk over under-par readers. One of these was Don—in school a poor reader, out of school an "I won't" reader. The coach reports: "Last week Don broke a record getting dressed to be first in line for a book. He walked out of the gym with that book under his coat. Today he told about it. Maybe I've changed an attitude, created an interest. That's all I wanted to do—just create an interest. You reading teachers won't go out and think you can coach basketball. And I don't want you to think that I'm a reading teacher. But working together, we can do the job."

# INDEX